E.J. PRATT

Selected Poems

This volume of E.J. Pratt's selected poems introduces Pratt's poems to the college and university student and to the general reader, providing the background necessary for an informed reading of the poems. The volume offers a full sampling of Pratt's poems chosen both for their representativeness and for their intrinsic value. Included are the major long poems, *The Witches' Brew, The Iron Door, The Titanic, Brébeuf and His Brethren,* and *Towards the Last Spike,* and important shorter lyrics such as 'Newfoundland,' 'Come Away, Death,' and 'From Stone to Steel.'

The editorial approach is historical, chronological, and biographical. The introduction locates E.J. Pratt in his Newfoundland and Canadian contexts, and discusses the development of his work in relation to his early modernist contemporaries, concluding that Pratt remains the most important and influential Canadian poet up to the mid-fifties. As such, he has been a key figure in shaping the Canadian literary imagination of his day and the later poetics of landscape adopted by Earle Birney and Margaret Atwood.

The editors provide newly edited versions of each poem, annotations, textual notes, and a biographical chronology. The printed volume is supplemented by the electronic resources of the *Selected Pratt* website at www.trentu.ca/pratt/selected.

SANDRA DJWA is a professor of English, at Simon Fraser University.
W.J. KEITH is a retired professor of English at the University of Toronto.
ZAILIG POLLOCK is professor emeritus of English Literature at Trent University.

E.J. PRATT

Selected Poems

Edited by
Sandra Djwa, W.J. Keith,
and Zailig Pollock

UNIVERSITY OF TORONTO PRESS
Toronto Buffalo London

© University of Toronto Press Incorporated 2000
Toronto Buffalo London
Printed in Canada

ISBN 0-8020-4335-6 (cloth)
ISBN 0-8020-8155-X (paper)

∞

Printed on acid-free paper

Canadian Cataloguing in Publication Data

Pratt, E.J. (Edwin John), 1882–1964
Selected poems

Includes bibliographical references and index.
ISBN 0-8020-4335-6 (bound)   ISBN 0-8020-8155-X (pbk.)

I. Djwa, Sandra, 1939– . II. Keith, W.J. (William John), 1934– .
III. Pollock, Zailig.   IV. Title.

PS8531.R23A17 2000   C811'.52   C99-932118-8
PR9199.3.P7A17 2000

University of Toronto Press acknowledges the financial assistance to its
publishing program of the Canada Council for the Arts and the Ontario Arts
Council.

University of Toronto Press acknowledges the financial support for its
publishing activities of the Government of Canada through the Book
Publishing Industry Development Program (BPIDP).

Contents

Acknowledgments

Many individuals have contributed to the development of this volume. We would especially like to thank our fellow-members of the Pratt Editorial Committee (Susan Gingell, Lila Laakso, Perry Millar, D.G. Pitt, and Beth Popham) and our Advisory Board (David Bentley, Claude Bissell, Robert Brandeis, Peter Buitenhuis, Michael Darling, Douglas Lochhead, Jay Macpherson, Malcolm Ross, David Staines, and Brian Trahearne) for their suggestions in establishing the list of poems to be reprinted and for their advice in general. We are especially grateful to Lila Laakso for bibliographical sources, to D.G. Pitt for biographical and textual information, and to Susan Gingell and Elizabeth Popham, who helped develop an earlier version of this book. Professor Gingell's work in transcribing and editing the Pratt collection has been invaluable. We also wish to thank Perry Millar, who worked with Sandra Djwa on the Introduction. Research assistance was provided by Tim Freeborn, Smoki Musaraj, Brian Saunders, Chris Turnbull, and Monica Weymer.

Editors' Introduction

E.J. Pratt grew up on the Newfoundland seacoast, where the poet is most often a storyteller and where the poem, like the folk song, has a public function in affirming community, celebrating heroes, and lamenting death. Although he left Newfoundland in his mid-twenties, his poetic imagination continually returned to the seascapes of his childhood. He believed that poetry should express the speech and emotions of ordinary men and women, yet he knew poetry to be 'an exacting, difficult craft, and it takes years of hard work, and education, and a sense of the language. Rhyme and meter do not make a poem ... The real flesh and blood of poetry lies in turns of phrases, vivid images, new and unusual thoughts and manners of expressing them.'[1] He also understood that a poem is, above all, a verbal structure and spoke of 'the poet's ability to shape his material, to adjust word to word, line to line, canto to canto, scene to scene, act to act ...'[2]

He was born Edwin John Pratt on 4 February 1882 in Western Bay, Newfoundland, to Fanny Knight, the daughter of a sea captain, and the Reverend John Pratt, an English Methodist minister. There he was raised in a series of small fishing villages, where life was harsh and nature intractable. It was a barter economy in which codfish and seals were exchanged for flour, sugar, and tea. Existence was always precarious. As a boy, he often accompanied his clergyman father, whose task it was to bring the tragic news of the loss at sea of a father or brother to unsuspecting families. In 1898, when he was sixteen and attending school in St John's, he was present when the *Greenland* steamed into harbour bearing on her decks, stacked like so many cords of wood, the bodies of sealers who had frozen to death on the ice when they became separated from their ship. He never forgot the memorial service at the Anglican cathedral: 'The words burned into our souls as they described the struggle of the men on the floes, the pitched battle with the elements at their worst, and the ironic enigma of Nature and its relation to the Christian view of the world.'[3]

The 'ironic enigma' suggests Thomas Hardy's sense of an ironic and incomprehensible universe, or, nearer to home, tales like 'The Young Ravens That Call upon Him,' from Charles G.D. Roberts's *Earth's Enigmas* (1896). It implies the gulf between the Christian ideal of a nature reflecting a God of love (the nature found in much Romantic poetry) and Darwin's nature as interpreted by Herbert Spencer and confirmed by Hardy's pessimism – the cruel Newfoundland nature that Pratt knew.[4] His early verse sprang from the attempt to explore this Hardyesque 'enigma,' a troubling question for the young man because he had entered the Methodist ministry, which emphasized God's love and man's redemption. In 1904, as a student probationer, he taught and preached in the Newfoundland outports, and in 1907 he was accepted for study in theology at Victoria College at the University of Toronto.

Pratt had first thought science could help man in his battle against nature. As a schoolboy in 1901, he had met Marconi shortly before the first wireless message was sent to England. Wireless seemed a miracle, for it appeared that man could conquer nature.[5] But only a decade later, in 1912, the inconceivable happened. The 'unsinkable' *Titanic* hit an iceberg and, despite wireless, sank with an appalling loss of life. Because the ship had gone down just off the coast of Newfoundland, this disaster took its place in Pratt's catalogue of Newfoundland disasters. It was followed by still greater personal losses: in 1912 his young fiancée, Lydia Trimble, died, and his friend and professor at Victoria College, George Blewett, drowned. Four years later, at the Battle of the Somme, a generation of his younger Newfoundland contemporaries were killed. In 1918 several classmates were lost when a ship went aground; in 1924 Pratt's older brother committed suicide; and in 1925 his mother died.

Not surprisingly, death rather than love became the primary subject of Pratt's poetry. Many of his personal losses are reflected in the early lyrics and *The Iron Door: An Ode* (1927), and he seriously questioned religious belief, at first in the unpublished verse-drama 'Clay' (1917–18). Although he completed an M.A. in 1912, a B.D. in 1913, and his Ph.D. in theology in 1917, he chose not to take up a Methodist pastoral charge but continued at the University of Toronto as a tutor and demonstrator in Wilhelm Wundt's stimulus-response psychology, then in the Department of Philosophy. At Victoria College he was introduced to Pelham Edgar's poetry reading group by Viola Whitney, the daughter of a Methodist clergyman, whom he married in 1918. Edgar, then Head of the English department at Victoria, became a mentor, and for the first time Pratt began to read English poetry seriously, and to try his hand at verse.

A poet like Pratt, who began to write in the early twentieth century, could draw upon three streams: the English literary tradition, the older Canadian tradition introduced by the poets of the Confederation, and the new poetry issuing from Great Britain and the United States. These literary sources were augmented by the Newfoundland ballad and, in the 1920s, by the Group of Seven's visual images of Canada as a vital northern land. Underlying all these factors were the intellectual currents of the period, especially the modernist urge to secularize, to find new human-centred explanations for older conceptions of God, the universe, and man's place in it.[6] Finally, there was the new Canadian nationalism generated by the Great War. All these strains are found in Pratt's poetry.

His place in the modern movement is best understood chronologically. He was born three years after John Masefield, two years before Siegfried Sassoon (who, with Isaac Rosenberg and Wilfred Owen, constituted the British war generation), and six years before T.S. Eliot. In terms of the poetic forms of his contemporaries, this situates him between the longer realistic narrative, the shorter war lyric, and the allusive, discontinuous poem. Like Masefield's sea poem *Dauber* (1913), with its oral narrative and realistic diction, Pratt's narratives move towards what Northrop Frye called a 'flexible, unpretentious speaking style.'[7] Pratt also developed a new, seemingly objective lyric, taking as his subjects war and nature. This lyric was often impersonal: it featured a persona, a controlled pose, and often an ambiguous, ironic reversal at the end of the poem. The form of the poem indicates repressed passion.[8] In several poems written in the 1940s, notably 'Come Away, Death,' he experimented with the allusive, elliptic, and symbolic narrative associated with later modernist poetry.[9]

These changes in his poetry spanned a quarter of a century. Although he began to write in imitation of traditional English poetry, by 1915–18 he had been introduced by a classmate, Arthur Phelps, to the new poetry, largely British and American imagism and free verse.[10] In 1918 Pratt published 'Dawn,' his first imagist poem. However, he considered the imagist poem too choppy and recognized that his talent lay in more ambitious, epic-size subjects. In the same year, in response to Duncan Campbell Scott's *Lundy's Lane and Other Poems* (1916), Pratt wrote Scott telling him how much he admired his long poems, such as 'The Height of Land,'[11] with its northern Canadian nature and an evolutionary sense of man's progress.

In Pratt's own practice, imagism and free verse take their place within the long poem, although his first narrative, *Rachel: A Sea Story of Newfoundland in Verse* (1917), owed more to Wordsworth than to the moderns. He saw himself as a public poet and wanted to celebrate a Newfoundland as yet 'not charactered ... by History's pen' (*Rachel*, 245). But his decision to remain in Toronto, confirmed in 1920 by his appointment as a part-time instructor in English at Victoria College, provided him with an institutional niche which allowed him 'a favourable stance from which to survey a situation most unfavourable to poetry.'[12] With the exception of D.C. Scott, the Confederation poets had dispersed, their successors made little impact, and Canadians tended to look elsewhere for their poetry. But post-war nationalism had led to Bliss Carman's return to Canada for a cross-country tour in 1921; this, in turn, helped spark the founding of the Canadian Authors' Association. At McGill University, Carman encouraged the young A.J.M. Smith, who brought him a poem, 'O when the winds of April.'[13] Charles G.D. Roberts also returned to Canada in the mid-1920s to become president of the Canadian Authors' Association. Smith soon became the leader of a group of younger poets at McGill, including F.R. Scott, A.M. Klein, and Leo Kennedy. However, the *McGill Fortnightly* group had no national audience until the mid-1930s, and Pratt became the principal Canadian poet from 1923 to 1955.

Pratt vitalized the Canadian scene in April 1922 with publication of 'The Ice-Floes' in the *Canadian Forum*, a poem illustrated with a woodcut by Thoreau MacDonald.[14] In this poem he developed his memories of the *Greenland* tragedy with modernist irony, structuring the poem to draw repeated parallels between man and the other animals, between the 'mother' seal and the 'mother' ship. What is most striking about this poem is its stark realism: a harsh northern nature, the irony of the human situation, and the curious interpenetration of man and nature. As a post-Darwinian, Pratt sees man as an animal, a part of nature. The tragedy of the poem is the struggle for survival, laconically expressed as the loss of sixty men 'to help to lower the price of bread' (146).

Newfoundland Verse, published a year later, contains 'Newfoundland,' selections from the earlier 'Clay,' and some shorter poems, including the imagist lyrics 'The Shark' and 'The Fog.' Pratt had discovered that poetry 'came best out of the imagination working upon the material of actual experience. My aim was to get the emotional effect out of the image or the symbol operating on the facts of sense perception ...'[15] Like the imagists, Pratt wanted to achieve Ezra Pound's 'intellectual and emotional complex in an instant of time ...,'[16] but, unlike the imagists, he wanted to retain the symbol with its implications of a reality beyond the physical.

'Newfoundland' is structured in terms of the interaction of the three basics of the Newfoundland seascape: tide, wind, and crag. Ironically, however, this interaction has a darker side: the tides flow with great energy, metaphorically running within the veins of man in his lifetime, physically running through his veins after shipwreck and death by drowning. Similarly the winds bring 'the bread of life' for they regulate the movement of schools of fish, but they also produce 'the waters of death' when a high gale dashes a ship against the rocks: thus the crags 'guard too well.' The free verse form gives movement to wind and tide as they sweep against the rocks. The tides flow 'not with that dull, unsinewed tread of waters' (3) but rather 'with a lusty stroke of life / Pounding at stubborn gates' (8–9). This poem is printed with italicized alternate stanzas, which function very much like the chorus in a New-foundland folk song or – with Pratt's turn towards tragedy – like the chorus in a Greek drama interpreting the action and directing our atten-tion to nature's darker side.

In 1925 Pratt turned to parody with a long, carnivalesque poem, *The Witches' Brew,* replete with allusions and historical personages, and written to celebrate his fifth wedding anniversary. For over fourteen years he had studied and written on scholarly and theological topics; now, responding to the 1920s urge to 'debunk,' he parodied. The poem satirizes a hypocritical Canadian puritanism – implicitly, members of the Toronto Temperance Union:

Puritans to whom the chance
Had never come in life to dance
Save when the dreadful circumstance
Of death removed their maiden aunts. (267–70)

In the largest sense, his parody is directed at religious themes: the poem alludes to an infernal trinity, a new fishy world to be saved or damned, and a new version of the apple – 'the witches' brew.'[17] This satire is reinforced by his form, the rollicking tetrameter of the Newfoundland ballad.

In his revolt against Canada's delayed Victorianism, Pratt had drawn heavily upon satire and parody. In retrospect, he recognized 'Clay' had been too serious and *The Witches' Brew* too ridiculous,[18] but he admired the combination of romance and science in Roberts's evolutionary tale *In the Morning of Time* (1919). By the mid-1920s, he began to associate himself with the new realists, notably Masefield, Carl Sandburg, and Roy Campbell.[19] A visit to England in 1924 introduced Pratt to Campbell's poetry and seems to have reinforced his interest in the long narrative sea poem, an impulse continued in both *The Roosevelt and the Antinoe* and *The Titanic*. For his next poem, 'The Cachalot' (1925), Pratt drew on the American Museum of Natural History and the whaling history found in Herman Melville's *Moby Dick*. 'The Great Feud,' its companion poem in *Titans* (1926), is an allegorical fantasy depicting a feud between the creatures of the land and the creatures of the sea which, like World War I, is occasioned by a struggle over a boundary strip, in this case the tidal flats which separate both. With *The Roosevelt and the Antinoe* (1930), the story of a rescue of a ship at sea, Pratt abandons fantasy for realism – but contemporary fact is now positioned within a larger mythological framework which evokes the terror of nature and the frailty of human response.

With the publication of *Titans*, Pratt was recognized as the first 'Canadian' voice in poetry. Barker Fairley, then literary editor of the *Canadian Forum*, commented: 'Take any previous Canadian poet and you have to admit that an Englishman residing in Canada might have written his work. No Englishman could have written *Titans*.'[20] Pratt's vision of nature and his original poetic voice were important qualities in a decade characterized by a persistent call for an authentic Canadian poetry. Despite his Newfoundland birth (the province did not join Confederation until 1949), Pratt soon became recognized as Canada's national poet.

During the 1930s, Pratt continued to identify with the new realists. Like most of his contemporaries, he had been convinced that to be modern was to be anti-Romantic, failing to see that modernism continued aspects of Romanticism. In a lecture given at Harvard in the 1940s, Pratt explained that the influence of Hardy and the writings of Thomas Huxley (who saw 'the ethical and the cosmic in perpetual struggle') had led poets like himself to lose 'the habit of interrogating nature as a kind mother.'[21] Supporting the realist attack on Wordsworthian nature poetry was the New Humanism as expounded by the American critic Irving Babbitt, who had delivered the Alexander Lectures at the University of Toronto in 1930.[22] Pratt attended Babbitt's lectures and appears to have read his book *Rousseau and Romanticism* (1919), which presented man as both good and evil, engaged in 'the civil war in the cave.' In response to this dilemma of consciousness, Babbitt urged ethical decisions.[23] A year later, in 1931, Pratt wrote 'The Highway,' and two years later he completed 'From Stone to Steel,' suggesting that human progress was situated 'between the temple and the cave' (13). These two poems and his next work, *The Titanic*, stress man's duality and the ambiguity of progress. These were particularly appropriate themes for the 1930s, a period of growing unrest and threatening war.

Pratt explores these questions in *The Titanic*, where the ship itself is a microcosm of twentieth-century technology and the iceberg a symbol of the inexplicable power of nature. Pratt saw the collision between the two as 'a study in irony ... So completely involved was the ship in what we call the web of Fate, that it seemed as if the order of events had been definitely contrived against a human arrangement.'[24] Elsewhere he speaks of 'some power with intelligence and resource [which] had organized and directed a conspiracy,'[25] and in the poem itself Pratt marshals his narrative to foreground the inevitable collision of ship and iceberg when man's 'judgment stood in little need / Of reason' (234–5).

The section entitled 'The Iceberg,' with its realist foreground and symbolic overtones, provides a clear example of Pratt's poetic technique. The description of the iceberg is built up from his own experience as a young man, from a journal in *After Icebergs with a Painter* (1861), a book kept in the family because his grandfather, William Knight, had been the ship's captain on this expedition,[26] and very probably from a painting by A.Y. Jackson, *Iceberg, at Godhaven* (1930). This physical portrayal of the iceberg is deepened by a clash of Christian and animal metaphors. At first a sea cathedral (as in his earlier treatment of an iceberg, 'The Sea-Cathedral'), it is suggestive of a beneficent universe. But the iceberg weathers under the effects of the sun and current, which shape it to an underwater 'claw' that rips through the *Titanic*, evoking nature 'red in tooth and claw.' Because the iceberg is developed through dual metaphors evoking both good and evil, it becomes in its last incarnation a symbol for the 'ironic enigma' of nature and man's inability to determine its moral nature.

The publishing of poetry lapsed in Canada during the Depression; consequently, Pratt established the *Canadian Poetry Magazine* in 1936, where Northrop Frye became his assistant. It was during the late 1930s that he began to write nationalist Canadian poems, taking as his subject the retrospective, myth-making topics of the period: the taming of the wilderness, the building of a nation, and the construction of a national railroad. American poets had celebrated the nation with epics such as Stephen Vincent Benét's *John Brown's Body* (1928) and Archibald MacLeish's *Conquistador* (1932). Strong public reception of these poems, both in the United States and Canada, post-war nationalism, the increasing threat of war, and Pratt's belief that the Canadian poets had not yet provided a sense of national myth may have encouraged the writing of both *Brébeuf and His Brethren* (1940) and *Towards the Last Spike* (1952).

In *Brébeuf and His Brethren*, Pratt hints obliquely at the Second World War in his account of the wars of the Huron and the Iroquois in seventeenth-century New France; his primary source was Francis Parkman's adaptation of *The Jesuits in North America in the Seventeenth Century* (1882), an account of the Jesuit mission to New France. Parkman had pointedly drawn attention to the ironic parallels between the Jesuits and their Indian brethren: and, in a version of Parkman prepared for Canadian use by Pelham Edgar, Brébeuf at the stake responds to the Iroquois 'roar for roar'; thus it was the defiance of the priest that Pratt emphasized.[27] He undoubtedly saw that the saga of Brébeuf (much like the figure of Thomas à Becket in T.S. Eliot's *Murder in the Cathedral*) provided a moral for the wartime present and brought together Canada's national past of French and English, Catholic and Protestant, priests and natives.

Pratt's attitude to his material is complex. He carefully researched the background and is deeply sympathetic to the mysticism of the Jesuits. Yet occasionally he follows Parkman's lead in discerning ironic similarities between priest and native, an irony implied in his title. When recruiting missionaries for New France, Brébeuf expresses the fundamental message of Christianity: 'You must sincerely love the savages / As brothers ...' (572–3). Yet in Pratt's tracing of ideological struggles between the two, the poem's controlling antithesis becomes that of 'savage' (heathen) versus 'civilized' (Christian), although both have the potential for movement forward and backward on an evolutionary scale. Pratt employs the narrative of *The Jesuit Relations*, but, as contemporary readers have agreed, he interpolates material and his treatment is sometimes ambiguous.[28]

His own 'story' begins with the Catholic story of conversion and Brébeuf's mission to the Hurons. Brébeuf's vision of a cross 'huge enough to crucify us all' (1161), and the metaphors of the breaking of the body and the drinking of the blood of the missionaries, become symbolic of a final sacrament. Although Pratt respects the faith animating the missionary endeavour, a tone conveyed by his symbols and the elevation of the language, he satirizes some aspects of the attempt to convert the Hurons, particularly when, as an inducement, pictures of suffering souls in hell are employed by the Jesuits. Moreover, when appalled by the treatment meted out by the Hurons to their captives, Pratt's Brébeuf is made to remark: 'a human art was torture' (683). Such descriptions were undoubtedly associated by Pratt's readers with then contemporary newspaper accounts of Nazi atrocities. Brébeuf's faith, which inspires him to endure torture unto death, seems to have been intended by Pratt as, in part, a parable for a nation then at war.

Shortly after concluding *Brébeuf*, Pratt turned to the kind of allusive, ironic, and complex poem associated with Pound and Eliot, possibly because his subject, the fearful omnipotence of death, and his sense of the way contemporary history was unfolding, demanded such treatment. The late lyric 'Come Away, Death,' from *Still Life and Other Verse* (1943), in which death comes, whether we wish it or not, unpredictably, illogically, is worth looking at in some detail. The poem's title and the first two lines incorporate allusions to clowns in two plays by Shakespeare: *Twelfth Night* and *Hamlet*. It is Feste, the clown of *Twelfth Night*, whose song 'Come away, death' supplies the title for the lyric. This song, which describes death as a sweet and easeful state, a cure for lovesickness, might imply that Pratt agrees – an impression supported by the surface statement of the first two stanzas. But on closer examination this message is undercut. The first words, 'Willy-nilly,' and the following references to the 'clown's logic' introduce a second pair of clowns, the gravediggers in *Hamlet*, who are preparing the drowned Ophelia's grave: 'If the man go to this water and drown himself, it is will he, nill he, he goes ...' This chop logic carries overtones of human will as a factor in causing death, a consideration that leads the poet to a discussion of war. This technique is consistent throughout the poem. Underneath the surface peace of death lies the horror unearthed by the poet, just as the clown-gravedigger in *Hamlet* unearths the skull of Yorick. In the searing last stanza, this emotion becomes overt when a bomb, falling, is a 'bolt / Outside the range and target of the thunder' as human speech curves back upon itself through 'Druid runways and the Piltdown scarps' (49–52).[29]

Pratt's poems struck a resonant note in the 1930s and early 1940s, signalling as they did the events that led up to the Second World War – Mussolini's attack on Ethiopia, the Spanish Civil War, the invasion of Poland, and the start of the phony war followed by the blitz on London. Throughout the Western world during the last months of 1940 there was a fear England would fall and, with it, Western civilization. It is in this context that Pratt wrote 'The Truant' (1942), about a struggle between man described as 'the truant' and cosmic nature, now personified as a totalitarian but ultimately ridiculous Grand Panjandrum with overtones of Hitler and the Old Testament Jehovah. Man differs from the rest of nature through the evolution of reason, which allows him to take the measure of the universe: thus he asserts his 'truancy' from the natural order presided over by the Grand Panjandrum. 'The Truant' is Pratt's strongest affirmation of human will, intelligence, and imagination and his repudiation of the threat posed by a determinist universe that now included not only Darwin's science but also Nazi totalitarianism.

All of the longer poems show Pratt's impulse to document his subject. In *Towards the Last Spike* (1952) it is Sir John A. Macdonald's promise in 1871 to build a transcontinental railroad on the condition that British Columbia enter Confederation. However, in this poem, Pratt is moving towards a narrative discontinuity more extreme than the effects in his earlier narratives:[30]

> It was the same world then as now – the same,
> Except for little differences of speed
> And power, and means to treat myopia
> To show an axe-blade infinitely sharp
> Splitting things infinitely small, or else
> Provide the telescopic sight to roam
> Through curved dominions never found in fables.
> The same, but for new particles of speech –
> Those algebraic substitutes for nouns ... (1–9)

Pratt's discontinuity implies progress. We see yesterday's technology, the 'axe-blade,' through the new electron microscope 'splitting things infinitely small,' a phrase that also reminds us of the splitting of the atom with its release of energy or power. The vision of the poem – the transformation of John A. Macdonald's vision into a railroad, uniting the scattered provinces into a nation – parallels Pratt's struggle in the poem to pull together the disparate elements of the story into a single work of art. The transformation of vision into a persuasive argument is as important as the story of the events themselves. Pratt's belief in the power of language as another form of energy – 'the battle of ideas and words' (470) – which can ultimately unite, demonstrates how Macdonald's national vision is brought into reality.

Pratt's first twelve lines also subtly introduce 'those algebraic substitutes for nouns' or $e = mc^2$, one of the tenets of the theory of relativity, that matter and energy are interconvertible: the splitting of the atom, for example, destroys 'mass' to create 'energy.' This metaphor, expressed as the conversion of mass to energy to mass again, structures the poem at a deeper metaphoric level than that of narrative or story. This 'energy' or 'power' Pratt attributes first to the Scots – the labourers, the financiers, and Sir John himself. 'This power,' Pratt tells us, 'lay in the custody of men' (57). Initially it is man's energy that transforms the landscape: in Pratt's metaphors, digested oatmeal releases the energy to allow men to prevail against rock. In this process, 'foreheads grew into cliffs, jaws into juts ...' (72). 'Energy' becomes 'mass' as the men take on the qualities of the landscape they oppose.

Nonetheless, nature remains a threat. The vast rock-bound terrain from northern Ontario to Great Slave Lake is personified as an enormous lizard. Into this 'scrimmage' come the railway labourers who 'massed, divided, subdivided' (834) – releasing their energy – but some are returned to mass again as the bodies of the Chinese and Scots railroad workers are reduced to the material elements from which the life cycle began. Many of the details of this poem coalesce to suggest the first law of thermodynamics, the concept that energy can never be destroyed or created. If all the elements of our world were present when it started – 'It was the same world then as now' – then, despite differences of technology, man and nature remain engaged in perpetual seesaw struggle. Despite the successful joining of the country by the CPR, the 'lizard' of nature is still there with the potential for reawakening.

Pratt's myth-making imagination was a bridge between the Confederation group and the younger poets of the 1940s. As he explained, 'I believe I share Eliot's creed of a developing tradition ... Duncan Campbell Scott, Carman, and Roberts did their job for their generation and did it well, and the fact that some of us have pursued other paths does not lessen the importance of their journeys.'[31] Although the older poets had created a nature poetry that reflected aspects of a national consciousness, they had not developed 'the larger human currents, the democratic visions, the creative impulses at work on myths and national origins.'[32] Pratt took up this role to show that the Canadian past could be transformed into a 'usable myth' for the political present and that the vast northern nature of Canadian landscape might be transplanted to poetry through metaphor and symbol.[33]

He also collaborated with younger poets such as A.J.M. Smith and

F.R. Scott in *New Provinces: Poems of Several Authors* (1936). This anthology was modelled on the British *New Signatures* (1932), which presented a group of British and American poets who wished to reject esotericism and 'find solidarity with others.'[34] Pratt rejected an early preface to *New Provinces* written by Smith (it attacked the older poets) but accepted a revised preface written by Scott stressing solidarity because he believed that the two generations of Canadian poets should work together. Pratt's poetry also influenced his contemporaries. His vernacular tone and documentary instinct[35] precede A.M. Klein's 'Barricade Smith: His Speeches' (1938) and are later reflected in Dorothy Livesay's radio docudrama *Call My People Home* (1949/1950). Indeed, the examples in Livesay's later essay on the documentary poem as a Canadian genre are culled largely from Pratt's poetry.[36] In the 1940s, his use of the longer narrative with a symbolic dimension strongly influenced Earle Birney's 'David' (1940). As Birney acknowledged, Pratt's 'example had encouraged [him] to adventure into the writing of a narrative poem with a Canadian wilderness setting.'[37] The metaphoric development from the 'crystal peaks' of Pratt's iceberg to the 'claw' that rips through the *Titanic* is echoed in the movement in Birney's poem from the 'sunlit spire' of the mountain peak to the 'cruel fang' that pierces David.[38]

The poets of the 1960s were influenced by Pratt's political nationalism, his depiction of man as animal, and his metaphors for the interpenetration of the human and the natural. In 1963, Margaret Atwood echoed Pratt's metamorphosis of man into nature ('Foreheads grew into cliffs, jaws into juts') when in 'Poor Tom' she writes of 'bedrock of his jawbone, rough redpine / of spine'[39] and continued a Prattian strain in poems like 'The Descent as Dissection.'[40] In 1964, the year of Pratt's death, James Reaney wrote an editorial for the little magazine *Alphabet* remarking that Pratt provided an example for Canadian poets: 'the young intellectual living in this country ... quite often ends up thinking he lives in a waste of surplus USA technology ... What our poets should be doing is to show us how to *identify* our society out of this depressing situation ... E.J. Pratt managed to do exactly that.'[41] Munro Beattie, writing on modern poetry in the *Literary History of Canada* (1965), concluded that Pratt's contribution to the modern movement was a breakthrough in tone and subject matter: 'Yet in the revitalization of Canadian poetry in the decades since 1920, Pratt's work has counted for more than any other man's – counted by virtue of its craftsmanship, its breadth of sub-ject-matter, its competence in dealing with ... the phenomena that engage the interest of twentieth-century men and women, its uninhib-ited and exhilarating vision of life.'[42]

In the 1970s and 1980s, younger poet-critics such as Frank Davey redefined Pratt's 'vision' restrictively in terms of power, rationality, and group action,[43] thus differentiating the aesthetics of Pratt's long poems from then contemporary practice, a judgment echoed by Smaro Kam-boureli.[44] However, concentrated readings of Pratt's poetry, which began with the Pratt Symposium in 1977, have reminded us that Pratt's poems cannot be wrenched from their historic or aesthetic contexts. At the Long-liners Conference in 1984, Magdalene Redekop argued: 'Pratt does celebrate faith and self-sacrifice. His great achievement is to do so while simultaneously accepting the world as a tissue of necessary fictions.'[45] Contemporary criticism has come to emphasize the highly crafted and sometimes ambiguous nature of Pratt's use of narrative and metaphor in the long poems.[46]

Pratt's epic themes – the pioneer struggle against the wilderness, and the building of Canada – were of paramount importance to Canadians between 1920 and 1967, who were preoccupied with questions of cultural identity. These themes were reinforced by the 1960s nationalism of such novelists as Margaret Laurence and of poets such as Margaret Atwood and Al Purdy, who translated them into the generic pioneer poem – Atwood's *The Journals of Susanna Moodie* (1970) or Purdy's *In Search of Owen Roblin* (1974) – both followed by numerous successors. Even poems inspired by different poetics – for example, bpNichol's *Continental Trance* (1983) – can be seen as a response to genre memory and *Towards the Last Spike*. Clearly, by the 1960s, Pratt had established a Canadian voice and a narrative mode, later classified as 'documentary,' which helped shape the English-Canadian poetic tradition of the twentieth century.

Sandra Djwa

TEXTUAL NOTE

In putting this volume together, the editors have tried to balance two important requirements: intrinsic merit and representativeness. We take ultimate responsibility for the final results, but in the process of arriving at our selection we consulted many colleagues, including the members of the Pratt Project editorial committee and advisory board. We have also taken into consideration the judgments that have emerged during many years of anthologizing and criticism of Pratt's poetry.

One decision which the editors arrived at early on was to include only complete poems. This inevitably resulted in a narrower selection of Pratt's longer narrative poems than we would have preferred. We regret, in particular, the exclusion of 'The Great Feud' because of its length; to have included it would have resulted in a bulkier and more expensive volume than we considered appropriate. However, we believe that the range of Pratt's achievement is well represented by the long poems which we have included: *The Witches' Brew, The Titanic, Brébeuf and His Brethren,* and *Towards the Last Spike.*

The texts published here are based on collations of all authoritative published versions, and of all unpublished versions which provide a complete text. To quote *Brébeuf and His Brethren,* 'all dots and commas were observed.' The collations have been undertaken as part of the ongoing hypertext edition of *E.J. Pratt: Complete Poems* (www.trentu.ca/ pratt).

The copy-texts for all of the poems in this volume are the versions in the second edition of the *Collected Poems* (Macmillan, 1958), edited by Northrop Frye. The following categories of accidentals have been regularized in accordance with the 'house' style of University of Toronto Press: capitalization of titles; quotation marks (single, with double quotation marks for interior quotes); ellipsis points (triple throughout). Apart from these regularizations, the accidentals of the copy-texts are followed, with two important exceptions:

1. Several of Pratt's poems originally included text set in the left margin (dates, speech headings, section headings). In the 1958 *Collected,* the left margin is reserved for section numbers; material that in earlier editions (including the 1944 *Collected*) had been placed in the left margin is now moved into the body of the page, set off from the main text by small caps or italics, by line spacing (in the case of section headings), and by punctuation (in the case of speech headings). The

poems in the *Selected* affected by this decision are *The Titanic* and *Brébeuf and His Brethren*. In both cases, we have restored the layout from the first editions, the 1935 and 1940 editions of *The Titanic* and of *Brébeuf and His Brethren* respectively, both published by Macmillan. We have done this for several reasons. These editions reflect Pratt's intentions (as is clear from the manuscripts); they are visually more attractive than the versions in the 1958 *Collected*; and they are clearer. Moreover, the compositors of the 1958 *Collected* made a number of mistakes in their placement of sub-headings.

2. In the 1958 *Collected*, speeches are enclosed in double quotation marks and are also set in italics, a practice which is followed in no other version of Pratt's poems. The effect is unpleasantly busy, especially when the speeches contain words or phrases that were originally set in italics and which in the *Collected* are either enclosed in single quotation marks or set in small caps. In this edition, speeches are set off only by quotation marks.

The *Selected Poems* follows a strictly chronological order of arrangement according to dates of composition. These dates, which inevitably involve some degree of speculation, are based primarily on the following sources:

1. D.G. Pitt. *E.J. Pratt: The Truant Years 1882–1927*. Toronto: University of Toronto Press 1984; and *E.J. Pratt: The Master Years 1927–1964*. Toronto: University of Toronto Press 1987
2. Lila Laakso. 'Descriptive Bibliography.' In *E.J. Pratt: Complete Poems*. 2 vols. Ed. Sandra Djwa and R.G. Moyles. Introd. Sandra Djwa. Toronto: University of Toronto Press 1989, 2:373–497
3. The letters of E.J. Pratt, currently being edited by D.G. Pitt and Elizabeth Popham (including annotations by Professor Pitt)
4. Materials deposited in the Victoria University Library (Toronto, Ontario), including the E.J. Pratt Collection, the Claire Pratt Collection, and back issues of *Acta Victoriana*

For each poem there is a textual note (at the back of the volume) indicating the date of composition, the date of first publication, and any emendations.

Where necessary, explanatory notes are also provided, immediately following the textual note. We have not glossed terms that are readily found in a good dictionary or atlas, but we have included historical references, literary references, and biblical and classical allusions. Pratt's own glosses are frequently cited, from the following volumes:

Verses of the Sea. Macmillan 1930 (*VS*)
Ten Selected Poems. Macmillan 1947 (*TSP*)
Poems for Upper School. Macmillan 1963 (*PUS*)
E.J. Pratt on His Life and Poetry. Ed. Susan Gingell. University of
  Toronto Press 1983 (*OHLP*)

For Pratt's more extensive comments, readers are directed, at the appropriate places, to the last of these volumes.

The footnotes to *Brébeuf and His Brethren* (pp. 96, 97, 111) and to *Towards the Last Spike* (pp. 158, 162) are Pratt's own.

The explanatory notes are drawn from the hypertext edition of the *Complete Poems.* Since the hypertext Pratt will not be completed for some time, we have prepared a site on the World Wide Web to accompany the *Selected Poems*, which includes much more extensive notes as well as a detailed timeline of Pratt's life and works (www.trentu.ca/pratt/selected).

Zailig Pollock

NOTES

1 [E.J. Pratt], 'Comment,' in *Pursuits Amateur and Academic: The Selected Prose of E.J. Pratt*, ed. Susan Gingell (Toronto: University of Toronto Press 1995), p. 114
2 'Principles of Poetic Art,' in *Pursuits Amateur and Academic*, p. 234
3 E.J. Pratt, 'Memories of Newfoundland,' in *E.J. Pratt on His Life and Poetry*, ed. Susan Gingell (Toronto: University of Toronto Press 1983), p. 8
4 Sandra Djwa, *E.J. Pratt: The Evolutionary Vision* (Toronto and Montreal: Copp Clark / McGill-Queen's University Press 1974), p. 20
5 Pratt writes: 'the sense of conquest over Nature ... the trust in science for the

prevention of the grosser human calamities' ('Memories of Newfoundland,' p. 7).

6 Frederick J. Hoffman, 'The Temper of the Twenties,' in *Backgrounds to Modern Literature*, ed. John Oliver Perry (San Francisco: Chandler 1968), pp. 59–69

7 Northrop Frye, Introduction, *The Collected Poems of E.J. Pratt*, 2nd ed., ed. Northrop Frye (Toronto: Macmillan 1958), p. xv

8 See Edna Froese, 'E.J. Pratt as Lyricist,' *Canadian Poetry* 30 (Spring/Summer 1992), 19; Robert Gibbs, 'A True Voice: Pratt as a Lyric Poet,' in *The E.J. Pratt Symposium*, ed. Glenn Clever (Ottawa: University of Ottawa Press 1977); and Germaine Warkentin, 'The Aesthetics of E.J. Pratt's Shorter Poems,' in *The E.J. Pratt Symposium*.

9 David Perkins, *A History of Modern Poetry: Modernism and After* (Cambridge, Mass.: Harvard University Press 1987), p. v

10 Viola Pratt, interview by Sandra Djwa, 29 October 1978. See Arthur Phelps, 'Tendencies in Modern Poetry,' *Canadian Magazine* 48 (1917), 523.

11 E.J. Pratt to D.C. Scott, letter, 18 January 1918

12 Roy Daniells, 'The Special Quality,' *Canadian Literature* 21 (Summer 1964), 10

13 A.J.M. Smith to Sandra Djwa, letter, 27 November 1974

14 E.J. Pratt, 'The Ice-Floes,' *Canadian Forum* 2.19 (April 1922), 591–3

15 E.J. Pratt, 'On Publishing,' in *E.J. Pratt on His Life and Poetry*, p. 33

16 Ezra Pound, 'A Few Don'ts by an Imagiste,' *Poetry: A Magazine of Verse* 1.1 (Oct. 1912), 200

17 Djwa, *E.J. Pratt: The Evolutionary Vision*, p. 38

18 As he later said: 'My friends say that *The Witches' Brew* was a psychological reaction against the doctorate, that I had to get hell out of my system before I could do anything worthy of serious consideration' (Pratt, 'On Publishing,' p. 34).

19 E.J. Pratt, 'Address on Wordsworth,' in *Pursuits Amateur and Academic*, p. 220

20 Barker Fairley, 'Pratt,' *Canadian Forum* 7.77 (Feb. 1927), 148–9

21 E.J. Pratt, 'Address on Wordsworth,' p. 222

22 E.J. Pratt, 'Address on Wordsworth,' p. 222

23 Irving Babbitt, *Rousseau and Romanticism* (Boston: Houghton Mifflin 1957), p. 130

24 E.J. Pratt, *Ten Selected Poems, with Notes* (Toronto: Macmillan 1947), p. 133

25 E.J. Pratt, 'The Titanic,' in *E.J. Pratt on His Life and Poetry*, pp. 99–100

26 D.G. Pitt, *E.J. Pratt: The Truant Years 1882–1927* (Toronto: University of Toronto Press 1984), pp. 9–10

27 Viola Pratt recalls that she drew Pratt's attention to this phrase (Viola Pratt, interview by Sandra Djwa, 19 January 1976).

28 Magdalene Redekop, 'Authority and the Margins of Escape in *Brébeuf and His Brethren*,' *Open Letter* 6.2–3 (Summer/Fall 1985), 48–9

29 Sandra Djwa, 'E.J. Pratt: Transitional Modern,' in *The E.J. Pratt Symposium*, pp. 64–5

30 Sandra Djwa, 'Digging into the Strata: Pratt's Modernism,' in *Bolder Flights: Essays on the Canadian Long Poem*, ed. Frank Tierney and Angela Robbeson (Ottawa: University of Ottawa Press 1998), pp. 65–80

31 E.J. Pratt to F.R. Scott, letter, 7 December 1944, F.R. Scott Papers, National Archives, Ottawa

32 E.J. Pratt, 'Canadian Poetry: Past and Present,' *University of Toronto Quarterly* 8 (Oct. 1938), 3

33 Sandra Djwa, Introduction, *E.J. Pratt: Complete Poems*, ed. Sandra Djwa and R.G. Moyles (Toronto: University of Toronto Press 1989), p. xviii

34 Perkins, *A History of Modern Poetry*, p. 113

35 Found in such poems as his 'The Parable of Puffsky' and 'A Prayer Medley.'

36 Dorothy Livesay, 'The Documentary Poem: A Canadian Genre,' in *Contexts of Canadian Criticism*, ed. Eli Mandel (Chicago: University of Chicago Press 1971), pp. 267–81

37 Earle Birney, *The Cow Jumped over the Moon: The Writing and Reading of Poetry* (Toronto: Holt, Rinehart and Winston), p. 35

38 See Sandra Djwa, 'A Developing Tradition,' *Essays on Canadian Writing* 21 (Spring 1981), 32–52.

39 Margaret Atwood, 'Poor Tom,' *Alphabet* 6 (June 1963), 52

40 Margaret Atwood, 'The Descent as Dissection,' *Canadian Forum*, March 1964, p. 280

41 James Reaney, Editorial, *Alphabet* 8 (June 1964), 5

42 Munro Beattie, 'E.J. Pratt,' in *Literary History of Canada*, ed. Carl F. Klinck (Toronto: University of Toronto Press 1965), p. 750

43 Frank Davey, 'E.J. Pratt: Apostle of Corporate Man,' *Canadian Literature* 43 (Winter 1970), 54–66

44 Smaro Kamboureli, *On the Edge of Genre: The Contemporary Canadian Long Poem* (Toronto: University of Toronto Press 1991), pp. 37, 29–33

45 Redekop, 'Authority and the Margins of Escape,' p. 58

46 See Frank Davey, 'Fort and Forest: Instability in the Symbolic Code in E.J. Pratt's *Brébeuf and His Brethren*,' in *Reading Canadian Reading* (Winnipeg:

Turnstone 1988), p. 167; and *Canadian Literary Power* (Edmonton: NeWest 1994), p. 283. See also Gwendolyn Guth, 'Virtu(e)al History: Interpolation in Pratt's *Brébeuf and His Brethren*,' in *Bolder Flights: Essays on the Canadian Long Poem*, p. 82.

Biographical Chronology

1882	born at Western Bay, Newfoundland, 4 February; third child of eight of the Rev. John Pratt, Yorkshire-born clergyman, and Fanny Pitts Knight, daughter of a Newfoundland sea captain
1888–1902	educated in outport schools and at the Methodist College, St John's, with a three-year intermission, 1897–1900, as a clerk in a dry-goods store
1902–4	teacher at Moreton's Harbour, a fishing village in Notre Dame Bay
1904–7	probationary minister in the Methodist ministry at Clarke's Beach–Cupids and Bell Island–Portugal Cove
1907–11	student in philosophy, Victoria College, University of Toronto; B.A., 1911
1912	received M.A. degree, University of Toronto
1913	received B.D. degree; ordained into the Methodist ministry
1913–20	demonstrator-lecturer in psychology, University of Toronto; assistant minister in a number of churches around Streetsville, Ontario
1917	received Ph.D. from University of Toronto – thesis, *Studies in Pauline Eschatology and Its Background*, published in Toronto; *Rachel: A Sea Story of Newfoundland in Verse* printed privately in New York
1918	married Viola Whitney (B.A., Victoria College, 1913), 20 August
1920	joined Department of English, Victoria College

1921	birth of only child, Mildred Claire
1923	*Newfoundland Verse,* first commercially published book of poems
1925	*The Witches' Brew* published in London
1926	*Titans* published in London; *The Witches' Brew,* in Toronto
1927	*The Iron Door (An Ode)* published in Toronto
1930	appointed professor, Department of English, Victoria College; elected fellow of the Royal Society of Canada; *The Roosevelt and the Antinoe* published in New York; *Verses of the Sea,* with introduction by Charles G.D. Roberts, published in Toronto
1930–52	taught summer school at Dalhousie, Queen's, and the University of British Columbia
1932	*Many Moods* published in Toronto
1935	*The Titanic* published in Toronto
1936	one of the founders and first editor, from January 1936 to August 1943, of *Canadian Poetry Magazine*
1937	*The Fable of the Goats and Other Poems* published in Toronto, winner of the Governor-General's Award
1938	appointed senior professor, Victoria College
1940	*Brébeuf and His Brethren* published in Toronto, winner of the Governor-General's Award; awarded the Royal Society's Lorne Pierce Gold Medal for distinguished service to Canadian literature
1941	*Dunkirk* published in Toronto
1943	*Still Life and Other Verse* published in Toronto
1944	*Collected Poems* published in Toronto
1945	*Collected Poems,* with introduction by William Rose Benét, published in New York; *They Are Returning* published in Toronto; received D. Litt. from University of Manitoba, first honorary degree (others: LL. D., Queen's 1948; D.C.L., Bishop's 1949; D. Litt., McGill 1949; D. Litt., Toronto 1953; D. Litt., Assumption 1955; D. Litt., New Brunswick 1957; D. Litt., Western Ontario 1957; D. Litt., Memorial 1961)
1946	created Companion of the Order of St Michael and St George in the King's Honours List
1947	*Behind the Log* and *Ten Selected Poems* published in Toronto

1952	*Towards the Last Spike* published in Toronto, winner of the Governor-General's Award; awarded the University of Alberta Gold Medal for distinguished service to Canadian literature; member of the editorial board, from 20 December 1952 to 13 September 1958, of *Saturday Night*
1953	retired from Victoria College; appointed professor emeritus of English
1955	elected honorary president of the Canadian Authors' Association
1957	received Canada Council award on seventy-fifth birthday
1958	*The Collected Poems of E.J. Pratt*, 2nd edition, edited by Northrop Frye, published in Toronto
1959	received Civic Award of Merit from the City of Toronto
1961	received the Canada Council Medal for distinction in the field of literature
1963	elected honorary member of the Empire Club of Canada; elected first honorary member of the Arts and Letters Club
1964	died in Toronto, 26 April

E.J. PRATT

Selected Poems

THE ICE-FLOES

Dawn from the Foretop! Dawn from the Barrel!
    A scurry of feet with a roar overhead;
The master-watch wildly pointing to Northward,
    Where the herd in front of *The Eagle* was spread!

Steel-planked and sheathed like a battleship's nose,
She battered her path through the drifting floes;
. Past slob and growler we drove, and rammed her
Into the heart of the patch and jammed her.
There were hundreds of thousands of seals, I'd swear,
In the stretch of that field – 'white harps' to spare   10
For a dozen such fleets as had left that spring
To share in the general harvesting.
The first of the line, we had struck the main herd;
The day was ours, and our pulses stirred
In that brisk, live hour before the sun,
At the thought of the load and the sweepstake won.

We stood on the deck as the morning outrolled
On the fields its tissue of orange and gold,
And lit up the ice to the north in the sharp,
Clear air; each mother-seal and its 'harp'   20
Lay side by side; and as far as the range
Of the patch ran out we saw that strange,
And unimaginable thing
That sealers talk of every spring –
The 'bobbing-holes' within the floes
That neither wind nor frost could close;
Through every hole a seal could dive,
And search, to keep her brood alive,
A hundred miles it well might be,
For food beneath that frozen sea.   30
Round sunken reef and cape she would rove,
And though the wind and current drove
The ice-fields many leagues that day,

We knew she would turn and find her way
Back to the hole, without the help
Of compass or log, to suckle her whelp –
Back to that hole in the distant floes,
And smash her way up with her teeth and nose.
But we flung those thoughts aside when the shout
Of command from the master-watch rang out.   40

Assigned to our places in watches of four –
    Over the rails in a wild carouse,
    Two from the port and starboard bows,
Two from the broadsides – off we tore,
In the breathless rush for the day's attack,
With the speed of hounds on a caribou's track.
With the rise of the sun we started to kill,
A seal for each blow from the iron bill
Of our gaffs. From the nose to the tail we ripped them,
    And laid their quivering carcasses flat   50
On the ice; then with our knives we stripped them·
    For the sake of the pelt and its lining of fat.
With three fathoms of rope we laced them fast,
    With their skins to the ice to be easy to drag,
With our shoulders galled we drew them, and cast
    Them in thousands around the watch's flag.
Then, with our bodies begrimed with the reek
    Of grease and sweat from the toil of the day,
    We made for *The Eagle*, two miles away,
At the signal that flew from her mizzen peak.   60
And through the night, as inch by inch
    She reached the pans with the 'harps' piled high,
    We hoisted them up as the hours filed by
To the sleepy growl of the donkey-winch.

Over the bulwarks again we were gone,
With the first faint streaks of a misty dawn;
Fast as our arms could swing we slew them,
Ripped them, 'sculped' them, roped and drew them

To the pans where the seals in pyramids rose
Around the flags on the central floes,   70
Till we reckoned we had nine thousand dead
By the time the afternoon had fled;
And that an added thousand or more
Would beat the count of the day before.
So back again to the patch we went
To haul, before the day was spent,
Another load of four 'harps' a man,
To make the last the record pan.
And not one of us saw, as we gaffed, and skinned,
And took them in tow, that the north-east wind   80
Had veered off-shore; that the air was colder;
    That the signs of recall were there to the south,
The flag of *The Eagle*, and the long, thin smoulder
    That drifted away from her funnel's mouth.
Not one of us thought of the speed of the storm
    That hounded our tracks in the day's last chase
(For the slaughter was swift, and the blood was warm),
    Till we felt the first sting of the snow in our face.
We looked south-east, where, an hour ago,
    Like a smudge on the sky-line, someone had seen   90
The Eagle, and thought he had heard her blow
    A note like a warning from her sirene.
We gathered in knots, each man within call
    Of his mate, and slipping our ropes, we sped,
Plunging our way through a thickening wall
    Of snow that the gale was driving ahead.
We ran with the wind on our shoulder; we knew
That the night had left us this only clue
Of the track before us, though with each wail
That grew to the pang of a shriek from the gale,   100
Some of us swore that *The Eagle* screamed
Right off to the east; to others it seemed
On the southern quarter and near, while the rest
    Cried out with every report that rose
    From the strain and the rend of the wind on the floes

That *The Eagle* was firing her guns to the west.
And some of them turned to the west, though to go
    Was madness – we knew it and roared, but the notes
Of our warning were lost as a fierce gust of snow
    Eddied, and strangled the words in our throats.   110
Then we felt in our hearts that the night had swallowed
    All signals, the whistle, the flare, and the smoke
To the south; and like sheep in a storm we followed
    Each other; like sheep we huddled and broke.
Here one would fall as hunger took hold
Of his step; here one would sleep as the cold
Crept into his blood, and another would kneel
Athwart the body of some dead seal,
And with knife and nails would tear it apart,
To flesh his teeth in its frozen heart.   120
And another dreamed that the storm was past,
    And raved of his bunk and brandy and food,
And *The Eagle* near, though in that blast
    The mother was fully as blind as her brood.
Then we saw, what we feared from the first – dark places
Here and there to the left of us, wide, yawning spaces
Of water; the fissures and cracks had increased
    Till the outer pans were afloat, and we knew,
As they drifted along in the night to the east,
    By the cries we heard, that some of our crew   130
Were borne to the sea on those pans and were lost.
    And we turned with the wind in our faces again,
    And took the snow with its lancing pain,
Till our eye-balls cracked with the salt and the frost;
Till only iron and fire that night
    Survived on the ice as we stumbled on;
As we fell and rose and plunged – till the light
    In the south and east disclosed the dawn,
And the sea heaving with floes – and then,
The Eagle in wild pursuit of her men.   140

And the rest is as a story told,
    Or a dream that belonged to a dim, mad past,
Of a March night and a north wind's cold,
    Of a voyage home with a flag half-mast;
Of twenty thousand seals that were killed
    To help to lower the price of bread;
Of the muffled beat ... of a drum ... that filled
    A nave ... at our count of sixty dead.

THE TOLL OF THE BELLS

I

We gave them at the harbour every token –
    The ritual of the guns, and at the mast
    The flag half-high, and as the cortege passed,
All that remained by our dumb hearts unspoken.
And what within the band's low requiem,
    In footfall or in head uncovered fails
    Of final tribute, shall at altar-rails
Around a chancel soon be offered them.

And now a throbbing organ-prelude dwells
    On the eternal story of the sea;   10
    Following in undertone, the Litany
Ends like a sobbing wave; and now begins
A tale of life's fore-shortened days; now swells
The tidal triumph of Corinthians.

II

But neither trumpet-blast, nor the hoarse din
    Of guns, nor the drooped signals from those mute
    Banners, could find a language to salute
The frozen bodies that the ship brought in.
To-day the vaunt is with the grave. Sorrow

Has raked up faith and burned it like a pile   20
    Of driftwood, scattering the ashes while
Cathedral voices anthemed God's To-morrow.

Out from the belfries of the town there swung
    Great notes that held the winds and the pagan roll
    Of open seas within their measured toll,
Only the bells' slow ocean tones, that rose
And hushed upon the air, knew how to tongue
That Iliad of Death upon the floes.

COME NOT THE SEASONS HERE

Comes not the springtime here,
    Though the snowdrop came,
And the time of the cowslip is near,
    For a yellow flame
Was found in a tuft of green;
    And the joyous shout
    Of a child rang out
That a cuckoo's eggs were seen.

Comes not the summer here,
    Though the cowslip be gone,   10
Though the wild rose blow as the year
    Draws faithfully on;
Though the face of the poppy be red
    In the morning light,
    And the ground be white
With the bloom of the locust shed.

Comes not the autumn here,
    Though someone said
He found a leaf in the sere
    By an aster dead;   20
And knew that the summer was done,

For a herdsman cried
That his pastures were brown in the sun,
    And his wells were dried.

Nor shall the winter come,
    Though the elm be bare,
And every voice be dumb
    On the frozen air;
But the flap of a waterfowl
    In the marsh alone,   30
Or the hoot of a horned owl
    On a glacial stone.

THE DROWNING

The rust of hours,
    Through a year of days,
Has dulled the edge of the pain;
    But at night
    A wheel in my sleep
Grinds it smooth and keen.

By day I remember
    A face that was lit
With the softness of human pattern;
    But at night   10
    It is changed in my sleep
To a bygone carved in chalk.

A cottage inland
    Through a year of days
Has latched its doors on the sea;
    But at night
    I return in my sleep
To the cold, green lure of the waters.

THE FOG

It stole in on us like a foot-pad,
Somewhere out of the sea and air,
Heavy with rifling Polaris
And the Seven Stars.
It left our eyes untouched,
But took our sight,
And then,
Silently,
It drew the song from our throats,
And the supple bend from our ash-blades;
For the bandit,   10
With occult fingering,
Had tangled up
The four threads of the compass,
And fouled the snarl around our dory.

THE GROUND SWELL

Three times we heard it calling with a low,
        Insistent note; at ebb-tide on the noon;
        And at the hour of dusk, when the red moon
    Was rising and the tide was on the flow;
    Then, at the hour of midnight once again,
        Though we had entered in and shut the door
        And drawn the blinds, it crept up from the shore
    And smote upon a bedroom window-pane;
Then passed away as some dull pang that grew
Out of the void before Eternity   10
        Had fashioned out an edge for human grief;
    Before the winds of God had learned to strew
    His harvest-sweepings on a winter sea
        To feed the primal hungers of a reef.

THE SHARK

He seemed to know the harbour,
So leisurely he swam;
His fin,
Like a piece of sheet-iron,
Three-cornered,
And with knife-edge,
Stirred not a bubble
As it moved
With its base-line on the water.

His body was tubular
And tapered   10
And smoke-blue,
And as he passed the wharf
He turned,
And snapped at a flat-fish
That was dead and floating.
And I saw the flash of a white throat,
And a double row of white teeth,
And eyes of metallic grey,
Hard and narrow and slit.

Then out of the harbour,   20
With that three-cornered fin
Shearing without a bubble the water
Lithely,
Leisurely,
He swam –
That strange fish,
Tubular, tapered, smoke-blue,
Part vulture, part wolf,
Part neither – for his blood was cold.

BEFORE AN ALTAR
(*After Gueudecourt*)

Break we the bread once more,
    The cup we pass around –
No, rather let us pour
    This wine upon the ground;

And on the salver lay
    The bread – there to remain.
Perhaps, some other day,
    Shrovetide will come again.

Blurred is the rubric now,
    And shadowy the token,   10
When blood is on the brow,
    And the frail body broken.

NEWFOUNDLAND

Here the tides flow,
And here they ebb;
Not with that dull, unsinewed tread of waters
Held under bonds to move
Around unpeopled shores –
Moon-driven through a timeless circuit
Of invasion and retreat;
But with a lusty stroke of life
Pounding at stubborn gates,
That they might run   10
Within the sluices of men's hearts,
Leap under throb of pulse and nerve,
And teach the sea's strong voice
To learn the harmonies of new floods,
The peal of cataract,
And the soft wash of currents

Against resilient banks,
Or the broken rhythms from old chords
Along dark passages
That once were pathways of authentic fires.   20

Red is the sea-kelp on the beach,
Red as the heart's blood,
Nor is there power in tide or sun
To bleach its stain.
It lies there piled thick
Above the gulch-line.
It is rooted in the joints of rocks,
It is tangled around a spar,
It covers a broken rudder,
It is red as the heart's blood,   30
And salt as tears.

Here the winds blow,
And here they die,
Not with that wild, exotic rage
That vainly sweeps untrodden shores,
But with familiar breath
Holding a partnership with life,
Resonant with the hopes of spring,
Pungent with the airs of harvest.
They call with the silver fifes of the sea,   40
They breathe with the lungs of men,
They are one with the tides of the sea,
They are one with the tides of the heart,
They blow with the rising octaves of dawn,
They die with the largo of dusk,
Their hands are full to the overflow,
In their right is the bread of life,
In their left are the waters of death.

Scattered on boom
And rudder and weed   50
Are tangles of shells;

Some with backs of crusted bronze,
And faces of porcelain blue,
Some crushed by the beach stones
To chips of jade;
And some are spiral-cleft
Spreading their tracery on the sand
In the rich veining of an agate's heart;
And others remain unscarred,
To babble of the passing of the winds.   60

Here the crags
Meet with winds and tides –
Not with that blind interchange
Of blow for blow
That spills the thunder of insentient seas;
But with the mind that reads assault
In crouch and leap and the quick stealth,
Stiffening the muscles of the waves.
Here they flank the harbours,
Keeping watch   70
On thresholds, altars and the fires of home,
Or, like mastiffs,
Over-zealous,
Guard too well.

Tide and wind and crag,
Sea-weed and sea-shell
And broken rudder –
And the story is told
Of human veins and pulses,
Of eternal pathways of fire,   80
Of dreams that survive the night,
Of doors held ajar in storms.

THE WITCHES' BREW

Perched on a dead volcanic pile,
Now charted as a submerged peak,
Near to a moon-washed coral isle,
A hundred leagues from Mozambique,
Three water-witches of the East,
Under the stimulus of rum,
Decided that the hour had come
To hold a Saturnalian feast,
In course of which they hoped to find
For their black art, once and for all,   10
The true effect of alcohol
Upon the cold, aquatic mind.
From two Phoenicians who were drowned,
The witches three (whose surnames ran
Lulu, Ardath, Maryan)
Had by an incantation found
A cavern near the coast of Crete,
And saw, when they had entered in,
A blacksmith with a dorsal fin,
Whose double pectorals and webbed feet   20
Proved – while his dusky shoulders swung –
His breed to be of land and water,
Last of great Neptune's stock that sprung
From Vulcan's union with his daughter.
The sisters' terms accepted, he,
Together with his family,
Left his native Cretan shore
To dig the witches' copper ore
Out of their sub-aquaceous mines
In the distant Carolines,   30
And forge a cauldron that might stand,
Stationary and watertight,
A thousand cubits in its height,
Its width a thousand breadths as spanned

By the smith's gigantic hand,
So that each fish, however dry,
Might have, before the Feast was through,
His own demonstrable supply
Of this Pan-Oceanic brew.
A thousand leagues or so away   40
Down the Pacific to Cape Horn,
And Southwards from Magellan lay
A table-land to which was borne
This cauldron from the Carolines,
For here, as well the sisters knew,
The Spanish conquerors of Peru
Had stored their rich and ancient wines,
About the time the English burst
Upon their galleons under Drake,
Who sank or captured them to slake   50
A vast Elizabethan thirst.
With pick and bar the Cretan tore
His way to the interior
Of every sunken ship whose hold
Had wines almost four centuries old.
Upon the broad Magellan floors,
Great passage-way from West to East,
Were also found more recent stores,
The products of a stronger yeast.
For twenty years or thereabout,   60
The Bacchanals of Western nations,
Scenting universal drought,
Had searched the ocean to find out
The most secluded ports and stations,
Where unmolested they might go
'To serve their god while here below,'
With all the strength of their libations.
So to the distant isles there sailed,
In honour of the ivy god,
Scores of log-loaded ships that hailed   70
From Christiania to Cape Cod

With manifests entitled *ham,*
Corn beef, molasses, chamois milk,
Cotton, Irish linen, silk,
Pickles, dynamite and *jam,*
And myriad substances whose form
Dissolved into quite other freights,
Beneath the magic of a storm
That scattered them around the Straits;
For this is what the blacksmith read,   80
While raking up the ocean bed: –
Budweiser, Guinness, Schlitz (in kegs),
Square Face Gin and *Gordon's Dry,*
O'Brien's, Burke's and *Johnny Begg's,*
Munich, Bock, and *Seagram's Rye,*
Dewar's, Hennessey's 3 Star,
Glenlivet, White Horse and *Old Parr,*
With *Haig and Haig, Canadian Club,*
Jamaica Rum, and other brands
Known to imbibers in all lands   90
That stock from Brewery or Pub.
All these the Cretan, with the aid
Of his industrious progeny,
Drew to the cauldron, and there laid,
By order of the witches three,
The real foundation for the spree.

OTHER INGREDIENTS

To make a perfect fish menu,
The witches found they had to place
Upon this alcoholic base
Great stacks of food and spices too.   100
Of all the things most edible
On which the souls of fish have dined,
That fish would sell their souls to find,
Most gracious to their sense of smell,

Is flesh exotic to their kind: –
Cold-blooded things yet not marine,
And not of earth, but half-between,
That live enclosed within the sand
Without the power of locomotion,
And mammal breeds whose blood is hot,   110
That court the sea but love it not,
That need the air but not the land, –
The Laodiceans of the ocean.
So in this spacious cauldron went
Cargoes of food and condiment.
Oysters fished from Behring Strait
Were brought and thrown in by the crate;
Spitzbergen scallops on half-shell,
Mussels, starfish, clams as well,
Limpets from the Hebrides,   120
Shrimps and periwinkles, these,
So celebrated as a stew,
Were meant to flavour up the brew.
Then for the more substantial fare,
The curried quarter of a tail
Hewn from a stranded Greenland whale,
A liver from a Polar bear,
A walrus' heart and pancreas,
A blind Auk from the coast of Java,
A bull moose that had died from gas   130
While eating toadstools near Ungava,
One bitter-cold November day;
Five sea-lion cubs were then thrown in,
Shot by the Cretan's javelin
In a wild fight off Uruguay,
With flippers fresh from the Azores,
Fijian kidneys by the scores,
Together with some pollywogs,
And kippered hocks of centipedes,
And the hind legs of huge bull frogs   140
Raked by the millions from the reeds
Of slimy Patagonian bogs.

Then before the copper lid
Was jammed upon the pyramid,
The sisters scattered on the top
Many a juicy lollipop;
Tongues from the Ganges crocodile,
Spawn from the delta of the Nile,
Hoofs of sheep and loins of goats,
Raised from foundered cattle-boats –   150
Titbits they knew might blend with hops,
Might strengthen rum or season rye,
From Zulu hams and Papuan chops
To filets mignons from Shanghai.
Now while volcanic fires burned,
Making the cauldron fiercely hot,
Lulu with her ladle churned
The pungent contents of the pot,
From which distinctive vapours soon
Rose palpably before the view.   160
Then Ardath summoned a typhoon
Which as it swooped upon the stew,
And swept around the compass, bore
To every sea and every shore
The tidings of the witches' Feast.
And from the West and from the East,
And from the South and from the North,
From every bay and strait and run,
From the Tropics to the Arctic sun,
The Parliament of fish came forth,   170
Lured by a smell surpassing far
The potencies of boiling tar,
For essences were in this brew
Unknown to blubber or to glue,
And unfamiliar to the nose
Of sailors hardened as they are
To every unctuous wind that blows

From Nantucket to Baccalieu.
The crudest oil one ever lit
Was frankincense compared to it.   180
It entered Hades, and the airs
Resuscitated the Immortals;
It climbed the empyrean stairs
And drove St. Peter from the portals.

DEFENSIVE MEASURES

According to the witches' plan,
All life whose blood did not run true
Must be excluded from the brew;
Each earthly thing from snail to man,
And every mammal of the sea
Was for that night an enemy.   190
And so the smith from ocean hoards
Had gathered masts and spars and boards
Of ships, with cutlasses and swords,
And countless pikes and spears, and made
With them a towering palisade.
And to the top thereof was sent,
To guard the brew, a warrior, –
The bravest of the ranks of war,
And deaf to bribe or argument.
To neither shark nor swordfish fell   200
The honours of the sentinel,
For of all fighters there, the star
Was Tom the cat from Zanzibar.

THE SEA-CAT

It's not for us to understand
How life on earth began to be,
How forms that lived within the sea
Should leave the water for the land;

Or how – (Satan alone may trace
The dark enigma of this race)
When feline variants, so far   210
Removed as tabs and tigers are,
Preferred, when they had left the shore,
The jungle and the kitchen floor –
That this uncouth, primordial cat
Should keep his native habitat.
Yet here he was, and one might find
In crouch and slink and instant spring
Upon a living, moving thing,
The common genus of his kind.
But there were qualities which he   220
Derived not from his family tree.
No leopard, lynx or jaguar
Could match this cat from Zanzibar
For whiskers that from ear to chin
Ran round to decorate his grin.
And something wilder yet than that
Lay in the nature of this cat.
It's said that mariners by night,
When near a dangerous coast-line, might
Recover bearings from the light   230
Of some strange thing that swam and gleamed;
A Salamander it might be,
They said, or Lucifer that streamed
His fiery passage through the sea.
But in this banquet place not one
Of all the revellers could fail
To solve the riddle when Tom spun
A vast ecliptic as his tail,
A fiery comet, and his fur
Electrified each banqueter.   240
So the three beldams there agreed
No alien could invade the hall
If one of such a fighting breed
Were placed upon the fortress wall;

For who, they asked, of mortal creatures
Could claim more fearful derivation
Than Tom with his Satanic features
And his spontaneous conflagration?

THE FLIGHT OF THE IMMORTALS

Close to the dunnest hour of night,
Sniffing the odour of the brew,   250
Their bat-wings oiled for water flight,
The Devil and his legions flew,
Smashing the record from Hell's Gates
By plumbline to Magellan Straits.
Far in their wake, but hurrying fast
For fear the odour might not last
Till morning, came a spectral band
Weary from Hades – that dry land.

INVENTORY OF HADES

1. Statesmen and apothecaries,
   Poets, plumbers, antiquaries,   260
   Premiers with their secretaries,
   Home and foreign missionaries,
   And writers of obituaries.

2. Mediaeval disputants,
   Mystics in perpetual trance,
   Philosophers in baggy pants,
   Puritans to whom the chance
   Had never come in life to dance
   Save when the dreadful circumstance
   Of death removed their maiden aunts.   270

3. Scribes with wide phylacteries,
   Publicists and Sadducees,
   Scholars, saints and Ph.D.'s.

4. Doctors, auctioneers and bakers,
   Dentists, diplomats and fakirs,
   Clergymen and undertakers.

5. Rich men, poor men, fools and sots,
   Logicians, tying Shades in knots,
   Pagans, Christians, Hottentots,
   Deacons good and bad in spots,   280
   Farmers with their Wyandots.

AN HOUR LATER

Not since the time the sense of evil
Caught our first parents by surprise,
While eating fruit in Paradise,
One fateful morning, had the Devil,
Used as he was to steam and smoke,
Beheld such chaos as now broke
Upon his horny, bloodshot eyes.
Prince of the Power of the air,
Lord of terrestrial things as well   290
As subterranean life in Hell,
He had till now not been aware
How this great watery domain
Might be enclosed within his reign;
Such things as fish, cold-blooded, wet,
Had served no end of his as yet.
The serpent could be made to lie,
And hence fit agent to deceive
A trustful female such as Eve;
But he, though cold, at least was dry.   300
For all his wily strategy
Since time began, the Devil saw
No way to circumvent the sea.
The fish transgressed no moral law,
They had no principles, no creed,

No prayers, no Bibles, and no Church,
No Reason's holy light to read
The truth and no desire to search.
Hence from Dame Nature's ancient way
Their fins had never learned to stray.   310
They ate and drank and fought, it's true,
And when the zest was on they slew;
But yet their most tempestuous quarrels
Were never prejudiced by morals;
As Nature had at the beginning
Created them, so they remained –
Fish with cold blood no skill had trained
To the warm arts of human sinning.

THE MIDNIGHT REVELS AS OBSERVED BY THE SHADES

'The witches' device for the equitable distribution of
the liquor consisted in the construction of tens of   320
thousands of stopcocks and bungs which were fitted
into the perforations of the cauldron, and graded so
nicely in calibre that every species of fish from a sar-
dine to a shark might find perfect oral adjustment. To
provide against all contingencies they had, in addi-
tion, furnished each amphibious member of the Cre-
tan family with a ladle so that the weaker fish, unable
to reach the taps and bung-holes, might be supplied
at the surface of the water. But notwithstanding all
their powers of divination, the scheme came very near   330
to being wrecked, first, by the tremendous congrega-
tion of fish, and secondly, by the advent of the wild
hordes from Hades. Now it was not within the coun-
sels of either the witches or the Devil that the test
should be prejudiced by the Shades. If they arrived at
all, their rôle would be severely restricted to that of
an audience. But the momentum of their rush carried
them up against the sides of the cauldron with such a

terrific impact that a vertical crack, one hundred
cubits long, was made near the top. Fortunately, how-   340
ever, for the experiment, the Shades were immedi-
ately driven back to the rear by a battalion of imps,
and the crack served the purpose of allowing suffi-
cient liquor to trickle through into the sea to account
for the inebriation of such fish as those whose ner-
vous constitution could not stand the undiluted
draughts.'

Byron:
Now what the devil can be hid
In whisky straight, or punch or sherbet,
To give the doldrums to that squid,   350
Or plant the horrors in that turbot?
I never dreamed a calamary
Could get so dead stiff on Canary.

Wolsey:
I've watched the effect of many a dram
On Richmond and on Buckingham;
And with good reasons have I mourned
To see my Royal Henry corned;
And many a noble prelate losing
His benefice by one night's boozing.
But till this hour I never knew   360
What alcoholic draughts could do
To change a salmon or a hake
Into a paralytic rake;
Or how a drunken sturgeon felt
When fever burned inside his pelt.

Campeggio:
Now by my Hat and Clement's foot,
What kind of devil must have dwelt
Inside a liquor that could put
Delirium tremens in a smelt?

Pepys:
What maddening impulse makes that shark,   370
Which ought, by its own nature, choose a
Mate of its own kind, to spark
With that gelatinous Medusa?

Paracelsus:
They say that mortals may go mad
Beneath thy beams, Divinest Luna;
But how canst thou debauch a shad,
Create an epileptic tuna?

Gulliver:
I saw a sardine just now glut
His hunger on a halibut.

Samuel Butler:
How could a thing like rye or hops stir   380
The turgid corpus of a lobster?
And thus induce an inflammation
Within the shell of a crustacean?

Samson:
I saw a small phlegmatic mullet
Holding a dogfish by the gullet.

Saint Patrick:
Such crimes as from the sea arise
Beat out the days of old Gomorrah;
Had I not seen it with my eyes
I would not have believed, begorra!

THE CHARGE OF THE SWORDFISH

Now when, beneath the riotous drinking,   390
The witches found the liquor sinking

So low their ladles couldn't reach it,
The blacksmith with a blazing larynx
Organized a swordfish phalanx
And charged the cauldron plate to breach it.
Back from its copper flanks they fell,
The smith had done his work too well.

A Greek:
From such a race of myrmidons
Our heroes and our Marathons.

Fabius Maximus:
It's but the fury of despair.   400

A French General:
Magnifique! mais ce n'est pas la guerre.

Napoleon:
By some such wild demonic means
My astral promise was undone.

Nelson:
By spirits like to such marines
Trafalgar and the Nile were won.

Carlyle:
Full ten feet thick that plate was wrought,
And yet those swordfish tried to ram it;
Unthinking fools! I never thought
The sea so full of numskulls, dammit!

Satan:
Now by my hoof, this recipe   410
Is worth a million souls to me;
But lo! what mortal creature there
Grins, haunched upon the parapet,
Whose fierce, indomitable stare
I long have dreamed of, but not met?

Maryan:
Most sovereign and most sulphurous lord!
We, with the help of Cretans, made
This circumambient palisade
Of this great height and strength, to ward
Off such invaders as might mar   420
Our feast, and then as sentinel –
Chief vigilante out of hell –
We stationed HIM from Zanzibar.

Satan:
Good! From such audacious seed
Sprang Heaven's finest, fallen breed,
Maryan! Ardath! Lulu!
Try out upon this cat, the brew.

THE SUPREME TEST

Now it was clear to every Shade
That some great wonder was before them,
As Tom upon the palisade   430
Emptied, as fast as Lulu bore them,
The flasks upon the ocean wagon.
And clear it was when Tom had cleaned
The liquor from the hundredth flagon,
The Shades then saw Hell's darkest fiend, –
A sea-cat with an awful jag-on.

Up to this time, he did not see
Upon the wide expanse of grey
A single thing approach his way
Which he might call his enemy.   440
He spent the hours upon the rim,
Leaping, dancing, rarely sitting,
Always grinning, always spitting,
Waiting for a foe to swim

Within his range, but through the night
Not a walrus offered fight, –
A most unusual night for him.
But with the hundredth flagon drink,
He spat at his inactive fate,
And moving closer to the brink,   450
Began more madly to gyrate.
Upon his face, ironic, grim,
A resolution was ingrained,
If fish would not come unto him
To offer battle, what remained
But that his fighting blood would freeze
Unless he were allowed to go,
Ranging at will upon the seas,
To fight and conquer every foe?
With that, into the cavernous deep   460
He took a ghastly, flying leap.

Gaping, breathless, every Shade
Watched the course of the wild-cat's raid;
And never was an errand run
With means and end so much at one.
For from his birth he was imbued
With hatred of his racial kind;
A more inveterate, blasting feud
Within the world one could not find.
His stock were traitors to the sea,   470
Had somehow learned the ways of earth,
The need of air, the mystery
Of things warm-blooded, and of birth.
To avenge this shameful derogation,
He had, upon his final flask,
Resolved to carry out his task, –
To wit: – the full extermination,
First, of his nearest order, male
And female, then the breed cetacean;
Grampus, porpoise, dolphin, whale, –   480

Humpback, Rorqual, Black and White;
Then the walrus, lion, hood,
Seals of all orders; these he would
Just as they came, in single fight,
Or in the fortunes of mêlée,
Challenge as his lawful prey.

The Blacksmith:
I never knew an ocean steed
Develop such demonic speed.

Sir Isaac Newton:
How he maintains that lightning rate,
Now in air and now in water,   490
And carries on such heavy slaughter,
Is more than I can formulate.

Blake:
The tiger, though in stretch of limb
And heft of bone is larger; still,
For straight uxoricidal will
Is but a lamb compared to him.

Bottom:
What humour is it makes him flail
His tawny quarters with that tail?

Owen Glendower:
Did any electrician mark
The explosive nature of that spark?   500

Benjamin Franklin:
I did in truth, but cannot quite
See, on the basis of my kite,
How such a flame should always sit
Upon a wild-cat's caudal tip.

Aesop:
Or what blind fury makes him whip
His smoking sides to capture it –
An ignis fatuus that eludes
The cat's most sanguinary moods.

Euclid:
The reasons for the circles lie
Within the nature of the thing;   510
This cat must run around a ring
If he would catch his tail. But why
So bloodily he chaseth it
Is past the compass of my wit.

Johnny Walker:
Just why this wild-cat should revolve,
Leaving his nether tip uncaught,
And spend his energy for naught,
The denser Shades will never solve;
But (granting that the speed is quicker)
All we discerning spirits know   520
It's just the way a man would go,
Grant the night and grant the liquor.

Calvin:
If I had known that such mad brutes
Had found, before the world began,
A place within the cosmic plan,
They would have dished my Institutes.

THE RETURN OF THE CAT
Time – Morning

A half-point Nor'ard from the West,
A bluish-tinted spot of light,
Now deep below, now on the crest
Of a high wave, hove into sight;   530

And by the curves and speed it made,
Conviction came to every Shade
That here the monster was returning
With all those inner fires burning
That no destruction could assuage;
Though through the hours of the night
The floating victims of the fight
Showed how the wild-cat could engage
His foes; achieve his victories;
For those he could not kill outright   540
Had either died from heart-disease
Or passed out through a haemorrhage.
An unexpected wonder met
His rolling, unabated eye –
For when he reached the parapet
He found the witches' cauldron dry.
And there was something which surprised
Him even more; the drunken riot
Was followed by a holy quiet;
The fish lay dead or paralysed;   550
No witch this time came forth to serve
His inbred hunger for assault
With either rum or wine or malt.
The thing told heavily on his nerve,
That near that massive banquet place
Not one lone member of his race,
Outside the fortress or within,
Survived to give him grin for grin,
Or swish a tail across his face.
And so this wild-cat, now bereft   560
Of all of life's amenities,
Took one blood-curdling leap and left
Magellan's for the vacant seas.
Sullen and dangerous he ripped
A gleaming furrow through the water,
Magnificently still equipped
For combat with rapine and slaughter.

Now with his tail electro-tipped,
Swiftly but leisurely he made
Around the steaming palisade   570
A blazing spiral which outshone
The fiercest glow of Acheron.
Then suddenly, as if aware,
By a deep ferment in his soul
Or something psychic in his hair,
Of some ulterior, mystic goal,
He sharply turned, began a lonely
Voyage pregnant of immortal raids
And epic plunder. But the Shades
Saw him no more in the flesh. Only   580
To Satan and the witches three
(In touch with his galvanic tail,
By more occulted masonry)
Appeared a phosphorescent trail
That headed for the Irish Sea.

SEA-GULLS

For one carved instant as they flew,
The language had no simile –
Silver, crystal, ivory
Were tarnished. Etched upon the horizon blue,
The frieze must go unchallenged, for the lift
And carriage of the wings would stain the drift
Of stars against a tropic indigo
Or dull the parable of snow.

Now settling one by one
Within green hollows or where curled   10
Crests caught the spectrum from the sun,
A thousand wings are furled.
No clay-born lilies of the world

Could blow as free
As those wild orchids of the sea.

THE SEA-CATHEDRAL

Vast and immaculate! No pilgrim bands,
In ecstasy before the Parian shrines,
Knew such a temple built by human hands,
With this transcendent rhythm in its lines;
Like an epic on the North Atlantic stream
It moved, and fairer than a Phidian dream.

Rich gifts unknown to kings were duly brought
At dawn and sunset and at cloudless noons,
Gifts from the sea-gods and the sun who wrought
Cascades and rainbows; flung them in festoons   10
Over the spires, with emerald, amethyst,
Sapphire and pearl out of their fiery mist.

And music followed when a litany,
Begun with the ring of foam bells and the purl
Of linguals as the edges cut the sea,
Crashed upon a rising storm with whirl
Of floes from far-off spaces where Death rides
The darkened belfries of his evening tides.

Within the sunlight, vast, immaculate!
Beyond all reach of earth in majesty,   20
It passed on southwards slowly to its fate –
To be drawn down by the inveterate sea
Without one chastening fire made to start
From altars built around its polar heart.

THE IRON DOOR
(An Ode)

Its features half-revealed in passing gleams
Which had no origin in earthly light,
Half-buried in a shifting mass of gloom
Which had no kinship with the face of night,
It had its station in the cliffs to stand
Against the clamour of eternal storm.
A giant hand
Had wrought it cruciform,
And placed deep shadows on the sunken panels,
Then in ironic jest,   10
Had carven out the crest
Of death upon the lintel.
Out of some Plutonian cave
It had been brought, and hung
Within its granite architrave.
I saw no latch or knocker on the door;
It seemed the smith designed it to be swung
But once, then closed forevermore.

The noise as of stubborn waters
Came in from a distant tide   20
To the beat of Time with slow,
Immeasurable stride.
From an uncharted quarter,
A wind began to blow,
And clouds to rise,
And underneath I saw the forms of mortals
Come and go,
And heard their cries, –
Fragments of speech, bewildered pleas,
That rose upon the pauses of the wind,   30
To hush upon the thunder of great seas.
And I thought what vain credulities

Should lure those human souls before
This vast inexorable door.

A music which the earth has only known
In the drab hours of its emptiness,
Or in the crisis of a fiery stress
Fell on my ear
In broken chord and troubled undertone.
For in this scale were tragic dreams   40
Awaiting unfulfilled decrees,
Some brighter than the purest gleams
Of seraphic ecstasies;
And some with hopes and fears
Which ran their paling way
Beyond the boundaries of availing prayer,
To dim-illumined reaches where the frore,
Dumb faces of despair
Gazed at their natural mirror in the door.
Then with the intermittent lull   50
Of wind and the dull
Break of transitory light,
Where rents in the shawl of the darkness
Revealed star-bursts and clouds in flight,
The cries were winged into language,
And forms which were featureless grew
Into the shapes of persons I knew
Who had tasted of life and had died.

Standing, anxious-eyed,
So small against the drift of space,   60
Enveloped by the gloom,
A boy searched for his father's face,
With that unvoiced appeal,
Which I remember, when he brought
A water-spaniel home one day,
Crushed beneath an engine-wheel;
And could not, by a rational way,

Be fully made to understand
That the mending of a lifeless body lay
Beyond the surgery of his father's hand.   70

A master mariner
Stood looking at the dull
Outline of a basalt spur,
Which in the fall and lift of fog,
Took on the shape of a gigantic hull.
He was old and travel-stained,
And his face grained
With rebel questionings
Urged with unsurrendered dignity;
For he had lost three sons at sea,   80
In a work of rescue known
To the high Atlantic records of that year.
Then as the crag took on the heaving motion
Of the fog, and the roar beat in his ear
Of surge afar off, he hallooed
The unknown admiral of the unknown ocean: –

Ahoy! The latitude and longitude?
Within these parts do the stars fail?
Is the sextant in default?
What signals and what codes prevail?   90
And is the taste of the water salt
About your reefs? Do you bury your dead
In the national folds?
Is the blood of your sailors red
When songs are sung
At the capstan bars? Are davits swung
At a call from the bridge when the night is dark,
And life like wine is spilled at a word to retrieve
The ravage of gales? Do courage and honour receive
On the wastes of your realm, their fair name and title?   100
As they do at our sea grey altars, – by your leave.

The fog closed in upon the spur,
The moving hull became a rock
Beneath the undulations, and the shock
Of winds from an unknown compass point cut short
The seaman's challenge till that sound again
From the hinter-sea broke through, and the swart
Impress on his face was stirred
By that insurgent flash
It once had known when after the report   110
Of his sons' loss on the High Seas, he had heard,
With a throb of pride,
The authentic word
From the Captain's lips,
Of the way the lads had died.

Another form appeared,
One whom I knew so well, – endeared
To me by all the natural ties which birth
And life and much-enduring love impose.
There was no trace   120
Of doubt or consternation on her face,   ·
Only a calm reliance that the door
Would open and disclose
Those who by swifter strides had gone ahead.
It was the same expression that she wore,
One evening, when with life-work done,
She went to bed,
In the serene belief that she could borrow
Sufficient strength out of the deep
Resources of a final sleep,   130
To overtake the others by the morrow.

A young man struck against the door
Demanding with his sanguine prime,
If the eternal steward registered
The unrecorded acts of time;
Not for himself insisting, but for one –

A stranger at his side –
For whom he had staked his life,
And on the daring odds had died.
No one had seen this young man go,   140
Or watched his plunge,
To save another whom he did not know.
Men only guessed the grimness of the struggle,
The body-tug, the valour of the deed,
For both were wrapped in the same green winding-sheet,
And blood-red was the colour of the weed
That lay around their feet.
Life for a life! The grim equivalent
Was vouched for by a sacred precedent;
But why the one who should have been redeemed   150
Should also pay the price
In the mutual sacrifice,
Was what he wished to know,
And urged upon the iron, blow by blow.

One who had sought for beauty all his days,
In form and colour, symphony and phrase,
Who had looked on gods made perfect by man's hand,
And Nature's glories on the sea and land, –
Now paused and wondered if the Creator's power,
Finding itself without a plan, was spent,   160
Leaving no relic at this vacant hour,
But a grave-stone and iron monument.

One who had sought for truth, but found the world
Outside the soul betray the one within,
Knew beacon signals but as casual fires,
And systems dead but for their power to spin,
Laid deeply to his heart his discipline,
Looked at the door where all the roadways closed,
And took it as the clench of evidence,
That the whole cosmic lie was predisposed,   170
Yet faced it with a fine indifference.

From somewhere near the threshold of the door,
A sharp insistent cry,
Above all other notes, arose, –
A miserere flung out to the sky,
Accompanied by a knocking
So importunate,
It might have been the great
Crescendo from the world of human souls,
Gathering strength to assail   180
The unhearing ears of God, or else to hail
His drowsy warders at the stellar poles.
Then through a rift
In a storm-cloud's eddying,
A greyness as of drift
Of winter snow in a belated spring,
Appeared upon a woman's face,
Eroded with much perishing.
The same dark burden under which the race
Reaches old age lay strapped upon her soul: –   190
That which collects in silence all the shame,
Through hidden passages of time and blood,
Then puts the open stigma of the blame
Upon a spotless name.

Why all the purchase of her pain,
And all her love could not atone
For that incalculable stain:
Why from that tortuous stream, –
Flesh of her flesh, bone of her bone, –
Should issue forth a Cain;   200
Were queries rained upon the iron plates.
'Twas not enough, it seemed, that her one gift
To life should be returned
To death, but that the Fates
Should so conspire
To have this one devoted offering burned
At such an altar, and by such a fire!

But what availed
A woman's cry against the arrest
Of hope when every rubric paled   210
Before the Theban mockery of the crest?

And at this darkest moment, as I dreamed,
The world with its dead weight of burdens seemed
To pause before the door, in drifts of sand,
And catacombs of rock and burial turf:
For every wind that raged upon the land
Had fled the nescient hollow of God's hand.
And all the music left upon its waters
Lay in the grey rotation of the surf,
With calls of seamen in great weariness   220
At their unanswered signals of distress;
And all the light remaining was bereft
Of colour and design in full eclipse;
No fragrance in the fields; no flowers left
But poppies with their charred autumnal lips.

Then with a suddenness beyond surprise,
When life was sinking in its cosmic trial,
And time was running down before my eyes,
New lights and shadows leaped upon the dial.

I have often heard it said that by some token,   230
As fragile as a shell,
Or a wish thrice-spoken,
The direst spell,
Though old and ringed of iron, might be broken;
That a fool's belief in the incredible,
Joined to the sounding magic of a name,
Makes up the stuff of miracle.
From such a source, it well might be,
Came this supreme authority.
It may have been the young man's claim   240
On life; or the old captain calling stormily

From sea to sea;
Or that root faith within a woman's heart;
Perhaps it was the white face of the child;
Or that last argument so wild
Of wing, of such tumultuous breath,
Its strange unreason might be made to prove
The case for life before the throne of death,
I do not know;
But in the dream the door began to move.   250

A light shot through the narrow cleft,
And shattered into hurrying gleams that rode
Upon the backs of clouds, and through deep hollows,
Like couriers with weird, prophetic code.
And as the door swung forward slowly,
A sound was heard, now like the beat
Of tides under the drive of winds,
Now like the swift deck-tread of feet,
Steadying to a drum
Which marshalled them to quarters, or the hum   260
Of multitudinous voices that would tell
Of the move of life invincible.

Then as the opening widened,
And the sound became more clear, I tried
With an insatiate hunger, to discover
The fountain of that light and life inside;
And with an exultation which outrode
The vaunt of raw untutored strength, I cried; –
Now shall be read
The faded symbols of the page which keeps   270
This hoary riddle of the dead.

But something heavy and as old as clay,
Which mires a human soul,
Laid hold upon the quest so that it fell,
Just baffled of its goal.

Beyond the threshold of the door,
I could not see; I only knew
That those who had been standing, waiting there,
Were passing through;
And while it was not given me to know   280
Whither their journey led, I had caught the sense
Of life with high auroras and the flow
Of wide majestic spaces;
Of light abundant; and of keen impassioned faces,
Transfigured underneath its vivid glow.

Then the door moved to its close with a loud,
Relentless swing, as backed by ocean power;
But neither gird of hinges, nor the feel of air
Returning with its drizzled weight of cloud,
Could cancel half the meaning of that hour, –   290
Not though the vision passed away,
And I was left alone, aware
Of blindness falling with terrestrial day
On sight enfeebled by the solar glare.

EROSION

It took the sea a thousand years,
A thousand years to trace
The granite features of this cliff,
In crag and scarp and base.

It took the sea an hour one night,
An hour of storm to place
The sculpture of these granite seams
Upon a woman's face.

THE HIGHWAY

What aeons passed without a count or name,
Before the cosmic seneschal,
Succeeding with a plan
Of weaving stellar patterns from a flame,
Announced at his high carnival
An orbit – with Aldebaran!

And when the drifting years had sighted land,
And hills and plains declared their birth
Amid volcanic throes,
What was the lapse before the marshal's hand   10
Had found a garden on the earth,
And led forth June with her first rose?

And what the gulf between that and the hour,
Late in the simian-human day,
When Nature kept her tryst
With the unfoldment of the star and flower –
When in her sacrificial way
Judaea blossomed with her Christ!

But what made *our* feet miss the road that brought
The world to such a golden trove,   20
In our so brief a span?
How may we grasp again the hand that wrought
Such light, such fragrance, and such love,
O star! O rose! O Son of Man?

THE MAN AND THE MACHINE

By right of fires that smelted ore
Which he had tended years before,
The man whose hands were on the wheel

Could trace his kinship through her steel,
Between his body warped and bent
In every bone and ligament,
And this 'eight-cylinder' stream-lined,
The finest model yet designed.
He felt his lesioned pulses strum
Against the rhythm of her hum,   10
And found his nerves and sinews knot
With sharper spasm as she climbed
The steeper grades, so neatly timed
From storage tank to piston shot –
This creature with the cougar grace,
This man with slag upon his face.

FROM STONE TO STEEL

From stone to bronze, from bronze to steel
Along the road-dust of the sun,
Two revolutions of the wheel
From Java to Geneva run.

The snarl Neanderthal is worn
Close to the smiling Aryan lips,
The civil polish of the horn
Gleams from our praying finger tips.

The evolution of desire
Has but matured a toxic wine,   10
Drunk long before its heady fire
Reddened Euphrates or the Rhine.

Between the temple and the cave
The boundary lies tissue-thin:
The yearlings still the altars crave
As satisfaction for a sin.

The road goes up, the road goes down –
Let Java or Geneva be –
But whether to the cross or crown,
The path lies through Gethsemane.   20

THE PRIZE CAT

Pure blood domestic, guaranteed,
Soft-mannered, musical in purr,
The ribbon had declared the breed,
Gentility was in the fur.

Such feline culture in the gads
No anger ever arched her back –
What distance since those velvet pads
Departed from the leopard's track!

And when I mused how Time had thinned
The jungle strains within the cells,   10
How human hands had disciplined
Those prowling optic parallels;

I saw the generations pass
Along the reflex of a spring,
A bird had rustled in the grass,
The tab had caught it on the wing:

Behind the leap so furtive-wild
Was such ignition in the gleam,
I thought an Abyssinian child
Had cried out in the whitethroat's scream.   20

SILENCES

There is no silence upon the earth or under the earth like the
    silence under the sea;
No cries announcing birth,
No sounds declaring death.
There is silence when the milt is laid on the spawn in the
    weeds and fungus of the rock-clefts;
And silence in the growth and struggle for life.
The bonitoes pounce upon the mackerel,
And are themselves caught by the barracudas,
The sharks kill the barracudas
And the great molluscs rend the sharks,
And all noiselessly –   10
Though swift be the action and final the conflict,
The drama is silent.

There is no fury upon the earth like the fury under the sea.
For growl and cough and snarl are the tokens of spend-
    thrifts who know not the ultimate economy of rage.
Moreover, the pace of the blood is too fast.
But under the waves the blood is sluggard and has the
    same temperature as that of the sea.
There is something pre-reptilian about a silent kill.

Two men may end their hostilities just with their battle-
    cries.
'The devil take you,' says one.
'I'll see you in hell first,' says the other.   20
And these introductory salutes followed by a hail of gut-
    turals and sibilants are often the beginning of friend-
    ship, for who would not prefer to be lustily damned
    than to be half-heartedly blessed?
No one need fear oaths that are properly enunciated, for
    they belong to the inheritance of just men made
    perfect, and, for all we know, of such may be the King-
    dom of Heaven.

But let silent hate be put away for it feeds upon the heart
    of the hater.
Today I watched two pairs of eyes. One pair was black
    and the other grey. And while the owners thereof,
    for the space of five seconds, walked past each other,
    the grey snapped at the black and the black riddled
    the grey.
One looked to say – 'The cat,'
And the other – 'The cur.'
But no words were spoken;
Not so much as a hiss or a murmur came through the
    perfect enamel of the teeth; not so much as a gesture
    of enmity.
If the right upper lip curled over the canine, it went
    unnoticed.
The lashes veiled the eyes not for an instant in the   30
    passing.
And as between the two in respect to candour of inten-
    tion or eternity of wish, there was no choice, for the
    stare was mutual and absolute.
A word would have dulled the exquisite edge of the feel-
    ing,
An oath would have flawed the crystallization of the
    hate.
For only such culture could grow in a climate of silence, –
Away back before the emergence of fur or feather, back to
    the unvocal sea and down deep where the darkness
    spills its wash on the threshold of light, where the
    lids never close upon the eyes, where the inhabitants
    slay in silence and are as silently slain.

FIRE

Wiser than thought, more intimate than breath,
More ancient than the plated rust of Mars,
Beyond the light geometry of stars,

Yet closer than our web of life and death –
This sergeant of the executing squads
Calls night from dawn no less than dawn from night;
This groom that teams the wolf and hare for flight
Is obstetrician at the birth of gods.
Around this crimson source of human fears,
Where rites and myths have built their scaffoldings,   10
With smoke of hecatombs upon her wings,
And chased by shadows of the coming years,
Our planet-moth tries blindly to survive
Her spinning vertigo as fugitive.

But stronger than its terror is the deep
Allurement, primary to our blood, which holds
Safety and warmth in unimpassioned folds,
Night and the candle-quietness of sleep;
With the day's bugles silent, when the will,
That feeds the tumult of our natures, rests   20
Along the broken arteries of its quests.
So, let the yellowing world revolve until
The old Sun's ultimate expatriate
On this exotic hearth leans forth to claim
Promethean virtue from a dying flame,
His fingers tapered – less to mitigate
The chilling accident of his sojourn
Than to invoke his ultimate return.

THE TITANIC

Harland &
Wolff
Works,
Belfast,
May 31,
1911

The hammers silent and the derricks still,
And high-tide in the harbour! Mind and will
In open test with time and steel had run
The first lap of a schedule and had won.
Although a shell of what was yet to be
Before another year was over, she,
Poised for the launching signal, had surpassed

The dreams of builder or of navigator.
The Primate of the Lines, she had out-classed
That rival effort to eliminate her   10
Beyond the North Sea where the air shots played
The laggard rhythms of their fusillade
Upon the rivets of the *Imperator*.
The wedges in, the shores removed, a girl's
Hand at a sign released a ribbon braid;
Glass crashed against the plates; a wine cascade,
Netting the sunlight in a shower of pearls,
Baptized the bow and gave the ship her name;
A slight push of the rams as a switch set free
The triggers in the slots, and her proud claim   20
On size – to be the first to reach the sea –
Was vindicated, for whatever fears
Stalked with her down the tallow of the slips
Were smothered under by the harbour cheers,
By flags strung to the halyards of the ships.

March 31, Completed! Waiting for her trial spin–
1912   Levers and telegraphs and valves within
Her intercostal spaces ready to start
The power pulsing through her lungs and heart.
An ocean lifeboat in herself – so ran   30
The architectural comment on her plan.
No wave could sweep those upper decks – unthinkable!
No storm could hurt that hull – the papers said so.
The perfect ship at last – the first unsinkable,
Proved in advance – had not the folders read so?
Such was the steel strength of her double floors
Along the whole length of the keel, and such
The fine adjustment of the bulkhead doors
Geared to the rams, responsive to a touch,
That in collision with iceberg or rock   40
Or passing ship she could survive the shock,
Absorb the double impact, for despite
The bows stove in, with forward holds aleak,
Her aft compartments buoyant, watertight,

Would keep her floating steady for a week.
And this belief had reached its climax when,
Through wireless waves as yet unstaled by use,
The wonder of the ether had begun
To fold the heavens up and reinduce
That ancient *hubris* in the dreams of men,   50
Which would have slain the cattle of the sun,
And filched the lightnings from the fist of Zeus.
What mattered that her boats were but a third
Of full provision – caution was absurd:
Then let the ocean roll and the winds blow
While the risk at Lloyds remained a record low.

The Iceberg   Calved from a glacier near Godhaven coast,
It left the fiord for the sea – a host
Of white flotillas gathering in its wake,
And joined by fragments from a Behring floe,   60
Had circumnavigated it to make
It centre of an archipelago.
Its lateral motion on the Davis Strait
Was casual and indeterminate,
And each advance to southward was as blind
As each recession to the north. No smoke
Of steamships nor the hoist of mainsails broke
The polar wastes – no sounds except the grind
Of ice, the cry of curlews and the lore
Of winds from mesas of eternal snow;   70
Until caught by the western undertow,
It struck the current of the Labrador
Which swung it to its definite southern stride.
Pressure and glacial time had stratified
The berg to the consistency of flint,
And kept inviolate, through clash of tide
And gale, façade and columns with their hint
Of inward altars and of steepled bells
Ringing the passage of the parallels.
But when with months of voyaging it came   80
To where both streams – the Gulf and Polar – met,

The sun which left its crystal peaks aflame
In the sub-arctic noons, began to fret
The arches, flute the spires and deform
The features, till the batteries of storm,
Playing above the slow-eroding base,
Demolished the last temple touch of grace.
Another month, and nothing but the brute
And palaeolithic outline of a face
Fronted the transatlantic shipping route.   90
A sloping spur that tapered to a claw
And lying twenty feet below had made
It lurch and shamble like a plantigrade;
But with an impulse governed by the raw
Mechanics of its birth, it drifted where
Ambushed, fog-grey, it stumbled on its lair,
North forty-one degrees and forty-four,
Fifty and fourteen west the longitude,
Waiting a world-memorial hour, its rude
Corundum form stripped to its Greenland core.   100

South-   An omen struck the thousands on the shore –
ampton,   A double accident! And as the ship
Wednes-
day, April Swung down the river on her maiden trip,
10, 1912 Old sailors of the clipper decades, wise
To the sea's incantations, muttered fables
About careening vessels with their cables
Snapped in their harbours under peaceful skies.
Was it just suction or fatality
Which caused the *New York* at the dock to turn,
Her seven mooring ropes to break at the stern   110
And writhe like anacondas on the quay,
While tugs and fenders answered the collision
Signals with such trim margin of precision?
And was it backwash from the starboard screw
Which, tearing at the big *Teutonic*, drew
Her to the limit of her hawser strain,
And made the smaller tethered craft behave

Like frightened harbour ducks? And no one knew
For many days the reason to explain
The rise and wash of one inordinate wave,   120
When a sunken barge on the Southampton bed
Was dragged through mire eight hundred yards ahead,
As the *Titanic* passed above its grave.
But many of those sailors wise and old,
Who pondered on this weird mesmeric power,
Gathered together, lit their pipes and told
Of portents hidden in the natal hour,
Told of the launching of some square-rigged ships,
When water flowed from the inverted tips
Of a waning moon, of sun-hounds, of the shrieks   130
Of whirling shags around the mizzen peaks.
And was there not this morning's augury
For the big one now heading for the sea?
So long after she passed from landsmen's sight,
They watched her with their Mother Carey eyes
Through Spithead smoke, through mists of Isle of Wight,
Through clouds of sea-gulls following with their cries.

Wednes- Electric elements were glowing down
day In the long galley passages where scores
evening Of white-capped cooks stood at the oven doors   140
To feed the population of a town.
Cauldrons of stock, purées and consommés,
Simmered with peppercorns and marjoram.
The sea-shore smells from bisque and crab and clam
Blended with odours from the fricassées.
Refrigerators, hung with a week's toll
Of the stockyards, delivered sides of lamb
And veal, beef quarters to be roasted whole,
Hundreds of capons and halibut. A shoal
Of Blue-Points waited to be served on shell.   150
The boards were loaded with pimolas, pails
Of lobster coral, jars of Béchamel,
To garnish tiers of rows of chilled timbales

And aspics. On the shelves were pyramids
Of truffles, sprigs of thyme and water-cress,
Bay leaf and parsley, savouries to dress
Shad roes and sweetbreads broiling on the grids.
And then in diamond, square, crescent and star,
Hors d'oeuvres were fashioned from the toasted bread,
With paste of anchovy and caviare,   160
Paprika sprinkled and pimento spread,
All ready, for the hour was seven!
                                        Meanwhile,
Rivalling the engines with their steady tread,
Thousands of feet were taking overhead
The fourth lap round the deck to make the mile.
Squash racquet, shuffle board and quoits; the cool
Tang of the plunge in the gymnasium pool,
The rub, the crisp air of the April night,
The salt of the breeze made by the liner's rate,
Worked with an even keel to stimulate   170
Saliva for an ocean appetite;
And like storm troops before a citadel,
At the first summons of a bugle, soon
The army massed the stairs towards the saloon,
And though twelve courses on the cards might well
Measure themselves against Falstaffian juices,
But few were found presenting their excuses,
When stewards offered on the lacquered trays
The Savoy chasers and the canapés.

The dinner gave the sense that all was well: 180
That touch of ballast in the tanks; the feel
Of peace from ramparts unassailable,
Which, added to her seven decks of steel,
Had constituted the *Titanic* less
A ship than a Gibraltar under heel.
And night had placed a lazy lusciousness
Upon a surfeit of security.
Science responded to a button press.

The three electric lifts that ran through tiers
Of decks, the reading lamps, the brilliancy   190
Of mirrors from the tungsten chandeliers,
Had driven out all phantoms which the mind
Had loosed from ocean closets, and assigned
To the dry earth the custody of fears.
The crowds poured through the sumptuous rooms
        and halls,
And tapped the tables of the Regency;
Smirked at the caryatids on the walls;
Talked Jacobean-wise; canvassed the range
Of taste within the Louis dynasty.
Grey-templed Caesars of the world's Exchange   200
Swallowed liqueurs and coffee as they sat
Under the Georgian carved mahogany,
Dictating wireless hieroglyphics that
Would on the opening of the Board Rooms rock
The pillared dollars of a railroad stock.

In the   A group had gathered round a mat to watch
gymna-   The pressure of a Russian hammerlock,
sium   A Polish scissors and a German crotch,
Broken by the toe-hold of Frank Gotch;
Or listened while a young Y.M.C.A.   210
Instructor demonstrated the left-hook,
And that right upper-cut which Jeffries took
From Johnson in the polished Reno way.
By midnight in the spacious dancing hall,
Hundreds were at the Masqueraders' Ball,
The high potential of the liner's pleasures,
Where mellow lights from Chinese lanterns glowed
Upon the scene, and the *Blue Danube* flowed
In andantino rhythms through the measures.

By three the silence that proceeded from   220
The night-caps and the soporific hum
Of the engines was far deeper than a town's:

The starlight and the low wash of the sea
Against the hull bore the serenity
Of sleep at rural hearths with eiderdowns.

The quiet on the decks was scarcely less
Than in the berths: no symptoms of the toil
Down in the holds; no evidence of stress
From gears drenched in the lubricating oil.
She seemed to swim in oil, so smooth the sea.   230
And quiet on the bridge: the great machine
Called for laconic speech, close-fitting, clean,
And whittled to the ship's economy.
Even the judgment stood in little need
Of reason, for the Watch had but to read
Levels and lights, metre or card or bell
To find the pressures, temperatures, or tell
Magnetic North within a binnacle,
Or gauge the hour of docking; for the speed
Was fixed abaft where under the Ensign,   240
Like a flashing trolling spoon, the log rotator
Transmitted through a governor its fine
Gradations on a dial indicator.

Morning of Sunday promised cool and clear,
Flawless horizon, crystal atmosphere;
Not a cat's paw on the ocean, not a guy
Rope murmuring: the steamer's columned smoke
Climbed like extensions of her funnels high
Into the upper zones, then warped and broke
Through the resistance of her speed – blue sky,   250
Blue water rifted only by the wedge
Of the bow where the double foam line ran
Diverging from the beam to join the edge
Of the stern wake like a white unfolding fan.
Her maiden voyage was being sweetly run,
Adding a half-knot here, a quarter there,
Gliding from twenty into twenty-one.

She seemed so native to her thoroughfare,
One turned from contemplation of her size,
Her sixty thousand tons of sheer flotation,   260
To wonder at the human enterprise
That took a gamble on her navigation –
Joining the mastiff strength with whippet grace
In this head-strained, world-watched Atlantic race:
Her less than six days' passage would combine
Achievement with the architect's design.

9 a.m.   *A message from Caronia: advice*
From ships proceeding west; sighted field ice
And growlers; forty-two north; forty-nine
To fifty-one west longitude. S.S.   270
Mesaba of Atlantic Transport Line
Reports encountering solid pack: would guess
The stretch five miles in width from west to east,
And forty-five to fifty miles at least
In length.

1 p.m.   *Amerika* obliged to slow
Down: warns all steamships in vicinity
Presence of bergs, especially of three
Upon the southern outskirts of the floe.

1.42 p.m.   The *Baltic* warns *Titanic*: so *Touraine*;
Reports of numerous icebergs on the Banks,   280
The floe across the southern traffic lane.

5 p.m.   The *Californian* and *Baltic* again
Present their compliments to Captain.

Titanic   *Thanks.*

Three men
talking on   'That spark's been busy all the afternoon –
deck   Warnings! The Hydrographic charts are strewn
With crosses showing bergs and pack-ice all

Along the routes, more south than usual
For this time of the year.'
                          'She's hitting a clip
Instead of letting up while passing through
This belt. She's gone beyond the twenty-two.'   290

'Don't worry – Smith's an old dog, knows his ship,
No finer in the mercantile marine
Than Smith with thirty years of service, clean
Record, honoured with highest of all commands,
Majestic, then *Olympic* on his hands,
Now the *Titanic*.'
                          ''Twas a lucky streak
That at Southampton dock he didn't lose her,
And the *Olympic* had a narrow squeak
Some months before rammed by the British Cruiser,
The *Hawke*.'   300
                          'Straight accident. No one to blame:
'Twas suction – Board absolved them both. The same
With the *Teutonic* and *New York*. No need
To fear she's trying to out-reach her speed.
There isn't a sign of fog. Besides by now
The watch is doubled at crow's nest and bow.'
'People are talking of that apparition,
When we were leaving Queenstown – that head showing
Above the funnel rim, and the fires going!
A stoker's face – sounds like a superstition.
But he was there within the stack, all right;   310
Climbed up the ladder and grinned. The explanation
Was given by an engineer last night –
A dummy funnel built for ventilation.'

'That's queer enough, but nothing so absurd
As the latest story two old ladies heard
At a rubber o' bridge. They nearly died with fright;
Wanted to tell the captain – of all things!
The others sneered a bit but just the same

It did the trick of breaking up the game.
A mummy from The Valley of the Kings   320
Was brought from Thebes to London. Excavators
Passed out from cholera, black plague or worse.
Egyptians understood – an ancient curse
Was visited on all the violators.
One fellow was run over, one was drowned,
And one went crazy. When in time it found
Its way to the Museum, the last man
In charge – a mothy Aberdonian –
Exploding the whole legend with a laugh,
Lost all his humour when the skeleton   330
Appeared within the family photograph,
And leered down from a corner just like one
Of his uncles.'
                'Holy Hades!'
                        'The B.M.
Authorities themselves were scared and sold
It to New York. That's how the tale is told.'
'The joke is on the Yanks.'
                        'No, not on them,
Nor on The Valley of the Kings. What's rummy
About it is – we're carrying the mummy.'

7.30 p.m.   *Green Turtle!*

At a table   *Potage Romanoff!*
in the din-
ing saloon   'White Star
Is out this time to press Cunarders close,   340
Got them on tonnage – fifty thousand gross.
Preferred has never paid a dividend.
The common's down to five – one hundred par.
The double ribbon – size and speed – would send
Them soaring.'
                'Speed is not in her design,
But comfort and security. The Line
Had never advertised it – 'twould be mania
To smash the record of the *Mauretania*.'

Sherry!
    'The rumour's out.'
                'There's nothing in it.'
'Bet you she docks on Tuesday night.'   350
                   'I'll take it.'
'She's hitting twenty-two this very minute.'
'That's four behind – She hasn't a chance to make it.'
Brook Trout!
          Fried Dover Sole!
                 'Her rate will climb
From twenty-two to twenty-six in time.
The Company's known never to rush their ships
At first or try to rip the bed-bolts off.
They run them gently half-a-dozen trips,
A few work-outs around the track to let
Them find their breathing, take the boiler cough
Out of them. She's not racing for a cup.'   360
Claret!
    'Steamships like sprinters have to get
Their second wind before they open up.'

'That group of men around the captain's table,
Look at them, count the aggregate – the House
Of Astor, Guggenheim, and Harris, Straus,
That's Frohman, isn't it? Between them able
To halve the national debt with a cool billion!
Sir Hugh is over there, and Hays and Stead.
That woman third from captain's right, it's said,
Those diamonds round her neck – a quarter million!' 370
Mignon of Beef!
        Quail!
            'I heard Phillips say
He had the finest outfit on the sea;
The new Marconi valve; the range by day,
Five hundred miles, by night a thousand. Three
Sources of power. If some crash below
Should hit the engines, flood the dynamo,

He had the batteries: in emergency,
He could switch through to the auxiliary
On the boat deck.'
                    Woodcock and *Burgundy!*
'Say waiter, I said *rare*, you understand.'   380
Escallope of Veal!
                    Roast Duckling!
                              Snipe! More *Rhine!*
'Marconi made the sea as safe as land:
Remember the *Republic* – White Star Line –
Rammed off Nantucket by the *Florida*,
One thousand saved – the *Baltic* heard the call.
Two steamers answered the *Slavonia*,
Disabled off the Azores. They got them all,
And when the *Minnehaha* ran aground
Near Bishop's Rock, they never would have found
Her – not a chance without the wireless. Same   390
Thing happened to that boat – what was her name?
The one that foundered off the Alaska Coast –
Her signals brought a steamer in the nick
Of time. Yes, sir – Marconi turned the trick.'

The *Barcelona salad*; no, *Beaucaire*;
That *Russian dressing*;
                    Avocado pear!

'They wound her up at the Southampton dock,
And then the tugs gave her a push to start
Her off – as automatic as a clock.'

Moselle!   400
          'For all the hand work there's to do
Aboard this liner up on deck, the crew
Might just as well have stopped ashore. Apart
From stokers and the engineers, she's run
By gadgets from the bridge – a thousand and one
Of them with a hundred miles of copper wire.

A filament glows at the first sign of fire,
A buzzer sounds, a number gives the spot,
A deck-hand makes a coupling of the hose.
That's all there's to it; not a whistle; not
A passenger upon the ship that knows   410
What's happened. The whole thing is done without
So much as calling up the fire brigade.
They don't need even the pumps – a gas is sprayed,
Carbon dioxide – and the blaze is out.'

A Cherry Flan!
                    Champagne!
                                    Chocolate parfait!

'How about a poker crowd to-night?
Get Jones, an awful grouch – no good to play,
But has the coin. Get hold of Larry.'
                                    'Right.'
'You fetch Van Raalte: I'll bring in MacRae.
In Cabin D, one hundred seventy-nine.   420
In half-an-hour we start playing.'
                                    'Fine.'

On deck   The sky was moonless but the sea flung back
With greater brilliance half the zodiac.
As clear below as clear above, the Lion
Far on the eastern quarter stalked the Bear:
Polaris off the starboard beam – and there
Upon the port the Dog-star trailed Orion.
Capella was so close, a hand might seize
The sapphire with the silver Pleiades.
And further to the south – a finger span,   430
Swam Betelgeuse and red Aldebaran.
Right through from east to west the ocean glassed
The billions of that snowy caravan
Ranging the highway which the Milkmaid passed.

9.05 p.m. *I say, old man, we're stuck fast in this place,*
Californian *More than an hour. Field ice for miles about.*
flashing

Titanic *Say,* Californian, *shut up, keep out,*
You're jamming all my signals with Cape Race.

10 p.m. A group of boys had gathered round a spot
Upon the rail where a dial registered   440
The speed, and waiting each three minutes heard
The taffrail log bell tallying off a knot.

11.20 p.m. First act to fifth act in a tragic plan,
Behind a Stage time, real time – a woman and a man,
deck house
Entering a play within a play, dismiss
The pageant on the ocean with a kiss.
Eleven-twenty curtain! Whether true
Or false the pantomimic vows they make
Will not be known till at the *fifth* they take
Their mutual exit twenty after two.   450

11.25 p.m. Position half-a-mile from edge of floe,
Hove-to for many hours, bored with delay,
The *Californian* fifteen miles away,
And fearful of the pack, has now begun
To turn her engines over under slow
Bell, and the operator, his task done,
Unclamps the 'phones and ends his dullest day.

The ocean sinuous, half-past eleven;
A silence broken only by the seven
Bells and the look-out calls, the log-book showing   460
Knots forty-five within two hours – not quite
The expected best as yet – but she was going
With all her bulkheads open through the night,
For not a bridge induction light was glowing.
Over the stern zenith and nadir met
In the wash of the reciprocating set.

The foam in bevelled mirrors multiplied
And shattered constellations. In between,
The pitch from the main drive of the turbine
Emerged like tuna breaches to divide   470
Against the rudder, only to unite
With the converging wake from either side.
Under the counter, blending with the spill
Of stars – the white and blue – the yellow light
Of Jupiter hung like a daffodil.

D-179   'Ace full! A long time since I had a pot.'

'Good boy, Van Raalte. That's the juiciest haul
To-night. Calls for a round of roodles, what?
Let's whoop her up. Double the limit. All
In.' (Jones, heard muttering as usual,   480
Demurs, but over-ruled.) 'Jones sore again.'

Van Raalte   'Ten dollars and all in!
(dealer)   The sea's like glass
To-night. That fin-keel keeps her steady.'

Jones   'Pass.'
        (Not looking at his hand.)

Larry   'Pass.'

Cripps   'Open for ten.'
        (Holding a pair of aces.) 'Say, who won
The sweep to-day?'

                    'A Minnesota guy
With olive-coloured spats and a mauve tie.
Five hundred and eighty miles – Beat last day's run.'

Mac   'My ten.'

Harry   (Taking a gamble on his four

Spades for a flush) 'I'll raise the bet ten more.'   490

Van R.   (Two queens) '*And* ten.'

Jones   (Discovering three kings)
         'Raise you to forty' (face expressing doubt.)

Larry   (Looking hard at a pair of nines) 'I'm out.'

Cripps   (Flirts for a moment with his aces, flings
         His thirty dollars to the pot.)

Mac   (The same.)

Harry   'My twenty. Might as well stay with the game.'

Van R.   'I'm in. Draw! Jones, how bloody long you wait.'

Jones   (Withholds an eight) 'One.' (And then draws an eight.)

Cripps   'Three.' (Gets another pair.)
                             'How many, Mac?'

Mac   'Guess I'll take two, no, three.' (Gets a third Jack.)   500

Harry   'One.' (Draws the ace of spades.)

Van R.   'Dealer takes three.'

Cripps   (Throws in a dollar chip.)
(the opener)
Mac   (The same.)

Harry   'I'll raise
         You ten.'

Van R.   'I'll see you.'

Jones   (Hesitates, surveys
          The chips.) 'Another ten.'

Cripps   'I'll call you.'

Mac   'See.'

Harry   'White livers! Here she goes to thirty.'

Van R.   'Just
          The devil's luck.' (Throws cards down in disgust.)

Jones   'Might as well raise.' (Counts twenty sluggishly,
          Tosses them to the centre.)
                              'Staying, Cripps?'

Cripps   'No, and be damned to it.'

Mac   'My ten.' (With groans.)

Harry   (Looks at the pyramid and swears at Jones,   510
          Then calls, pitching ten dollars on the chips.)

Jones   (Cards down.) 'A full house tops the flush.' (He spreads
          His arms around the whites and blues and reds.)

Mac   'As the Scotchman once said of the Sphinx,
             I'd like just to know what he thinks,
             I'll ask him, he cried,
             And the Sphinx – he replied,
             It's the hell of a time between drinks.'

Cripps   'Time? Eleven forty-four, to be precise.'
(watch in
hand)

Harry   'Jones – that will fatten up your pocket-book.   520
          My throat's like charcoal. Ring for soda and ice.'

Van R. 'Ice: God! Look – take it through the port-hole – look!'

11.45 p.m. A signal from the crow's nest. Three bells pealed:
The look-out telephoned – *Something ahead,*
Murdoch
holding the
bridge-
watch *Hard to make out, sir; looks like ... iceberg dead*
On starboard bow!
         Starboard your helm: ship heeled
To port. From bridge to engine-room the clang
Of the telegraph. *Danger. Stop.* A hand sprang
To the throttle; the valves closed, and with the churn
Of the reverse the sea boiled at the stern.   530
Smith hurried to the bridge and Murdoch closed
The bulkheads of the ship as he supposed,
But could not know that with those riven floors
The electro-magnets failed upon the doors.
No shock! No more than if something alive
Had brushed her as she passed. The bow had missed.
Under the vast momentum of her drive
She went a mile. But why that ominous five
Degrees (within five minutes) of a list?

In a cabin 'What was that, steward?'   540
        'Seems like she hit a sea, sir.'
'But there's no sea; calm as a landlocked bay
It is; lost a propeller blade?'
        'Maybe, sir.'
'She's stopped.'
      'Just cautious like, feeling her way,
There's ice about. It's dark, no moon to-night,
Nothing to fear, I'm sure, sir.'

      For so slight
The answer of the helm, it did not break
The sleep of hundreds: some who were awake
Went up on deck, but soon were satisfied
That nothing in the shape of wind or tide
Or rock or ice could harm that huge bulk spread   550
On the Atlantic, and went back to bed.

Captain in
wireless
room

'We've struck an iceberg – glancing blow: as yet
Don't know extent; looks serious; so get
Ready to send out general call for aid;
I'll tell you when – having inspection made.'

Report of
ship's
carpenter
and fourth
officer

A starboard cut three hundred feet or more
From foremast to amidships. Iceberg tore
Right at the bilge turn through the double skin:
Some boiler rooms and bunkers driven in;
The forward five compartments flooded – mail   560
Bags floating. Would the engine power avail
To stem the rush?

Wireless
room, First
officer Phil-
lips at key

Titanic, C.Q.D.
Collision: iceberg: damaged starboard side:
Distinct list forward. (Had Smith magnified
The danger? Over-anxious certainly.)
The second (joking) – 'Try new call, maybe
Last chance you'll have to send it.'
S.O.S.
Then back to older signal of distress.

On the same instant the *Carpathia* called,
The distance sixty miles – *Putting about,*   570
And heading for you; double watch installed
In engine-room, in stokehold and look-out.
Four hours the run, should not the ice retard
The speed; but taking chances: Coming hard!

The Bridge

As leaning on her side to ease a pain,
The tilted ship had stopped the captain's breath:
The inconceivable had stabbed his brain,
This thing unfelt – her visceral wound of death?
Another message – this time to report her
Filling, taxing the pumps beyond their strain.   580

Had that blow rent her from the bow to quarter?
Or would the aft compartments still intact
Give buoyancy enough to counteract
The open forward holds?
                              The carpenter's
Second report had offered little chance,
And panic – heart of God – the passengers,
The fourteen hundred – seven hundred packed
In steerage – seven hundred immigrants!
Smith thought of panic clutching at their throats,
And feared that Balkan scramble for the boats.   590

No call from bridge, no whistle, no alarm
Was sounded. Have the stewards quietly
Inform the passengers: no vital harm,
Precautions merely for emergency;
Collision? Yes, but nature of the blow
Must not be told: not even the crew must know:
Yet all on deck with lifebelts, and boats ready,
The sailors at the falls, and all hands steady.

Wireless   The lilac spark was crackling at the gap,
room   Eight ships within the radius of the call   600
From fifteen to five hundred miles, and all
But one answering the operator's tap.
Olympic twenty hours away had heard;
The *Baltic* next and the *Virginian* third;
Frankfurt and *Burma* distant one-half day;
Mount Temple nearer, but the ice-field lay
Between the two ships like a wall of stone;
The *Californian* deaf to signals though
Supreme deliverer an hour ago:
The hope was on *Carpathia* alone.   610

On the   So suave the fool-proof sense of life that fear
decks   Had like the unforeseen become a mere
Illusion – vanquished by the towering height

Of funnels pouring smoke through thirty feet
Of bore; the solid deck planks and the light
From a thousand lamps as on a city street;
The feel of numbers; the security
Of wealth; the placid surface of the sea,
Reflecting on the ship the outwardness
Of calm and leisure of the passengers;   620
Deck-hands obedient to their officers;
Pearl-throated women in their evening dress
And wrapped in sables and minks; the silhouettes
Of men in dinner jackets staging an act
In which delusion passed, deriding fact
Behind the cupped flare of the cigarettes.

Women and children first! Slowly the men
Stepped backward from the rails where number ten,
Its cover off, and lifted from the chocks,
Moved outward as the Welin davits swung.   630
The new ropes creaking through the unused blocks,'
The boat was lowered to B deck and hung
There while her load of sixty stepped inside,
Convinced the order was not justified.

Rockets, one, two, God! Smith – what does he mean?
The sounding of the bilges could not show
This reason for alarm – the sky serene
And not a ripple on the water – no
Collision. What report came from below?
No leak accounts for this – looks like a drill,   640
A bit of exhibition play – but still
Stopped in mid-ocean! and those rockets – *three!*
More urgent even than a tapping key
And more immediate as a protocol
To a disaster. *There!* An arrow of fire,
A fourth sped towards the sky, its bursting spire
Topping the foremast like a parasol
With fringe of fuchsia, – more a parody
Upon the tragic summons of the sea

Than the real script of unacknowledged fears   650
Known to the bridge and to the engineers.

Midnight! The Master of the ship presents
To the Master of the Band his compliments,
Desiring that the Band should play right through;
No intermission.

Conductor   'Bad?'

Officer   'Yes, bad enough,
The half not known yet even to the crew;
For God's sake, cut the sentimental stuff,
The *Blue Bells* and Kentucky lullabies.
Murdoch will have a barrel of work to do,
Holding the steerage back, once they get wise;   660
They're jumpy now under the rockets' glare;
So put the ginger in the fiddles – Zip
Her up.'

Conductor   'Sure, number forty-seven:' *E-Yip*
I Addy-I-A, I Ay ... I don't care ...

Number   Full noon and midnight by a weird design
ten goes   Both met and parted at the median line.
over the
side   Beyond the starboard gunwale was outspread
The jet expanse of water islanded
By fragments of the berg which struck the blow.
And further off towards the horizon lay   670
The loom of the uncharted parent floe,
Merging the black with an amorphous grey.
On the port gunwale the meridian
Shone from the terraced rows of decks that ran
From gudgeon to the stem nine hundred feet;
And as the boat now tilted by the stern,
Or now resumed her levels with the turn
Of the controlling ropes at block and cleat,

How easy seemed the step and how secure
Back to the comfort and the warmth – the lure   680
Of sheltered promenade and sun decks starred
By hanging bulbs, amber and rose and blue,
The trellis and palms lining an avenue
With all the vista of a boulevard:
The mirror of the ceilings with festoon
Of pennants, flags and streamers – and now through
The leaded windows of the grand saloon,
Through parted curtains and the open doors
Of vestibules, glint of deserted floors
And tables, and under the sorcery   690
Of light excelling their facsimile,
The periods returning to relume
The panels of the lounge and smoking-room,
Holding the mind in its abandonment
During those sixty seconds of descent.
Lower away! The boat with its four tons
Of freight went down with jerks and stops and runs
Beyond the glare of the cabins and below
The slanting parallels of port-holes, clear
Of the exhaust from the condenser flow: 700
But with the uneven falls she canted near
The water line; the stern rose; the bow dipped;
The crew groped for the link-releasing gear;
The lever jammed; a stoker's jack-knife ripped
The aft ropes through, which on the instant brought her
With rocking keel though safe upon the water.

The
Carpathia   Fifteen, sixteen, seventeen, eighteen – three
Full knots beyond her running limit, she
Was feeling out her port and starboard points,
And testing rivets on her boiler joints.   710
The needle on the gauge beyond the red,
The blow-offs feathered at the funnel head.
The draught-fans roaring at their loudest, now
The quartermaster jams the helm hard-over,

As the revolving searchlight beams uncover
The columns of an iceberg on the bow,
Then compensates this loss by daring gains
Made by her passage through the open lanes.

The Band   *East side, West side, all around the town,*
            The tots sang 'Ring-a-Rosie'   720
            'London Bridge is falling down,'
            Boys and girls together ...

The cranks turn and the sixth and seventh swing
Over and down, the 'tiller' answering
'Aye, Aye, sir' to the shouts of officers –
'Row to the cargo ports for passengers.'
The water line is reached, but the ports fail
To open, and the crews of the boats hail
The decks; receiving no response they pull
Away from the ship's side, less than half full.   730
The eighth caught in the tackle foul is stuck
Half-way. With sixty-five capacity,
Yet holding twenty-four, goes number three.

The sharp unnatural deflection, struck
By the sea-level with the under row
Of dipping port-holes at the forward, show
How much she's going by the head. Behind
The bulkheads, sapping out their steel control,
Is the warp of the bunker press inclined
By many thousand tons of shifting coal.   740

The smoothest, safest passage to the sea
Is made by number one – the next to go –
Her space is forty – twelve her company:
'Pull like the devil from her – harder – row!
The minute that she founders, not a boat
Within a mile around that will not follow.
What nearly happened at Southampton? So

Pull, pull, I tell you – not a chip afloat,
God knows how far, her suction will not swallow.'

Alexander's rag-time band ...   750
It's the best band in the land ...

Voices
from the
deck
'There goes the Special with the toffs. You'll make
New York to-night rowing like that. You'll take
Your death o' cold out there with all the fish
And ice around.'
                        'Make sure your butlers dish
You up your toddies now, and bring hot rolls
For breakfast.'
                        'Don't forget the finger bowls.'

The engineering staff of thirty-five
Are at their stations: those off-duty go
Of their free will to join their mates below   760
In the grim fight for steam, more steam, to drive
The pressure through the pumps and dynamo.
Knee-deep, waist-deep in water they remain,
Not one of them seen on the decks again.
The under braces of the rudder showing,
The wing propeller blades began to rise,
And with them, through the hawse-holes, water
        flowing –
The angle could not but assault the eyes.
A fifteen minutes, and the fo'c'sle head
Was under. And five more, the sea had shut   770
The lower entrance to the stairs that led
From C deck to the boat deck – the short cut
For the crew. Another five, the upward flow
Had covered the wall brackets where the glow
Diffusing from the frosted bulbs turned green
Uncannily through their translucent screen.

On the
Carpathia
White Star – Cunarder, forty miles apart,
Still eighteen knots! From coal to flame to steam –
Decision of a captain to redeem
Errors of brain by hazards of the heart!   780
Showers of sparks danced through the funnel smoke,
The firemen's shovels, rakes and slice-bars broke
The clinkers, fed the fires, and ceaselessly
The hoppers dumped the ashes on the sea.

As yet no panic, but none might foretell
The moment when the sight of that oblique
Breath-taking lift of the taffrail and the sleek
And foamless undulation of the swell
Might break in meaning on those diverse races,
And give them common language. As the throng   790
Came to the upper decks and moved along
The incline, the contagion struck the faces
With every lowering of a boat and backed
Them towards the stern. And twice between the hush
Of fear and utterance the gamut cracked,
When with the call for women and the flare
Of an exploding rocket, a short rush
Was made for the boats – fifteen and two.
'Twas nearly done – the sudden clutch and tear
Of canvas, a flurry of fists and curses met   800
By swift decisive action from the crew,
Supported by a quartermaster's threat
Of three revolver shots fired on the air.

But still the fifteenth went with five inside,
Who, seeking out the shadows, climbed aboard
And, lying prone and still, managed to hide
Under the thwarts long after she was lowered.

> *Jingle bells, jingle bells,*
> *Jingle all the way,*
> *O what fun ...*   810

'Some men in number two, sir!'
                              The boat swung
Back.
        'Chuck the fellows out.'
                              Grabbed by the feet,
The lot were pulled over the gunwale and flung
Upon the deck.
                    'Hard at that forward cleat!
A hand there for that after fall. Lower
Away – port side, the second hatch, and wait.'

With six hands of his watch, the bosun's mate,
Sent down to open up the gangway door,
Was trapped and lost in a flooded alley way,
And like the seventh, impatient of delay,   820
The second left with room for twenty more.

The fiddley leading from a boiler room
Lay like a tortuous exit from a tomb.
A stoker climbed it, feeling by the twist
From vertical how steep must be the list.
He reached the main deck where the cold night airs
Enswathed his flesh with steam. Taking the stairs,
He heard the babel by the davits, faced
The forward, noticed how the waters raced
To the break of the fo'c'sle and lapped   830
The foremast root. He climbed again and saw
The resolute manner in which Murdoch's rapped
Command put a herd instinct under law;
No life-preserver on, he stealthily
Watched Phillips in his room, bent at the key,
And thinking him alone, he sprang to tear
The jacket off. He leaped too soon. 'Take that!'
The second stove him with a wrench. 'Lie there,
Till hell begins to singe your lids – you rat!'

But set against those scenes where order failed,   840

Was the fine muster at the fourteenth where,
Like a zone of calm along a thoroughfare,
The discipline of sea-worn laws prevailed.
No women answering the repeated calls,
The men filled up the vacant seats: the falls
Were slipping through the sailors' hands,
When a steerage group of women, having fought
Their way over five flights of stairs, were brought
Bewildered to the rails. Without commands
Barked from the lips of officers; without   850
A protest registered in voice or face,
The boat was drawn up and the men stepped out
Back to the crowded stations with that free
Barter of life for life done with the grace
And air of a Castilian courtesy.

> *I've just got here through Paris,*
> *From the sunny Southern shore,*
> *I to Monte Carlo went ...*

Isidor and   At the sixteenth – a woman wrapped her coat
Ida Straus   Around her maid and placed her in the boat;   860
Was ordered in but seen to hesitate
At the gunwale, and more conscious of her pride
Than of her danger swiftly took her fate
With open hands, and without show of tears
Returned unmurmuring to her husband's side;
'We've been together now for forty years,
Whither you go, I go.'

          A boy of ten,
Ranking himself within the class of men,
Though given a seat, made up his mind to waive
The privilege of his youth and size, and piled   870
The inches on his stature as he gave
Place to a Magyar woman and her child.

And men who had in the world's run of trade,
Or in pursuit of the professions, made
Their reputation, looked upon the scene
Merely as drama in a life's routine:
Millet was studying eyes as he would draw them
Upon a canvas; Butt, as though he saw them
In the ranks; Astor, social, debonair,
Waved 'Good-bye' to his bride – 'See you to-morrow,'
And tapped a cigarette on a silver case;   880
Men came to Guggenheim as he stood there
In evening suit, coming this time to borrow
Nothing but courage from his calm, cool face.

And others unobserved, of unknown name
And race, just stood behind, pressing no claim
Upon priority but rendering proof
Of their oblation, quiet and aloof
Within the maelstrom towards the rails. And some
Wavered a moment with the panic urge,
But rallied to attention on the verge   890
Of flight as if the rattle of a drum
From quarters faint but unmistakable
Had put the stiffening in the blood to check
The impulse of the feet, leaving the will
No choice between the lifeboats and the deck.

The four collapsibles, their lashings ripped,
Half-dragged, half-lifted by the hooks, were slipped
Over the side. The first two luckily
Had but the forward distance to the sea.
Its canvas edges crumpled up, the third   900
Began to fill with water and transferred
Its cargo to the twelfth, while number four,
Abaft and higher, nose-dived and swamped its score.

The wireless cabin – Phillips in his place,
Guessing the knots of the Cunarder's race.

Water was swirling up the slanted floor
Around the chair and sucking at his feet.
Carpathia's call – the last one heard complete –
Expect to reach position half-past four.
The operators turned – Smith at the door   910
With drawn incredulous face. 'Men, you have done
Your duty. I release you. Everyone
Now for himself.' They stayed ten minutes yet,
The power growing fainter with each blue
Crackle of flame. Another stammering jet –
Virginian heard 'a tattering C.Q.'
Again a try for contact but the code's
Last jest had died between the electrodes.

Even yet the spell was on the ship: although
The last lifeboat had vanished, there was no   920
Besieging of the heavens with a crescendo
Of fears passing through terror into riot –
But on all lips the strange narcotic quiet
Of an unruffled ocean's innuendo.
In spite of her deformity of line,
Emergent like a crag out of the sea,
She had the semblance of stability,
Moment by moment furnishing no sign,
So far as visible, of that decline
Made up of inches crawling into feet.   930
Then, with the electric circuit still complete,
The miracle of day displacing night
Had worked its fascination to beguile
Direction of the hours and cheat the sight.
Inside the recreation rooms the gold
From Arab lamps shone on the burnished tile.
What hindered the return to shelter while
The ship clothed in that irony of light
Offered her berths and cabins as a fold?
And, was there not the *Californian*?   940
Many had seen her smoke just over there,

But two hours past – it seemed a harbour span –
So big, so close, she could be hailed, they said;
She must have heard the signals, seen the flare
Of those white stars and changed at once her course.
There under the *Titanic*'s foremast head,
A lamp from the look-out cage was flashing Morse.
No ship afloat unless deaf, blind and dumb
To those three sets of signals but would come.
And when the whiz of a rocket bade men turn   950
Their faces to each other in concern
At shattering facts upon the deck, they found
Their hearts take reassurance with the sound
Of the violins from the gymnasium, where
The bandsmen in their blithe insouciance
Discharged the sudden tension of the air
With the fox-trot's sublime irrelevance.

The fo'c'sle had gone under the creep
Of the water. Though without a wind, a lop
Was forming on the wells now fathoms deep.   960
The seventy feet – the boat deck's normal drop –
Was down to ten. Rising, falling, and waiting,
Rising again, the swell that edged and curled
Around the second bridge, over the top
Of the air-shafts, backed, resurged and whirled
Into the stokehold through the fiddley grating.

Under the final strain the two wire guys
Of the forward funnel tugged and broke at the eyes:
With buckled plates the stack leaned, fell and smashed
The starboard wing of the flying bridge, went through   970
The lower, then tilting at the davits crashed
Over, driving a wave aboard that drew
Back to the sea some fifty sailors and
The captain with the last of the bridge command.

Out on the water was the same display
Of fear and self-control as on the deck –
Challenge and hesitation and delay,
The quick return, the will to save, the race
Of snapping oars to put the realm of space
Between the half-filled lifeboats and the wreck.   980
The swimmers whom the waters did not take
With their instant death-chill struck out for the wake
Of the nearer boats, gained on them, hailed
The steersmen and were saved: the weaker failed
And fagged and sank. A man clutched at the rim
Of a gunwale, and a woman's jewelled fist
Struck at his face: two others seized his wrist,
As he released his hold, and gathering him
Over the side, they staunched the cut from the ring.
And there were many deeds envisaging   990
Volitions where self-preservation fought
Its red primordial struggle with the 'ought,'
In those high moments when the gambler tossed
Upon the chance and uncomplaining lost.

Aboard the ship, whatever hope of dawn
Gleamed from the *Carpathia*'s riding lights was gone,
For every knot was matched by each degree
Of list. The stern was lifted bodily
When the bow had sunk three hundred feet, and set
Against the horizon stars in silhouette   1000
Were the blade curves of the screws, hump of the rudder.
The downward pull and after buoyancy
Held her a minute poised but for a shudder
That caught her frame as with the upward stroke
Of the sea a boiler or a bulkhead broke.

Climbing the ladders, gripping shroud and stay,
Storm-rail, ringbolt or fairlead, every place
That might befriend the clutch of hand or brace
Of foot, the fourteen hundred made their way
To the heights of the aft decks, crowding the inches   1010

Around the docking bridge and cargo winches.
And now that last salt tonic which had kept
The valour of the heart alive – the bows
Of the immortal seven that had swept
The strings to outplay, outdie their orders – ceased.
Five minutes more, the angle had increased
From eighty on to ninety when the rows
Of deck and port-hole lights went out, flashed back
A brilliant second and again went black.
Another bulkhead crashed, then following   1020
The passage of the engines as they tore
From their foundations, taking everything
Clean through the bows from 'midships with a roar
Which drowned all cries upon the deck and shook
The watchers in the boats, the liner took
Her thousand fathoms journey to her grave.

*

And out there in the starlight, with no trace
Upon it of its deed but the last wave
From the *Titanic* fretting at its base,
Silent, composed, ringed by its icy broods,   1030
The grey shape with the palaeolithic face
Was still the master of the longitudes.

THE BARITONE

He ascended the rostrum after the fashion of the Caesars:
His arm, a baton raised oblique,
Answering the salute of the thunder,
Imposed a silence on the Square.
For three hours
A wind-theme swept his laryngeal reeds,
Pounded on the diaphragm of a microphone,
Entered, veered, ran round a coil,

Emerged, to storm the passes of the ether,
Until, impinging on a hundred million ear-drums,   10
It grew into the fugue of Europe.

Nickel, copper and steel rang their quotations to the skies,
And down through the diatonic scale
The mark hallooed the franc,
The franc bayed the lira,
With the three in full flight from the pound.
And while the diapasons were pulled
On the *Marseillaise,*
The *Giovinezza,*
And the *Deutschlandlied,*   20
A perfect stretto was performed
As the *Dead March* boomed its way
Through *God Save The King*
And the *Star Spangled Banner.*

Then the codetta of the clerics
(Chanting a ritual over the crosses of gold tossed into the
        crucibles to back the billion credit)
Was answered by
The clang of the North Sea against the bows of the
        destroyers,
The ripple of surf on the periscopes,
The grunt of the Mediterranean shouldering Gibraltar,   30
And the hum of the bombing squadrons in formation
        under Orion.

And the final section issued from the dials,
WHEN –
Opposed by contrapuntal blasts
From the Federated Polyphonic Leagues
Of Gynecologists,
Morticians,
And the Linen Manufacturers –
The great Baritone,

Soaring through the notes of the hymeneal register,   40
Called the brides and the grooms to the altar,
To be sent forth by the Recessional Bells
To replenish the earth,
And in due season to produce
Magnificent crops of grass on the battlefields.

BRÉBEUF AND HIS BRETHREN

I

The winds of God were blowing over France,
Kindling the hearths and altars, changing vows
Of rote into an alphabet of flame.
The air was charged with song beyond the range
Of larks, with wings beyond the stretch of eagles.
Skylines unknown to maps broke from the mists
And there was laughter on the seas. With sound
Of bugles from the Roman catacombs,
The saints came back in their incarnate forms.
Across the Alps St. Francis of Assisi   10
In his brown tunic girt with hempen cord,
Revisited the plague-infected towns.
The monks were summoned from their monasteries,
Nuns from their convents; apostolic hands
Had touched the priests; foundlings and galley slaves
Became the charges of Vincent de Paul;
Francis de Sales put his heroic stamp
Upon his order of the Visitation.
Out of Numidia by way of Rome,
The architect of palaces, unbuilt   20
Of hand, again was busy with his plans,
Reshaping for the world his *City of God*.
Out of the Netherlands was heard the call
Of Kempis through the *Imitatio*

To leave the dusty marts and city streets
And stray along the shores of Galilee.
The flame had spread across the Pyrenees –
The visions of Theresa burning through
The adorations of the Carmelites;
The very clouds at night to John of the Cross   30
Being cruciform – chancel, transept and aisle
Blazing with light and holy oracle.
Xavier had risen from his knees to drive
His dreams full-sail under an ocean compass.
Loyola, soldier-priest, staggering with wounds
At Pampeluna, guided by a voice,
Had travelled to the Montserrata Abbey
To leave his sword and dagger on an altar
That he might lead the *Company of Jesus.*

The story of the frontier like a saga   40
Sang through the cells and cloisters of the nation,
Made silver flutes out of the parish spires,
Troubled the ashes of the canonized
In the cathedral crypts, soared through the nave
To stir the foliations on the columns,
Roll through the belfries, and give deeper tongue
To the *Magnificat* in Notre Dame.
It brought to earth the prophets and apostles
Out of their static shrines in the stained glass.
It caught the ear of Christ, reveined his hands   50
And feet, bidding his marble saints to leave
Their pedestals for chartless seas and coasts
And the vast blunders of the forest glooms.
So, in the footsteps of their patrons came
A group of men asking the hardest tasks
At the new outposts of the Huron bounds
Held in the stern hand of the Jesuit Order.

And in Bayeux a neophyte while rapt
In contemplation saw a bleeding form

Falling beneath the instrument of death,   60
Rising under the quickening of the thongs,
Stumbling along the Via Dolorosa.
No play upon the fancy was this scene,
But the Real Presence to the naked sense.
The fingers of Brébeuf were at his breast,
Closing and tightening on a crucifix,
While voices spoke aloud unto his ear
And to his heart – *per ignem et per aquam.*
Forests and streams and trails thronged through his mind,
The painted faces of the Iroquois,   70
Nomadic bands and smoking bivouacs
Along the shores of western inland seas,
With forts and palisades and fiery stakes.
The stories of Champlain, Brulé, Viel,
Sagard and Le Caron had reached his town –
The stories of those northern boundaries
Where in the winter the white pines could brush
The Pleiades, and at the equinoxes
Under the gold and green of the auroras
Wild geese drove wedges through the zodiac.   80
The vows were deep he laid upon his soul.
'I shall be broken first before I break them.'
He knew by heart the manual that had stirred
The world – the clarion calling through the notes
Of the Ignatian preludes. On the prayers,
The meditations, points and colloquies,
Was built the soldier and the martyr programme.
This is the end of man – *Deum laudet,*
To seek and find the will of God, to act
Upon it for the ordering of life,   90
And for the soul's beatitude. This is
To do, this not to do. To weigh the sin;
The interior understanding to be followed
By the amendment of the deed through grace;
The abnegation of the evil thought
And act; the trampling of the body under;

The daily practice of the *counter virtues*.
'In time of desolation to be firm
And constant in the soul's determination,
Desire and sense obedient to the reason.'   100

The oath Brébeuf was taking had its root
Firm in his generations of descent.
The family name was known to chivalry –
In the Crusades; at Hastings; through the blood
Of the English Howards; called out on the rungs
Of the siege ladders; at the castle breaches;
Proclaimed by heralds at the lists, and heard
In Council Halls: – the coat-of-arms a bull
In black with horns of gold on a silver shield.
So on that toughened pedigree of fibre   110
Were strung the pledges. From the novice stage
To the vow-day he passed on to the priesthood,
And on the anniversary of his birth
He celebrated his first mass at Rouen.

And the first clauses of the Jesuit pledge
April 26   Were honoured when, embarking at Dieppe,
1625   Brébeuf, Massé and Charles Lalemant
Travelled three thousand miles of the Atlantic,
And reached the citadel in seven weeks.
A month in preparation at Notre Dame   120
Des Anges, Brébeuf in company with Daillon
Moved to Three Rivers to begin the journey.
Taking both warning and advice from traders,
They packed into their stores of altar-ware
And vestments, strings of coloured beads with knives,
Kettles and awls, domestic gifts to win
The Hurons' favour or appease their wrath.
There was a touch of omen in the warning,
For scarcely had they started when the fate
Of the Franciscan mission was disclosed –   130
News of Viel, delivered to Brébeuf, –

Drowned by the natives in the final league
Of his return at Sault-au-Récollet!

Back to Quebec by Lalemant's command;
A year's delay of which Brébeuf made use
By hardening his body and his will,
Learning the rudiments of the Huron tongue,
Mastering the wood-lore, joining in the hunt
For food, observing habits of speech, the ways
Of thought, the moods and the long silences.   140
Wintering with the Algonquins, he soon knew
The life that was before him in the cabins –
The troubled night, branches of fir covering
The floor of snow; the martyrdom of smoke
That hourly drove his nostrils to the ground
To breathe, or offered him the choice of death
Outside by frost, inside by suffocation;
The forced companionship of dogs that ate
From the same platters, slept upon his legs
Or neck; the nausea from sagamite,   150
Unsalted, gritty, and that bloated feeling,
The February stomach touch when acorns,
Turk's cap, bog-onion bulbs dug from the snow
And bulrush roots flavoured with eel skin made
The menu for his breakfast-dinner-supper.
Added to this, the instigated taunts
Common as daily salutations; threats
Of murderous intent that just escaped
The deed – the prologue to Huronia!

July 1626   Midsummer and the try again – Brébeuf,   160
Daillon, de Noué just arrived from France;
Quebec up to Three Rivers; the routine
Repeated; bargaining with the Indians,
Axes and beads against the maize and passage;
The natives' protest when they saw Brébeuf,
High as a totem-pole. What if he placed

His foot upon the gunwale, suddenly
Shifted an ounce of those two hundred pounds
Off centre at the rapids! They had visions
Of bodies and bales gyrating round the rocks,   170
Plunging like stumps and logs over the falls.
The Hurons shook their heads: the bidding grew;
Kettles and porcelain necklaces and knives,
Till with the last awl thrown upon the heap,
The ratifying grunt came from the chief.
Two Indians holding the canoe, Brébeuf,
Barefooted, cassock pulled up to his knees,
Planted one foot dead in the middle, then
The other, then slowly and ticklishly
Adjusted to the physics of his range   180
And width, he grasped both sides of the canoe,
Lowered himself and softly murmuring
An *Ave*, sat, immobile as a statue.

So the flotilla started – the same route
Champlain and Le Caron eleven years
Before had taken to avoid the swarm
Of hostile Iroquois on the St. Lawrence.
Eight hundred miles – along the Ottawa
Through the steep gorges where the river narrowed,
Through calmer waters where the river widened,   190
Skirting the island of the Allumettes,
Thence to the Mattawa through lakes that led
To the blue waters of the Nipissing,
And then southward a hundred tortuous miles
Down the French River to the Huron shore.
The record of that trip was for Brébeuf
A memory several times to be re-lived;
Of rocks and cataracts and portages,
Of feet cut by the river stones, of mud
And stench, of boulders, logs and tangled growths,   200
Of summer heat that made him long for night,
And when he struck his bed of rock – mosquitoes

That made him doubt if dawn would ever break.
'Twas thirty days to the Georgian Bay, then south
One hundred miles threading the labyrinth
Of islands till he reached the western shore
That flanked the Bay of Penetanguishene.
Soon joined by both his fellow priests he followed
The course of a small stream and reached Toanché,
Where for three years he was to make his home   210
And turn the first sod of the Jesuit mission.

'Twas ploughing only – for eight years would pass
Before even the blades appeared. The priests
Knew well how barren was the task should signs,
Gestures and inarticulate sounds provide
The basis of the converse. And the speech
Was hard. De Noüe set himself to school,
Unfalteringly as to his Breviary,
Through the long evenings of the fall and winter.
But as light never trickled through a sentence,   220
Either the Hurons' or his own, he left
With the spring's expedition to Quebec,
Where intermittently for twenty years
He was to labour with the colonists,
Travelling between the outposts, and to die
Snow-blind, caught in the circles of his tracks
Between Three Rivers and Fort Richelieu.

Daillon migrated to the south and west
To the country of the Neutrals. There he spent
The winter, fruitless. Jealousies of trade   230
Awoke resentment, fostered calumnies,
Until the priest under a constant threat
That often issued in assault, returned
Against his own persuasion to Quebec.

Brébeuf was now alone. He bent his mind
To the great end. The efficacious rites

Were hinged as much on mental apprehensions
As on the disposition of the heart.
For that the first equipment was the speech.
He listened to the sounds and gave them letters,   240
Arranged their sequences, caught the inflections,
Extracted nouns from objects, verbs from actions
And regimented rebel moods and tenses.
He saw the way the chiefs harangued the clans,
The torrent of compounded words, the art
Concealed within the pause, the look, the gesture.
Lacking all labials, the open mouth
Performed a double service with the vowels
Directed like a battery at the hearers.
With what forebodings did he watch the spell   250
Cast on the sick by the Arendiwans:
The sorcery of the Huron rhetoric
Extorting bribes for cures, for guarantees
Against the failure of the crop or hunt!
The time would come when steel would clash on steel,
And many a battle would be won or lost
With weapons from the armoury of words.
Three years of that apprenticeship had won
The praise of his Superior and no less
Evoked the admiration of Champlain.   260
That soldier, statesman, navigator, friend,
Who had combined the brain of Richelieu
With the red blood of Cartier and Magellan,
Was at this time reduced to his last keg
Of powder at the citadel. Blockade,
The piracy of Kirke on the Atlantic,
The English occupation of Quebec,
1629   And famine, closed this chapter of the Mission.

II

Four years at home could not abate his zeal.
Brébeuf, absorbed within his meditations,   270

Made ready to complete his early vows.
Each year in France but served to clarify
His vision. At Rouen he gauged the height
Of the Cathedral's central tower in terms
Of pines and oaks around the Indian lodges.
He went to Paris. There as worshipper,
His eyes were scaling transepts, but his mind,
Straying from window patterns where the sun
Shed rose ellipses on the marble floor,
Rested on glassless walls of cedar bark.   280
To Rennes – the Jesuits' intellectual home,
Where, in the *Summa* of Aquinas, faith
Laid hold on God's existence when the last
Link of the Reason slipped, and where Loyola
Enforced the high authoritarian scheme
Of God's vicegerent on the priestly fold.
Between the two nostalgic fires Brébeuf
Was swung – between two homes; in one was peace
Within the holy court, the ecstasy
Of unmolested prayer before the Virgin,   290
The daily and vicarious offering
On which no hand might dare lay sacrilege:
But in the other would be broken altars
And broken bodies of both Host and priest.
Then of which home, the son? From which the exile?
With his own blood Brébeuf wrote his last vow –
'Lord Jesus! Thou didst save me with thy blood;
By thy most precious death; and this is why
I make this pledge to serve thee all my life
In the Society of Jesus – never   300
To serve another than thyself. Hereby
I sign this promise in my blood, ready
To sacrifice it all as willingly
As now I give this drop.' – Jean de Brébeuf.

Nor did the clamour of the *Thirty Years*,
The battle-cries at La Rochelle and Fribourg,

Blow out the flame. Less strident than the names
Of Richelieu and Mazarin, Condé,
Turenne, but just as mighty, were the calls
Of the new apostolate. A century   310
Before had Xavier from the Indies summoned
The world to other colours. Now appeals
Were ringing through the history of New France.
Le Jeune, following the example of Biard
And Charles Lalemant, was capturing souls
By thousands with the fire of the *Relations*:
Noble and peasant, layman, priest and nun
Gave of their wealth and power and personal life.
Among his new recruits were Chastellain,
Pijart, Le Mercier, and Isaac Jogues,   320
The Lalemants – Jerome and Gabriel –
Jerome who was to supervise and write,
With Ragueneau, the drama of the Mission;
Who told of the survivors reaching France
When the great act was closed that 'all of them
Still hold their resolution to return
To the combat at the first sound of the trumpets.'
The other, Gabriel, who would share the crown
With Jean Brébeuf, pitting the frailest body
Against the hungers of the wilderness,   330
The fevers of the lodges and the fires
That slowly wreathed themselves around a stake.

Then Garnier, comrade of Jogues. The winds
Had fanned to a white heat the hearth and placed
Three brothers under vows – the Carmelite,
The Capuchin, and his, the Jesuit.
The gentlest of his stock, he had resolved
To seek and to accept a post that would
Transmit his nurture through a discipline
That multiplied the living martyrdoms   340
Before the casual incident of death.

To many a vow did Chabanel subject
His timid nature as the evidence
Of trial came through the Huronian records.
He needed every safeguard of the soul
To fortify the will, for every day
Would find him fighting, mastering his revolt
Against the native life and practices.
Of all the priests he could the least endure
The sudden transformation from the Chair   350
Of College Rhetoric to the heat and drag
Of portages, from the monastic calm
To the noise and smoke and vermin of the lodges,
And the insufferable sights and stinks
When, at the High Feast of the Dead, the bodies
Lying for months or years upon the scaffolds
Were taken down, stripped of their flesh, caressed,
Strung up along the cabin poles and then
Cast in a pit for common burial.
The day would come when in the wilderness,   360
The weary hand protesting, he would write
This final pledge – 'I, Noel Chabanel,
Do vow, in presence of the Sacrament
Of Thy most precious blood and body, here
To stay forever with the Huron Mission,
According to commands of my Superiors.
Therefore I do beseech Thee to receive me
As Thy perpetual servant and to make
Me worthy of so sublime a ministry.'

And the same spirit breathed on Chaumonot,   370
Making his restless and undisciplined soul
At first seek channels of renunciation
In abstinence, ill health and beggary.
His months of pilgrimages to the shrines
At Rome and to the Lady of Loretto,
The static hours upon his knees had sapped
His strength, turning an introspective mind
Upon the weary circuit of its thoughts,

Until one day a letter from Brébeuf
Would come to burn the torpors of his heart   380
And galvanize a raw novitiate.

III

1633   New France restored! Champlain, Massé, Brébeuf
Were in Quebec, hopes riding high as ever.
Davost and Daniel soon arrived to join
The expedition west. Midsummer trade,
The busiest the Colony had known,
Was over: forty-three canoes to meet
The hazards of return; the basic sense
Of safety, now Champlain was on the scene;
The joy of the Toanché Indians   390
As they beheld Brébeuf and heard him speak
In their own tongue, was happy augury.
But as before upon the eve of starting
The path was blocked, so now the unforeseen
Stepped in. A trade and tribal feud long-blown
Between the Hurons and the Allumettes
Came to a head when the Algonquin chief
Forbade the passage of the priests between
His island and the shore. The Hurons knew
The roughness of this channel, and complied.   400

In such delays which might have been construed
By lesser wills as exits of escape,
As providential doors on a light latch,
The Fathers entered deeper preparation.
They worked incessantly among the tribes
In the environs of Quebec, took hold
Of Huron words and beat them into order.
Davost and Daniel gathered from the store
Of speech, manners, and customs that Brébeuf
Had garnered, all the subtleties to make   410
The bargain for the journey. The next year

Seven canoes instead of forty! Fear
Of Iroquois following a recent raid
And massacre; growing distrust of priests;
The sense of risk in having men aboard
Unskilled in fire-arms, helpless at the paddles
And on the portages – all these combined
To sharpen the terms until the treasury
Was dry of presents and of promises.

1634   The ardours of his trip eight years before   420
Fresh in his mind, Brébeuf now set his face
To graver peril, for the native mood
Was hostile. On the second week the corn
Was low, a handful each a day. Sickness
Had struck the Huron, slowing down the blades,
And turning murmurs into menaces
Against the Blackrobes and their French companions.
The first blow hit Davost. Robbed of his books,
Papers and altar linens, he was left
At the Island of the Allumettes; Martin*   430
Was put ashore at Nipissing; Baron*
And Daniel were deserted, made to take
Their chances with canoes along the route,
Yet all in turn, tattered, wasted, with feet
Bleeding – broken though not in will – rejoined
Their great companion after he had reached
The forest shores of the Fresh Water Sea,
And guided by the sight of smoke had entered
The village of Ihonatiria.

A year's success flattered the priestly hope   440
That on this central field seed would be sown
On which the yield would be the Huron nation
Baptized and dedicated to the Faith;

*French assistants.

And that a richer harvest would be gleaned
Of duskier grain from the same seed on more
Forbidding ground when the arch-foes themselves
Would be re-born under the sacred rites.
For there was promise in the auspices.
Ihonatiria received Brébeuf
With joy. Three years he had been there, a friend   450
Whose visit to the tribes could not have sprung
From inspiration rooted in private gain.
He had not come to stack the arquebuses
Against the mountains of the beaver pelts.
He had not come to kill. Between the two –
Barter and battle – what was left to explain
A stranger in their midst? The name *Echon**
Had solved the riddle.

              So with native help
The Fathers built their mission house – the frame
Of young elm-poles set solidly in earth;   460
Their supple tops bent, lashed and braced to form
The arched roof overlaid with cedar-bark.
'No Louvre or palace is this cabin,' wrote
Brébeuf, 'no stories, cellar, garret, windows,
No chimney – only at the top a hole
To let the smoke escape. Inside, three rooms
With doors of wood alone set it apart
From the single long-house of the Indians.
The first is used for storage; in the second
Our kitchen, bedroom and refectory;   470
Our bedstead is the earth; rushes and boughs
For mattresses and pillows; in the third,
Which is our chapel, we have placed the altar,
The images and vessels of the Mass.'
It was the middle room that drew the natives,
Day after day, to share the sagamite

Echon – he who pulls the heavy load.

And raisins, and to see the marvels brought
From France – marvels on which the Fathers built
A basis of persuasion, recognizing
The potency of awe for natures nurtured   480
On charms and spells, invoking kindly spirits
And exorcising demons. So the natives
Beheld a mass of iron chips like bees
Swarm to a lodestone: was it gum that held
Them fast? They watched the handmill grind the corn;
Gaped at a lens eleven-faceted
That multiplied a bead as many times,
And at a phial where a captive flea
Looked like a beetle. But the miracle
Of all, the clock! It showed the hours; it struck   490
Or stopped upon command. Le Capitaine
Du Jour which moved its hands before its face,
Called up the dawn, saluted noon, rang out
The sunset, summoned with the count of twelve
The Fathers to a meal, or sent at four
The noisy pack of Indians to their cabins.
'What did it say?' 'Yo eiouahaoua –
Time to put on the cauldron.' 'And what now?'
'Time to go home at once and close the door.'
It was alive: an *oki* dwelt inside,   500
Peering out through that black hub on the dial.

As great a mystery was writing – how
A Frenchman fifteen miles away could know
The meaning of black signs the runner brought.
Sometimes the marks were made on peel of bark,
Sometimes on paper – in itself a wonder!
From what strange tree was it the inside rind?
What charm was in the ink that transferred thought
Across such space without a spoken word?

This growing confirmation of belief   510
Was speeded by events wherein good fortune

Waited upon the priestly word and act.
August 27
1635 A moon eclipse was due – Brébeuf had known it –
Had told the Indians of the moment when
The shadow would be thrown across the face.
Nor was there wastage in the prayers as night,
Uncurtained by a single cloud, produced
An orb most perfect. No one knew the lair
Or nest from which the shadow came; no one
The home to which it travelled when it passed.   520
Only the vague uncertainties were left –
Was it the dread invasion from the south?
Such portent was the signal for the braves
To mass themselves outside the towns and shoot
Their multitudes of arrows at the sky
And fling their curses at the Iroquois.
Like a crow's wing it hovered, broodily
Brushing the face – five hours from rim to rim
While midnight darkness stood upon the land.
This was prediction baffling all their magic.   530
Again, when weeks of drought had parched the land
And burned the corn, when dancing sorcerers
Brought out their tortoise shells, climbed on the roofs,
Clanging their invocation to the Bird
Of Thunder to return, day after day,
Without avail, the priests formed their processions,
Put on their surplices above their robes,
And the Bird of Thunder came with heavy rain,
Released by the nine masses at Saint Joseph.

Nor were the village warriors slow to see   540
The value of the Frenchmen's strategy
In war. Returning from the eastern towns,
They told how soldiers had rebuilt the forts,
And strengthened them with corner bastions
Where through the embrasures enfilading fire
Might flank the Iroquois bridging the ditches,
And scaling ramparts. Here was argument

That pierced the thickest prejudice of brain
And heart, allaying panic ever present,
When with the first news of the hated foe   550
From scouts and hunters, women with their young
Fled to the dubious refuge of the forest
From terror blacker than a pestilence.
On such a soil tilled by those skilful hands
Those passion flowers and lilies of the East,
The *Aves* and the *Paternosters* bloomed.
The *Credos* and the *Thou-shalt-nots* were turned
By Daniel into simple Huron rhymes
And taught to children, and when points of faith
Were driven hard against resistant rock,   560
The Fathers found the softer crevices
Through deeds which readily the Indian mind
Could grasp – where hands were never put to blows
Nor the swift tongues used for recrimination.

Acceptance of the common lot was part
Of the original vows. But that the priests
Who were to come should not misread the text,
Brébeuf prepared a sermon on the theme
Of Patience: – 'Fathers, Brothers, under call
Of God! Take care that you foresee the perils,   570
Labours and hardships of this Holy Mission.
You must sincerely love the savages
As brothers ransomed by the blood of Christ.
All things must be endured. To win their hearts
You must perform the smallest services.
Provide a tinder-box or burning mirror
To light their fires. Fetch wood and water for them;
And when embarking never let them wait
For you; tuck up your habits, keep them dry
To avoid water and sand in their canoes. Carry   580
Your load on portages. Always appear
Cheerful – their memories are good for faults.
Constrain yourselves to eat their sagamite

The way that they prepare it, tasteless, dirty.'

And by the priests upon the ground all dots
And commas were observed. They suffered smoke
That billowed from the back-draughts at the roof,
Smothered the cabin, seared the eyes; the fire
That broiled the face, while frost congealed the spine;
The food from unwashed platters where refusal   590
Was an offence; the rasp of speech maintained
All day by men who never learned to talk
In quiet tones; the drums of the Diviners
Blasting the night – all this without complaint!
And more – whatever sleep was possible
To snatch from the occasional lull of cries
Was broken by uncovenanted fleas
That fastened on the priestly flesh like hornets.
Carving the curves of favour on the lips,
Tailoring the man into the Jesuit coat,   600
Wrapping the smiles round inward maledictions,
And sublimating hoary Gallic oaths
Into the *Benedicite* when dogs
And squaws and reeking children violated
The hours of rest, were penances unnamed
Within the iron code of good Ignatius.
Was there a limit of obedience
Outside the jurisdiction of this Saint?
How often did the hand go up to lower
The flag? How often by some ringing order   610
Was it arrested at the halliard touch?
How often did Brébeuf seal up his ears
When blows and insults woke ancestral fifes
Within his brain, blood-cells, and viscera,
Is not explicit in the written story.

But never could the Indians infer
Self-gain or anything but simple courage
Inspired by a zeal beyond reproof,

As when the smallpox spreading like a flame
Destroying hundreds, scarifying thousands,   620
The Fathers took their chances of contagion,
Their broad hats warped by rain, their moccasins
Worn to the kibes, that they might reach the huts,
Share with the sick their dwindled stock of food –
A sup of partridge broth or raisin juice,
Inscribe the sacred sign of the cross, and place
A touch of moisture from the Holy Water
Upon the forehead of a dying child.

Before the year was gone the priests were shown
The way the Hurons could prepare for death   630
A captive foe. The warriors had surprised
A band of Iroquois and had reserved
The one survivor for a fiery pageant.
No cunning of an ancient Roman triumph,
Nor torment of a Medici confession
Surpassed the subtle savagery of art
Which made the dressing for the sacrifice
A ritual of mockery for the victim.
What visions of the past came to Brébeuf,
And what forebodings of the days to come,   640
As he beheld this weird compound of life
In jest and intent taking place before
His eyes – the crude unconscious variants
Of reed and sceptre, robe and cross, brier
And crown! Might not one day baptismal drops
Be turned against him in a rain of death?
Whatever the appeals made by the priests,
They could not break the immemorial usage
Or vary one detail. The prisoner
Was made to sing his death-song, was embraced,   650
Hailed with ironic greetings, forced to state
His willingness to die.

                    'See how your hands

Are crushed. You cannot thus desire to live.

No.

Then be of good courage – you shall die.

True! – What shall be the manner of my death?

By fire.

When shall it be?

Tonight.

What hour?

At sunset.

All is well.'

Eleven fires
Were lit along the whole length of the cabin.
His body smeared with pitch and bound with belts
Of bark, the Iroquois was forced to run   660
The fires, stopped at each end by the young braves,
And swiftly driven back, and when he swooned,
They carried him outside to the night air,
Laid him on fresh damp moss, poured cooling water
Into his mouth, and to his burns applied
The soothing balsams. With resuscitation
They lavished on him all the courtesies
Of speech and gesture, gave him food and drink,
Compassionately spoke of his wounds and pain.
The ordeal every hour was resumed   670
And halted, but, with each recurrence, blows
Were added to the burns and gibes gave place
To yells until the sacrificial dawn,
Lighting the scaffold, dimming the red glow
Of the hatchet collar, closed the festival.

Brébeuf had seen the worst. He knew that when
A winter pack of wolves brought down a stag
There was no waste of time between the leap
And the business click upon the jugular.
Such was the forthright honesty in death   680
Among the brutes. They had not learned the sport
Of dallying around the nerves to halt
A quick despatch. A human art was torture,
Where Reason crept into the veins, mixed tar
With blood and brewed its own intoxicant.
Brébeuf had pleaded for the captive's life,
But as the night wore on, would not his heart,
Colliding with his mind, have wished for death?
The plea refused, he gave the Iroquois
The only consolation in his power.   690
He went back to his cabin, heavy in heart.
To stem that viscous melanotic current
Demanded labour, time, and sacrifice.
Those passions were not altered over-night.
Two plans were in his mind – the one concerned
The seminary started in Quebec.
The children could be sent there to be trained
In Christian precepts, weaned from superstition
And from the savage spectacle of death.
He saw the way the women and their broods   700
Danced round the scaffold in their exaltation.
How much of this was habit and how much
Example? Curiously Brébeuf revolved
The facets of the Indian character.
A fighting courage equal to the French –
It could be lifted to crusading heights
By a battle speech. Endurance was a code
Among the braves, and impassivity.
Their women wailing at the Feast of Death,
The men sat silent, heads bowed to the knees.   710
'Never in nine years with but one exception,'
Wrote Ragueneau, 'did I see an Indian weep

For grief.' Only the fires evoked the cries,
And these like scalps were triumphs for the captors.
But then their charity and gentleness
To one another and to strangers gave
A balance to the picture. Fugitives
From villages destroyed found instant welcome
To the last communal share of food and land.
Brébeuf's stay at Toanché gave him proof   720
Of how the Huron nature could respond
To kindness. But last night upon that scaffold!
Could that be scoured from the heart? Why not
Try out the nurture plan upon the children
And send the boys east, shepherded by Daniel?

The other need was urgent – labourers!
The villages were numerous and were spread
Through such a vast expanse of wilderness
And shore. Only a bell with a bronze throat
Must summon missionaries to these fields.   730
With the last cry of the captive in his ears,
Brébeuf strode from his cabin to the woods
To be alone. He found his tabernacle
Within a grove, picked up a stone flat-faced,
And going to a cedar-crotch, he jammed
It in, and on this table wrote his letter.
'Herein I show you what you have to suffer.
I shall say nothing of the voyage – that
You know already. If you have the courage
To try it, that is only the beginning,   740
For when after a month of river travel
You reach our village, we can offer you
The shelter of a cabin lowlier
Than any hovel you have seen in France.
As tired as you may be, only a mat
Laid on the ground will be your bed. Your food
May be for weeks a gruel of crushed corn
That has the look and smell of mortar paste.

This country is the breeding place of vermin.
Sandflies, mosquitoes haunt the summer months.   750
In France you may have been a theologian,
A scholar, master, preacher, but out here
You must attend a savage school; for months
Will pass before you learn even to lisp
The language. Here barbarians shall be
Your Aristotle and Saint Thomas. Mute
Before those teachers you shall take your lessons.
What of the winter? Half the year is winter.
Inside your cabins will be smoke so thick
You may not read your Breviary for days.   760
Around your fireplace at mealtime arrive
The uninvited guests with whom you share
Your stint of food. And in the fall and winter,
You tramp unbeaten trails to reach the missions,
Carrying your luggage on your back. Your life
Hangs by a thread. Of all calamities
You are the cause – the scarcity of game,
A fire, famine or an epidemic.
There are no natural reasons for a drought
And for the earth's sterility. You are   770
The reasons, and at any time a savage
May burn your cabin down or split your head.
I tell you of the enemies that live
Among our Huron friends. I have not told
You of the Iroquois our constant foes.
Only a week ago in open fight
They killed twelve of our men at Contarea,
A day's march from the village where we live.
Treacherous and stealthy in their ambuscades,
They terrorize the country, for the Hurons   780
Are very slothful in defence, never
On guard and always seeking flight for safety.

'Wherein the gain, you ask, of this acceptance?
There is no gain but this – that what you suffer

Shall be of God: your loneliness in travel
Will be relieved by angels overhead;
Your silence will be sweet for you will learn
How to commune with God; rapids and rocks
Are easier than the steeps of Calvary.
There is a consolation in your hunger   790
And in abandonment upon the road,
For once there was a greater loneliness
And deeper hunger. As regards the soul
There are no dangers here, with means of grace
At every turn, for if we go outside
Our cabin, is not heaven over us?
No buildings block the clouds. We say our prayers
Freely before a noble oratory.
Here is the place to practise faith and hope
And charity where human art has brought   800
No comforts, where we strive to bring to God
A race so unlike men that we must live
Daily expecting murder at their hands,
Did we not open up the skies or close
Them at command, giving them sun or rain.
So if despite these trials you are ready
To share our labours, come; for you will find
A consolation in the cross that far outweighs
Its burdens. Though in many an hour your soul
Will echo – "Why hast Thou forsaken me?",   810
Yet evening will descend upon you when,
Your heart too full of holy exultation,
You call like Xavier – "Enough, O Lord!"'

This letter was to loom in history,
For like a bulletin it would be read
In France, and men whose bones were bound for dust
Would find that on those jagged characters
Their names would rise from their oblivion
To flame on an eternal Calendar.
Already to the field two young recruits   820

Had come – Pijart, Le Mercier; on their way
Were Chastellain with Garnier and Jogues
Followed by Ragueneau and Du Peron.

On many a night in lonely intervals,
The priest would wander to the pines and build
His oratory where celestial visions
Sustained his soul. As unto Paul and John
Of Patmos and the martyr multitude
The signs were given – voices from the clouds,
Forms that illumined darkness, stabbed despair,   830
Turned dungeons into temples and a brand
Of shame into the ultimate boast of time –
So to Brébeuf had Christ appeared and Mary.
One night at prayer he heard a voice command –
'Rise, Read!' Opening the *Imitatio Christi*,
His eyes 'without design' fell on the chapter,
Concerning the royal way of the Holy Cross,
Which placed upon his spirit 'a great peace.'
And then, day having come, he wrote his vow –
'My God, my Saviour, I take from thy hand   840
The cup of thy sufferings. I invoke thy name;
I vow never to fail thee in the grace
Of martyrdom, if by thy mercy, thou
Dost offer it to me. I bind myself,
And when I have received the stroke of death,
I will accept it from thy gracious hand
With all pleasure and with joy in my heart;
To thee my blood, my body and my life.'

IV

The labourers were soon put to their tasks, –
The speech, the founding of new posts, the sick: 850
Ihonatiria, a phantom town,
Through plague and flight abandoned as a base,

The Fathers chose the site, Teanaostayé,
To be the second mission of St. Joseph.
But the prime hope was on Ossossané,
A central town of fifty cabins built
On the east shore of Nottawasaga Bay.
The native council had approved the plans.
The presence of the priests with their lay help
Would be defence against the Iroquois.   860
Under the supervision of Pijart
The place was fortified, ramparts were strengthened,
And towers of heavy posts set at the angles.
And in the following year the artisans
And labourers from Quebec with Du Peron,
Using broad-axe and whipsaw built a church,
The first one in the whole Huronian venture
To be of wood. Close to their lodge, the priests
Dug up the soil and harrowed it to plant
A mere handful of wheat from which they raised   870
A half a bushel for the altar bread.
From the wild grapes they made a cask of wine
For the Holy Sacrifice. But of all work
The hardest was instruction. It was easy
To strike the Huron sense with sound and colour –
The ringing of a bell; the litanies
And chants; the surplices worn on the cassocks;
The burnished ornaments around the altar;
The pageant of the ceremonial.
But to drive home the ethics taxed the brain   880
To the limit of its ingenuity.
Brébeuf had felt the need to vivify
His three main themes of God and Paradise
And Hell. The Indian mind had let the cold
Abstractions fall: the allegories failed
To quicken up the logic. Garnier
Proposed the colours for the homilies.
The closest student of the Huron mind,
He had observed the fears and prejudices

Haunting the shadows of their racial past;   890
Had seen the flaws in Brébeuf's *points*; had heard
The Indian comments on the moral law
And on the Christian scheme of Paradise.
Would Iroquois be there? Yes, if baptized.
Would there be hunting of the deer and beaver?
No. Then starvation. War? And Feasts? Tobacco?
No. Garnier saw disgust upon their faces,
And sent appeals to France for pictures – one
Only of souls in bliss: of *âmes damnées*
Many and various – the horned Satan,   900
His mastiff jaws champing the head of Judas;
The plummet fall of the unbaptized pursued
By demons with their fiery forks; the lick
Of flames upon a naked Saracen;
Dragons with scarlet tongues and writhing serpents
In ambush by the charcoal avenues
Just ready at the Judgment word to wreak
Vengeance upon the unregenerate.
The negative unapprehended forms
Of Heaven lost in the dim canvas oils   910
Gave way to glows from brazier pitch that lit
The visual affirmatives of Hell.

Despite the sorcerers who laid the blame
Upon the French for all their ills – the plague,
The drought, the Iroquois – the Fathers counted
Baptisms by the hundreds, infants, children
And aged at the point of death. Adults
In health were more intractable, but here
The spade had entered soil in the conversion
Of a Huron in full bloom and high in power   920
And counsel, Tsiouendaentaha
Whose Christian name – to aid the tongue – was Peter.
Being the first, he was the Rock on which
The priests would build their Church. He was baptized

With all the pomp transferable from France
Across four thousand miles combined with what
A sky and lake could offer, and a forest
Strung to the *aubade* of the orioles.
The wooden chapel was their Rheims Cathedral.
In stole and surplice Lalemant intoned –   930
'If therefore thou wilt enter into life,
Keep the commandments. Thou shalt love the Lord
Thy God with all thy heart, with all thy soul,
With all thy might, and thy neighbour as thyself.'
With salt and water and the holy chrism,
And through the signs made on his breast and forehead
The Huron was exorcised, sanctified,
And made the temple of the Living God.

The holy rite was followed by the Mass
Before the motliest auditory known   940
In the annals of worship, Oblates from Quebec,
Blackrobes, mechanics, soldiers, labourers,
With almost half the village packed inside,
Or jammed with craning necks outside the door.
The warriors lean, lithe, and elemental,
'As naked as your hand'* but for a skin
Thrown loosely on their shoulders, with their hair
Erect, boar-brushed, matted, glued with the oil
Of sunflower larded thickly with bear's grease;
Papooses yowling on their mothers' backs,   950
The squatting hags, suspicion in their eyes,
Their nebulous minds relating in some way
The smoke and aromatics of the censer,
The candles, crucifix and Latin murmurs
With vapours, sounds and colours of the Judgment.

*Lalemant's phrase.

V

(The Founding of Fort Sainte Marie)

1639   The migrant habits of the Indians
With their desertion of the villages
Through pressure of attack or want of food
Called for a central site where undisturbed
The priests with their attendants might pursue   960
Their culture, gather strength from their devotions,
Map out the territory, plot the routes,
Collate their weekly notes and write their letters.
The roll was growing – priests and colonists,
Lay brothers offering services for life.
For on the ground or on their way to place
Themselves at the command of Lalemant,
Superior, were Claude Pijart, Poncet,
Le Moyne, Charles Raymbault, René Menard
And Joseph Chaumonot: as oblates came   970
Le Coq, Christophe Reynaut, Charles Boivin,
Couture and Jean Guérin. And so to house
Them all the Residence – Fort Sainte Marie!
Strategic as a base for trade or war
The site received the approval of Quebec,
Was ratified by Richelieu who saw
Commerce and exploration pushing west,
Fulfilling the long vision of Champlain –
'Greater New France beyond those inland seas.'
The fort was built, two hundred feet by ninety,   980
Upon the right bank of the River Wye:
Its north and eastern sides of masonry,
Its south and west of double palisades,
And skirted by a moat, ran parallel
To stream and lake. Square bastions at the corners,
Watch-towers with magazines and sleeping posts,
Commanded forest edges and canoes
That furtively came up the Matchedash,

And on each bastion was placed a cross.
Inside, the Fathers built their dwelling house,   990
No longer the bark cabin with the smoke
Ill-trained to work its exit through the roof,
But plank and timber – at each end a chimney
Of lime and granite field-stone. Rude it was
But clean, capacious, full of twilight calm.
Across the south canal fed by the river,
Ringed by another palisade were buildings
Offering retreat to Indian fugitives
Whenever war and famine scourged the land.

The plans were supervised by Lalemant,   1000
Assigning zones of work to every priest.
He made a census of the Huron nation;
Some thirty villages – twelve thousand persons.
Nor was this all: the horizon opened out
On larger fields. To south and west were spread
The unknown tribes – the Petuns and the Neutrals.

VI

(*The mission to the Petuns and Neutrals*)

1640–1641   In late November Jogues and Garnier
Set out on snow-obliterated trails
Towards the Blue Hills south of the Nottawasaga,
A thirty mile journey through a forest   1010
Without a guide. They carried on their backs
A blanket with the burden of the altar.
All day confronting swamps with fallen logs,
Tangles of tamarack and juniper,
They made detours to avoid the deep ravines
And swollen creeks. Retreating and advancing,
Ever in hope their tread was towards the south,
Until, 'surprised by night in a fir grove,'

They took an hour with flint and steel to nurse
A fire from twigs, birch rind and needles of pine;   1020
And flinging down some branches on the snow,
They offered thanks to God, lay down and slept.
Morning – the packs reshouldered and the tramp
Resumed, the stumble over mouldering trunks
Of pine and oak, the hopeless search for trails,
Till after dusk with cassocks torn and 'nothing
To eat all day save each a morsel of bread,'
They saw the smoke of the first Indian village.

And now began a labour which for faith
And triumph of the spirit over failure   1030
Was unsurpassed in records of the mission.
Famine and pest had struck the Neutral tribes,
And fleeing squaws and children had invaded
The Petun villages for bread and refuge,
Inflicting on the cabins further pest
And further famine. When the priests arrived,
They found that their black cassocks had become
The symbols of the scourge. Children exclaimed –
'Disease and famine are outside.' The women
Called to their young and fled to forest shelters,   1040
Or hid them in the shadows of the cabins.
The men broke through a never-broken custom,
Denying the strangers right to food and rest.
Observing the two priests at prayer, the chief
Called out in *council voice* – 'What are these demons
Who take such unknown postures, what are they
But spells to make us die – to finish those
Disease had failed to kill inside our cabins?'
Driven from town to town with all doors barred,
Pursued by storms of threats and flying hatchets,   1050
The priests sought refuge through the forest darkness
Back to the palisades of Sainte Marie.

As bleak an outlook faced Brébeuf when he

And Chaumonot took their November tramp –
Five forest days – to the north shores of Erie,
Where the most savage of the tribes – the Neutrals –
Packed their twelve thousand into forty towns.
Evil report had reached the settlements
By faster routes, for when upon the eve
Of the new mission Chaumonot had stated   1060
The purpose of the journey, Huron chiefs,
Convinced by their own sorcerers that Brébeuf
Had laid the epidemic on the land,
Resolved to make the Neutral leaders agents
Of their revenge: for it was on Brébeuf,
The chieftain of the robes, that hate was centred.
They had the reason why the drums had failed
The hunt, why moose and deer had left the forest,
And why the Manitou who sends the sun
And rain upon the corn, lures to the trap   1070
The beaver, trains the arrow on the goose,
Had not responded to the chants and cries.
The magic of the 'breathings' had not cured
The sick and dying. Was it not the prayers
To the new God which cast malignant spells?
The rosary against the amulet?
The Blackrobes with that water-rite performed
Upon the children – with that new sign
Of wood or iron held up before the eyes
Of the stricken? Did the Indian not behold   1080
Death following hard upon the offered Host?
Was not *Echon* Brébeuf the evil one?
Still, all attempts to kill him were forestalled,
For awe and fear had mitigated fury:
His massive stature, courage never questioned,
His steady glance, the firmness of his voice,
And that strange nimbus of authority,
In some dim way related to their gods,
Had kept the bowstrings of the Hurons taut
At the arrow feathers, and the javelin poised   1090

And hesitant. But now cunning might do
What fear forbade. A brace of Huron runners
Were sped to the Neutral country with rich bribes
To put the priests to death. And so Brébeuf
And his companion entered the first town
With famine in their cheeks only to find
Worse than the Petun greetings – corn refused,
Whispers of death and screams of panic, flight
From incarnated plague, and while the chiefs
In closest council on the Huron terms   1100
Voted for life or death, the younger men
Outside drew nearer to the priests, cursed them,
Spat at them while convulsive hands were clutching
At hatchet helves, waiting impatiently
The issue of that strident rhetoric
Shaking the cabin bark. The council ended,
The feeling strong for death but ruled by fears,
For if those foreign spirits had the power
To spread the blight upon the land, what could
Their further vengeance not exact? Besides,   1110
What lay behind those regimental colours
And those new drums reported from Quebec?
The older men had qualified the sentence –
The priests at once must leave the Neutral land,
All cabins to be barred against admission,
No food, no shelter, and return immediate.
Defying threats, the Fathers spent four months,
Four winter months, besieging half the towns
In their pursuit of souls, for days their food
Boiled lichens, ground-nuts, star-grass bulbs and roots 1120
Of the wild columbine. Met at the doors
By screams and blows, they would betake themselves
To the evergreens for shelter over-night.
And often, when the body strength was sapped
By the day's toil and there were streaks of blood
Inside the moccasins, when the last lodge

Rejected them as lepers and the welts
Hung on their shoulders, then the Fathers sought
The balm that never failed. Under the stars,
Along an incandescent avenue   1130
The visions trembled, tender, placid, pure,
More beautiful than the doorway of Rheims
And sweeter than the Galilean fields.
For what was hunger and the burn of wounds
In those assuaging, healing moments when
The clearing mists revealed the face of Mary
And the lips of Jesus breathing benedictions?

At dawn they came back to the huts to get
The same rebuff of speech and club. A brave
Repulsed them at the palisade with axe   1140
Uplifted – 'I have had enough,' he said,
'Of the dark flesh of my enemies. I mean
To kill and eat the white flesh of the priests.'
So close to death starvation and assault
Had led them and so meagre of result
Were all their ministrations that they thought
This was the finish of the enterprise.
The winter ended in futility.
And on their journey home the Fathers took
A final blow when March leagued with the natives   1150
Unleashed a northern storm, piled up the snow-drifts,
Broke on the ice the shoulder of Brébeuf,
And stumbled them for weeks before she sent
Them limping through the postern of the fort.
Upon his bed that night Brébeuf related
A vision he had seen – a moving cross,
Its upright beam arising from the south –
The country of the Iroquois: the shape
Advanced along the sky until its arms
Cast shadows on the Huron territory,   1160
'And huge enough to crucify us all.'

VII

(*The story of Jogues*)

Bad days had fallen on Huronia.
A blight of harvest, followed by a winter
In which unusual snowfall had thinned out
The hunting and reduced the settlements
To destitution, struck its hardest blow
At Sainte Marie. The last recourse in need,
The fort had been a common granary
And now the bins were empty. Altar-ware,
Vessels, linens, pictures lost or damaged;   1170
Vestments were ragged, writing paper spent.
The Eucharist requiring bread and wine,
Quebec eight hundred miles away, a war
Freshly renewed – the Iroquois (Dutch-armed
And seething with the memories of Champlain)
Arrayed against the French and Huron allies.
The priests assessed the perils of the journey,
1642   And the lot fell on Jogues to lead it. He,
Next to Brébeuf, had borne the heaviest brunt –
The Petun mission, then the following year,   1180
The Ojibway where, after a hundred leagues,
Canoe and trail, accompanied by Raymbault,
He reached the shores of Lake Superior,
'And planted a great cross, facing it west.'
The soundest of them all in legs, he gathered
A band of Huron traders and set out,
His task made double by the care of Raymbault
Whose health was broken mortally. He reached
Quebec with every day of the five weeks
A miracle of escape. A few days there,   1190
With churches, hospitals, the Indian school
At Sillery, pageant and ritual,
Making their due impression on the minds
Of the Huron guides, Jogues with his band of forty

Packed the canoes and started back. Mohawks,
Enraged that on the east-bound trip the party
Had slipped their hands, awaited them, ambushed
Within the grass and reeds along the shore.

(The account of Jogues' capture and enslavement by the
Mohawks as taken from his letter to his Provincial, Jean
Filleau, dated August 5, 1643.)

'Unskilled in speech, in knowledge and not knowing
The precious hour of my visitation,   1200
I beg you, if this letter chance to come
Unto your hands that in your charity
You aid me with your Holy Sacrifices
And with the earnest prayers of the whole Province,
As being among a people barbarous
In birth and manners, for I know that when
You will have heard this story you will see
The obligation under which I am
To God and my deep need of spiritual help.
Our business finished at Quebec, the feast   1210
Of Saint Ignatius celebrated, we
Embarked for the Hurons. On the second day
Our men discovered on the shore fresh tracks
Thought by Eustache, experienced in war,
To be the footprints of our enemies.
A mile beyond we met them, twelve canoes
And seventy men. Abandoning the boats,
Most of the Hurons fled to a thick wood,
Leaving but twelve to put up the best front
We could, but seeing further Iroquois   1220
Paddling so swiftly from the other shore,
We ceased from our defence and fled to cover
Of tree and bulrush. Watching from my shelter
The capture of Goupil and Indian converts,
I could not find it in my mind to leave them;
But as I was their comrade on the journey,

And should be made their comrade in the perils,
I gave myself as prisoner to the guard.
Likewise Eustache, always devoted, valiant,
Returned, exclaiming "I praise God that He   1230
Has granted me my prayer – that I should live
And die with you." And then Guillaume Couture
Who, young and fleet, having outstripped his foe,
But finding flight intolerable came back
Of his free will, saying "I cannot leave
My father in the hands of enemies."
On him the Iroquois let loose their first
Assault for in the skirmish he had slain
A chief. They stripped him naked; with their teeth
They macerated his finger tips, tore off   1240
The nails and pierced his right hand with a spear,
Couture taking the pain without a cry.
Then turning on Goupil and me they beat
Us to the ground under a flurry of fists
And knotted clubs, dragging us up half-dead
To agonize us with the finger torture.
And this was just the foretaste of our trials:
Dividing up as spoils of war our food,
Our clothes and books and vessels for the church,
They led or drove us on our six weeks' journey,   1250
Our wounds festering under the summer sun.
At night we were the objects of their sport –
They mocked us by the plucking of our hair
From head and beard. And on the eighth day meeting
A band of warriors from the tribe on march
To attack the Richelieu fort, they celebrated
By disembarking all the captives, making
Us run the line beneath a rain of clubs.
And following that they placed us on the scaffolds,
Dancing around us hurling jests and insults.   1260
Each one of us attempted to sustain
The other in his courage by no cry
Or sign of our infirmities. Eustache,

His thumbs wrenched off, withstood unconquerably
The probing of a stick which like a skewer
Beginning with the freshness of a wound
On the left hand was pushed up to the elbow.
And yet next day they put us on the route
Again – three days on foot and without food.
Through village after village we were led   1270
In triumph with our backs shedding the skin
Under the sun – by day upon the scaffolds,
By night brought to the cabins where, cord-bound,
We lay on the bare earth while fiery coals
Were thrown upon our bodies. A long time
Indeed and cruelly have the wicked wrought
Upon my back with sticks and iron rods.
But though at times when left alone I wept,
Yet I thanked Him who always giveth strength
To the weary (I will glory in the things   1280
Concerning my infirmity, being made
A spectacle to God and to the angels,
A sport and a contempt to the barbarians)
That I was thus permitted to console
And animate the French and Huron converts,
Placing before their minds the thought of Him
Who bore against Himself the contradiction
Of sinners. Weak through hanging by my wrists
Between two poles, my feet not touching ground,
I managed through His help to reach the stage,   1290
And with the dew from leaves of Turkish corn
Two of the prisoners I baptized. I called
To them that in their torment they should fix
Their eyes on me as I bestowed the sign
Of the last absolution. With the spirit
Of Christ, Eustache then in the fire entreated
His Huron friends to let no thought of vengeance
Arising from this anguish at the stake
Injure the French hope for an Iroquois peace.
Onnonhoaraton, a youthful captive,   1300

They killed – the one who seeing me prepared
For torture interposed, offering himself
A sacrifice for me who had in bonds
Begotten him for Christ. Couture was seized
And dragged off as a slave. René Goupil,
While placing on a child's forehead the sign
Of the Cross was murdered by a sorcerer,
And then, a rope tied to his neck, was dragged
Through the whole village and flung in the River.'

(*The later account*)

A family of the Wolf Clan having lost   1310
A son in battle, Jogues as substitute
Was taken in, half-son, half-slave, his work
The drudgery of the village, bearing water,
Lighting the fires, and clad in tatters made
To join the winter hunt, bear heavy packs
On scarred and naked shoulders in the trade
Between the villages. His readiness
To execute his tasks, unmurmuring,
His courage when he plunged into a river
To save a woman and a child who stumbled   1320
Crossing a bridge made by a fallen tree,
Had softened for a time his master's harshness.
It gained him scattered hours of leisure when
He set his mind to work upon the language
To make concrete the articles of Faith.
At intervals he stole into the woods
To pray and meditate and carve the Name
Upon the bark. Out of the Mohawk spoils
At the first battle he had found and hid
Two books – *The Following of Christ* and one   1330
Of Paul's *Epistles*, and with these when 'weary
Even of life and pressed beyond all measure
Above his strength' he followed the 'running waters'
To quench his thirst. But often would the hate

Of the Mohawk foes flame out anew when Jogues
Was on his knees muttering the magic words,
And when a hunting party empty-handed
Returned or some reverse was met in battle,
Here was the victim ready at their door.
Believing that a band of warriors   1340
Had been destroyed, they seized the priest and set
His day of death, but at the eleventh hour,
With the arrival of a group of captives,
The larger festival of torture gave
Him momentary reprieve. Yet when he saw
The holocaust and rushed into the flames
To save a child, a heavy weight laid hold
Upon his spirit lasting many days –
'My life wasted with grief, my years with sighs;
Oh wherefore was I born that I should see   1350
The ruin of my people! Woe is me!
But by His favour I shall overcome
Until my change is made and He appear.'

This story of enslavement had been brought
To Montmagny, the Governor of Quebec,
And to the outpost of the Dutch, Fort Orange.
Quebec was far away and, short of men,
Could never cope with the massed Iroquois,
Besides, Jogues' letter begged the Governor
That no measures 'to save a single life'   1360
Should hurt the cause of France. To the Provincial
He wrote – 'Who in my absence would console
The captives? Who absolve the penitent?
Encourage them in torments? Who baptize
The dying? On this cross to which our Lord
Has nailed me with Himself am I resolved
To live and die.'
          And when the commandant
Of the Dutch fort sent notice that a ship
At anchor in the Hudson would provide
Asylum, Jogues delayed that he might seek   1370

Counsel of God and satisfy his conscience,
Lest some intruding self-preserving thought
Conflict with duty. Death was certain soon.
He knew it – for that mounting tide of hate
Could not be checked: it had engulfed his friends;
'Twould take him next. How close to suicide
Would be refusal? Not as if escape
Meant dereliction: no, his early vows
Were still inviolate – he would return.
He pledged himself to God there on his knees   1380
Before two bark-strips fashioned as a cross
Under the forest trees – his oratory.
And so, one night, the Indians asleep,
Jogues left the house, fumbling his darkened way,
Half-walk, half-crawl, a lacerated leg
Making the journey of one-half a mile
The toil of half a night. By dawn he found
The shore, and, single-handed, pushed a boat,
Stranded by ebb-tide, down the slope of sand
To the river's edge and rowed out to the ship,   1390
Where he was lifted up the side by sailors
Who, fearful of the risk of harbouring
A fugitive, carried him to the hatch
And hid him with the cargo in the hold.

The outcry in the morning could be heard
Aboard the ship as Indians combed the cabins,
Threatened the guards and scoured the neighbouring
        woods,
And then with strong suspicion of the vessel
Demanded of the officers their captive.
After two days Jogues with his own consent   1400
Was taken to the fort and hid again
Behind the barrels of a store. For weeks
He saw and heard the Mohawks as they passed,
Examining cordage, prying into casks,
At times touching his clothes, but missing him

As he lay crouched in darkness motionless.
With evidence that he was in the fort,
The Dutch abetting the escape, the chiefs
Approached the commandant – 'The prisoner
Is ours. He is not of your race or speech.   1410
The Dutch are friends: the Frenchmen are our foes.
Deliver up this priest into our hands.'
The cries were countered by the officer –
'He is like us in blood if not in tongue.
The Frenchman here is under our protection.
He is our guest. We treat him as you treat
The strangers in your cabins, for you feed
And shelter them. That also is our law,
The custom of our nation.' Argument
Of no avail, a ransom price was offered,   1420
Refused, but running up the bargain scale,
It caught the Mohawks at three hundred livres,
And Jogues at last was safely on the Hudson.

The tale of Jogues' first mission to the Hurons
Ends on a sequel briefly sung but keyed
To the tune of the story, for the stretch
Home was across a wilderness, his bed
A coil of rope on a ship's open deck
Swept by December surge. The voyage closed
At Falmouth where, robbed by a pirate gang,   1430
He wandered destitute until picked up
By a French crew who offered him tramp fare.
He landed on the shore of Brittany
On Christmas Eve, and by New Year he reached
The Jesuit establishment at Rennes.

The trumpets blew once more, and Jogues returned
With the spring expedition to Quebec.
Honoured by Montmagny, he took the post
Of peace ambassador to hostile tribes,
And then the orders came from Lalemant   1440

That he should open up again the cause
Among the Mohawks at Ossernenon.
Jogues knew that he was travelling to his death,
And though each hour of that former mission
Burned at his finger stumps, the wayward flesh
Obeyed the summons. Lalemant as well
Had known the peril – had he not re-named
Ossernenon, the Mission of the Martyrs?
So Jogues, accompanied by his friend Lalande
Departed for the village – his last letter   1450
To his Superior read: 'I will return
Cost it a thousand lives. I know full well
That I shall not survive, but He who helped
Me by His grace before will never fail me
Now when I go to do His holy will.'
And to the final consonant the vow
Was kept, for two days after they had struck
The town, their heads were on the palisades,
1646   And their dragged bodies flung into the Mohawk.

VIII

(*Bressani*)

The western missions waiting Jogues' return   1460
Were held together by a scarlet thread.
The forays of the Iroquois had sent
The fugitive survivors to the fort.
Three years had passed – and where was Jogues?
        The scant
Supplies of sagamite could never feed
The inflow from the stricken villages.
The sparse reports had filtered to Quebec
And the command was given to Bressani
To lead the rescue band to Sainte Marie.
Leaving Three Rivers in the spring when ice   1470
Was on the current, he was caught like Jogues,

With his six Hurons and a French oblate,
A boy of twelve; transferred to Iroquois'
Canoes and carried up the Richelieu;
Disbarked and driven through the forest trails
To Lake Champlain; across it; and from there
Around the rocks and marshes to the Hudson.
And every time a camp was built and fires
Were laid the torment was renewed; in all
The towns the squaws and children were regaled   1480
With evening festivals upon the scaffolds.
Bressani wrote one day when vigilance
Relaxed and his split hand was partly healed –
'I do not know if your Paternity
Will recognize this writing for the letter
Is soiled. Only one finger of the hand
Is left unburned. The blood has stained the paper.
My writing table is the earth; the ink
Gunpowder mixed with water.' And again –
This time to his Superior – 'I could   1490
Not have believed it to be possible
That a man's body was so hard to kill.'
The earlier fate of Jogues was his – enslaved,
But ransomed at Fort Orange by the Dutch;
Restored to partial health; sent to Rochelle
In the autumn, but in April back again
And under orders for the Huron mission,
Where he arrived this time unscathed to take
A loyal welcome from his priestly comrades.

Bressani's presence stimulated faith   1500
Within the souls of priests and neophytes.
The stories burned like fuel of the faggots –
Jogues' capture and his rock stability,
And the no less triumphant stand Eustache
Had made showing the world that native metal
Could take the test as nobly as the French.
And Ragueneau's letter to his General stated –
'Bressani ill-equipped to speak the Huron

Has speech more eloquent to capture souls:
It is his scars, his mutilated hands.   1510
"Only show us," the neophytes exclaim,
"The wounds, for they teach better than our tongues
Your faith, for you have come again to face
The dangers. Only thus we know that you
Believe the truth and would have us believe it."'

IX

In those three years since Jogues' departure doubts
Though unexpressed had visited the mission.
For death had come to several in the fold –
Raymbault, Goupil, Eustache, and worse than death
To Jogues, and winter nights were bleaker, darker   1520
Without the company of Brébeuf. Lion
Of limb and heart, he had entrenched the faith,
Was like a triple palisade himself.
But as his broken shoulder had not healed,
And ordered to Quebec by Lalemant,
He took the leave that seven years of work
Deserved. The city hailed him with delight.
For more than any other did he seem
The very incarnation of the age –
Champlain the symbol of exploring France,   1530
Tracking the rivers to their lairs, Brébeuf
The token of a nobler chivalry.
He went the rounds of the stations, saw the gains
The East had made in converts – Sillery
For Indians and Notre Dame des Anges
For the French colonists; convents and schools
Flourished. Why should the West not have the same
Yield for the sowing? It was labourers
They needed with supplies and adequate
Defence. St. Lawrence and the Ottawa   1540
Infested by the Iroquois were traps

Of death. Three bands of Hurons had been caught
That summer. Montmagny had warned the priest
Against the risk of unprotected journeys.
So when the reinforcements came from France,
Brébeuf set out under a guard of soldiers
Taking with him two young recruits – Garreau
And Chabanel – arriving at the fort
In the late fall. The soldiers wintered there
And supervised defensive strategy.   1550
Replaced the forlorn feelings with fresh hopes,
And for two years the mission enterprise
Renewed its lease of life. Rumours of treaties
Between the French and Mohawks stirred belief
That peace was in the air, that other tribes
Inside the Iroquois Confederacy
Might enter – with the Hurons sharing terms.
This was the pipe-dream – was it credible?
The ranks of missionaries were filling up:
At Sainte Marie, Brébeuf and Ragueneau,   1560
Le Mercier, Chastellain and Chabanel;
St. Joseph – Garnier and René Menard;
St. Michel – Chaumonot and Du Peron;
The others – Claude Pijart, Le Moyne, Garreau
And Daniel.
                 What validity the dream
Possessed was given by the seasonal
Uninterrupted visits of the priests
To their loved home, both fort and residence.
Here they discussed their plans, and added up
In smiling rivalry their tolls of converts: 1570
They loitered at the shelves, fondled the books,
Running their fingers down the mellowed pages
As if they were the faces of their friends.
They stood for hours before the saints or knelt
Before the Virgin and the crucifix
In mute transfiguration. These were hours
That put the bandages upon their hurts,

Making their spirits proof against all ills
That had assailed or could assail the flesh,
Turned winter into spring and made return   1580
To their far mission posts an exaltation.
The bell each morning called the neophytes
To Mass, again at evening, and the tones
Lured back the memories across the seas.
And often in the summer hours of twilight
When Norman chimes were ringing, would the
        priests
Forsake the fort and wander to the shore
To sing the *Gloria* while hermit thrushes
Rivalled the rapture of the nightingales.

The native register was rich in name   1590
And number. Earlier years had shown results
Mainly among the young and sick and aged,
Where little proof was given of the root
Of faith, but now the Fathers told of deeds
That flowered from the stems. Had not Eustache
Bequeathed his record like a Testament?
The sturdiest warriors and chiefs had vied
Among themselves within the martyr ranks: –
Stories of captives led to sacrifice,
Accepting scaffold fires under the rites,   1600
Enduring to the end, had taken grip
Of towns and clans. St. Joseph had its record
For Garnier reported that Totiri,
A native of high rank, while visiting
St. Ignace when a torture was in progress,
Had emulated Jogues by plunging through
The flaming torches that he might apply
The Holy Water to an Iroquois.
Garreau and Pijart added lists of names
From the Algonquins and the Nipissings,   1610
And others told of Pentecostal meetings
In cabins by the Manitoulin shores.

Not only was the faith sustained by hopes
Nourished within the bosom of their home
And by the wish-engendered talk of peace,
But there outside the fort was evidence
Of tenure for the future. Acres rich
In soil extended to the forest fringe.
Each year they felled the trees and burned the stumps,
Pushing the frontier back, clearing the land,   1620
Spading, hoeing. The stomach's noisy protest
At sagamite and wild rice found a rest
With bread from wheat, fresh cabbages and pease,
And squashes which when roasted had the taste
Of Norman apples. Strawberries in July,
October beechnuts, pepper roots for spice,
And at the bottom of a spring that flowed
Into a pond shaded by silver birches
And ringed by marigolds was water-cress
In chilled abundance. So, was this the West?   1630
The Wilderness? That flight of tanagers;
Those linguals from the bobolinks; those beeches,
Roses and water-lilies; at the pools
Those bottle-gentians! For a time the fields
Could hypnotize the mind to scenes of France.
Within five years the change was wrought. The cocks
Were crowing in the yards, and in the pasture
Were sheep and cows and pigs that had been brought
As sucklings that immense eight hundred miles
In sacks – canoed, and portaged on the shoulders.   1640
The traders, like the soldiers, too, had heard
Of a great ocean larger than the Huron.
Was it the western gateway to Cathay?
The Passage? Master-theme of song and ballad;
The *myth* at last resolved into the *fact*!
Along that route, it was believed, French craft
Freighted with jewels, spices, tapestries,
Would sail to swell the coffers of the Bourbons.
Such was the dream though only buffalo roamed
The West and autumn slept upon the prairies.   1650

This dream was at its brightest now, Quebec
Was building up a western citadel
In Sainte Marie. With sixty Frenchmen there,
The eastern capital itself had known
Years less auspicious. Might the fort not be
The bastion to one-half the continent,
New France expanding till the longitudes
Staggered the daring of the navigators?
The priests were breathless with another space
Beyond the measure of the astrolabe –   1660
A different empire built upon the pulses,
Where even the sun and moon and stars revolved
Around a Life and a redemptive Death.
They pushed their missions to the north and west
Further into Algonquin territories,
Among the Ottawas at Manitoulin,
And towards the Ojibways at Sault Sainte Marie.
New village groups were organized in stations –
St. Magdalen, St. Jean, and St. Matthias.
Had Chabanel, ecstatic with success,   1670
Not named one fort the Village of Believers?
Brébeuf was writing to his General –
'Peace, union and tranquillity are here
Between the members of our Order. We need
More workers for the apostolic field,
Which more than ever whitens for the harvest.'
And to this call came Gabriel Lalemant,
Bonin, Daran, Greslon, besides a score
Of labourers and soldiers. In one year
Twelve hundred converts, churches over-crowded,   1680
With Mass conducted in the open air!

And so the seasons passed. When the wild ducks
Forsook the Huron marshes for the south,
It was the signal for the priests to pack

Their blankets. Not until the juncos came,
And flickers tapped the crevices of bark,
And the bloodroot was pushing through the leaf-mould,
Would they reset their faces towards their home.

X

While Ragueneau's *Relations* were being sent
Homeward, picturing the promise of the west,   1690
The thunder clouds were massing in the east
Under the pounding drums. The treaty signed
Between the Iroquois and Montmagny
Was broken by the murder of Lalande
And Jogues. The news had drifted to the fort –
The prelude only to the heavier blows
And deeper treachery. The Iroquois,
Infesting lake and stream, forest and shore,
Were trapping soldiers, traders, Huron guides:
The whole confederacy was on the march.   1700
Both waterways were blocked, the quicker route –
St. Lawrence, and the arduous Ottawa.
They caught the Hurons at their camps, surprised
Canoe-fleets from the reeds and river bends
And robbed them, killed them on the portages.
So widespread were their forays, they encountered
Bands of Algonquins on the hunt, slew them,
Dispersed them from their villages and sent
Survivors to the northern wilderness.
So keen their lust for slaughter, they enticed   1710
The Huron chieftains under pledge of truce
And closed negotiations with their scalps.

As the months passed the pressure of attack
Moved grimly towards the west, making complete
The isolation of Huronia.
No commerce with Quebec – no traveller

For a whole year came to the Residence.
But constant was the stream of fugitives
From smaller undefended villages,
Fleeing west and ever west. The larger towns,   1720
The deluge breaking down their walls, drove on
The surplus to their neighbours which, in turn,
Urged on the panic herd to Sainte Marie.
This mother of the missions felt the strain
As one by one the buffers were destroyed,
And the flocks came nearer for their pasturage.
There could be only one conclusion when
The priests saw the migration of the missions –
That of St. Jean four times abandoning
Its stations and four times establishing   1730
New centres with a more improved defence;
That of St. Ignace where a double raid
That slaughtered hundreds, lifted bodily
Both town and mission, driving to their last
Refuge the ragged remnants. Yet Ragueneau
Was writing – 'We are here as yet intact
But all determined to shed blood and life
If need be. In this Residence still reigns
The peace and love of Heaven. Here the sick
Will find a hospital, the travellers   1740
A place of rest, the fugitives, asylum.
During the year more than three thousand persons
Have sought and found shelter under our roof.
We have dispensed the Bread of Life to all
And we have fed their bodies, though our fare
Is down to one food only, crushed corn boiled
And seasoned with the powder of smoked fish.'

Despite the perils, Sainte Marie was sending
Her missionaries afield, revisiting
The older sites, establishing the new,   1750
With that same measure of success and failure
Which tested courage or confirmed a faith.

Garreau, sick and expecting death, was brought
By Pijart and a French assistant back
From the Algonquin wastes, for thirteen days
Borne by a canoe and by his comrades' shoulders.
Recovering even after the last rites
Had been administered, he faced the task
Again. Fresh visits to the Petun tribes
Had little yield but cold and starving days,   1760
Unsheltered nights, the same fare at the doors,
Savoured by Jogues and Garnier seven years
Before. And everywhere the labourers worked
Under a double threat – the Iroquois,
And the Huron curse inspired by sorcerers
Who saw black magic in the Jesuit robes
And linked disaster with their ritual.
Between the hammer and the anvil now
Huronia was laid and the first priest
To take the blow was Daniel.   1770
                         Fourteen years
This priest had laboured at the Huron mission.
Following a week of rest at Sainte Marie
He had returned to his last post, St. Joseph,
Where he had built his church and for the year
Just gone had added to his charge the hundreds
Swarming from villages stormed by the foe.
And now in that inexorable order,
Station by station, town by town, it was
St. Joseph's turn. Aware that the main force
Of Huron warriors had left the town,   1780
The Iroquois had breached the palisade
And, overwhelming the defenders, sacked
And burned the cabins. Mass had just been offered,
When the war yells were heard and Daniel came
Outside. Seeing the panic, fully knowing
Extinction faced the town with this invasion,
And that ten precious minutes of delay
Might give his flock the refuge of the woods,

He faced the vanguard of the Iroquois,
And walked with firm selective dignity   1790
As in the manner of a parley. Fear
And wonder checked the Indians at the sight
Of a single dark-robed, unarmed challenger
Against arrows, muskets, spears and tomahawks.
That momentary pause had saved the lives
Of hundreds as they fled into the forest,
But not the life of Daniel. Though afraid
At first to cross a charmed circumference
To take a struggle hand-to-hand, they drove
Their arrows through him, then in frenzied rush   1800
Mastering their awe, they hurled themselves upon
The body, stripped it of its clothes and flung it
Into the burning church. By noon nothing
Remained but ashes of the town, the fort,
July 1648   The cabins and their seven hundred dead.

XI

Ragueneau was distraught. He was shepherd-priest.
Daniel was first to die under his care,
And nigh a score of missionaries were lost
In unprotected towns. Besides, he knew
He could not, if he would, resist that mob   1810
That clamoured at the stockades, day by day.
His moral supervision was bound up
With charity that fed and warmed and healed.
And through the winter following Daniel's death
Six thousand Indians sought shelter there.
The season's crops to the last grain were garnered
And shared. 'Through the kind Providence of God,
We managed, as it were, to draw both oil
And honey from the very stones around us.
The obedience, patience of our missionaries   1820
Excel reward – all with one heart and soul

Infused with the high spirit of our Order;
The servants, boys, and soldiers day and night
Working beyond their strength! Here is the service
Of joy, that we will take whatever God
Ordains for us whether it be life or death.'
The challenge was accepted, for the spring
Opened upon the hardest tragic blows
The iron in the human soul could stand.

St. Louis and St. Ignace still remained   1830
The flying buttresses of Sainte Marie.
From them the Residence received reports
Daily of movements of the Iroquois.
Much labour had been spent on their defence.
Ramparts of pine fifteen feet high enclosed
St. Louis. On three sides a steep ravine
Topped by the stakes made nigh impregnable
St. Ignace; then the palisaded fourth,
Subject alone to a surprise assault,
Could rally the main body of defenders.   1840
The Iroquois, alert as eagles, knew
The weakness of the Hurons, the effect
On the morale of unexpected raids
Committing towns to fire and pushing back
The eastern ramparts. Piece by piece, the rim
Was being cracked and fissures driven down
The bowl: and stroke by stroke the strategy
Pointed to Sainte Marie. Were once the fort
Now garrisoned by forty Frenchmen taken,
No power predicted from Quebec could save   1850
The Huron nation from its doom. St. Ignace
Lay in the path but during the eight months
After St. Joseph's fall the enemy
Had leisurely prepared their plans. Their scouts
Reported that one-half of the town's strength
Was lost by flight and that an apathy,
In spite of all the priests could do to stem it,

Had seized the invaded tribes. They knew that when
The warriors were hunting in the forest
This weaker palisade was scalable.   1860
And the day came in March when the whole fate
That overtook St. Joseph in July
Swept on St. Ignace – sudden and complete.
The Mohawks and the Senecas uniting,
A thousand strong, the town bereft of fighters,
Four hundred old and young inside the stakes,
The assault was made two hours before the dawn.
But half-aroused from sleep, many were killed
Within their cabins. Of the four hundred three
Alone managed to reach the woods to scream   1870
The alarm to the drowsed village of St. Louis.

At nine o'clock that morning – such the speed
Of the pursuit – a guard upon the hill
Behind the Residence was watching whiffs
Of smoke to the south, but a league away.
Bush fires? Not with this season's depth of snow.
The Huron bivouacs? The settlements
Too close for that. Camps of the Iroquois?
Not while cunning and stealth controlled their tactics.
The smoke was in the town. The morning air,   1880
Clearing, could leave no doubt of that, and just
As little that the darkening pall could spring
Out of the vent-holes from the cabin roofs.
Ragueneau rushed to the hill at the guard's call;
Summoned Bressani; sheets and tongues of flame
Leaping some fifty feet above the smoke
Meant to their eyes the capture and the torch –
St. Louis with Brébeuf and Lalemant!

Less than two hours it took the Iroquois
To capture, sack and garrison St. Ignace,   1890
And start then for St. Louis. The alarm
Sounded, five hundred of the natives fled

To the mother fort only to be pursued
And massacred in the snow. The eighty braves
That manned the stockades perished at the breaches;
And what was seen by Ragueneau and the guard
Was smoke from the massed fire of cabin bark.

Brébeuf and Lalemant were not numbered
In the five hundred of the fugitives.
They had remained, infusing nerve and will   1900
In the defenders, rushing through the cabins
Baptizing and absolving those who were
Too old, too young, too sick to join the flight.
And when, resistance crushed, the Iroquois
Took all they had not slain back to St. Ignace,
The vanguard of the prisoners were the priests.

March 16
1649 Three miles from town to town over the snow,
Naked, laden with pillage from the lodges,
The captives filed like wounded beasts of burden,
Three hours on the march, and those that fell   1910
Or slowed their steps were killed.
                                        Three days before
Brébeuf had celebrated his last mass.
And he had known it was to be the last.
There was prophetic meaning as he took
The cord and tied the alb around his waist,
Attached the maniple to his left arm
And drew the seamless purple chasuble
With the large cross over his head and shoulders,
Draping his body: every vestment held
An immediate holy symbol as he whispered –   1920
'Upon my head the helmet of Salvation.
So purify my heart and make me white;
With this cincture of purity gird me,
O Lord.
            May I deserve this maniple
Of sorrow and of penance.
                                Unto me

Restore the stole of immortality.
My yoke is sweet, my burden light.
                              Grant that
I may so bear it as to win Thy grace.'

Entering, he knelt before as rude an altar
As ever was reared within a sanctuary,   1930
But hallowed as that chancel where the notes
Of Palestrina's score had often pealed
The *Assumpta est Maria* through Saint Peter's.
For, covered in the centre of the table,
Recessed and sealed, a hollowed stone contained
A relic of a charred or broken body
Which perhaps a thousand years ago or more
Was offered as a sacrifice to Him
Whose crucifix stood there between the candles.
And on the morrow would this prayer be answered: –   1940
'Eternal Father, I unite myself
With the affections and the purposes
Of Our Lady of Sorrows on Calvary.
And now I offer Thee the sacrifice
Which Thy Beloved Son made of Himself
Upon the Cross and now renews on this,
His holy altar ...
                    Graciously receive
My life for His life as He gave His life
For mine ...
              This is my body.
                              In like manner ...
Take ye and drink – the chalice of my blood.'   1950

XII

No doubt in the mind of Brébeuf that this was the last
Journey – three miles over the snow. He knew
That the margins as thin as they were by which he escaped
From death through the eighteen years of his mission toil

Did not belong to this chapter: not by his pen
Would this be told. He knew his place in the line,
For the blaze of the trail that was cut on the bark by
    Jogues
Shone still. He had heard the story as told by writ
And word of survivors – of how a captive slave
Of the hunters, the skin of his thighs cracked with the   1960
    frost,
He would steal from the tents to the birches, make a
    rough cross
From two branches, set it in snow and on the peel
Inscribe his vows and dedicate to the Name
In 'litanies of love' what fragments were left
From the wrack of his flesh; of his escape from the tribes;
Of his journey to France where he knocked at the door
    of the College
Of Rennes, was gathered in as a mendicant friar,
Nameless, unknown, till he gave for proof to the priest
His scarred credentials of faith, the nail-less hands
And withered arms – the signs of the Mohawk fury.   1970
Nor yet was the story finished – he had come again
Back to his mission to get the second death.
And the comrades of Jogues – Goupil, Eustache and
    Couture,
Had been stripped and made to run the double files
And take the blows – one hundred clubs to each line –
And this as the prelude to torture, leisured, minute,
Where thorns on the quick, scallop shells to the joints
    of the thumbs,
Provided the sport for children and squaws till the end.
And adding salt to the blood of Brébeuf was the thought
Of Daniel – was it months or a week ago?   1980
So far, so near, it seemed in time, so close
In leagues – just over there to the south it was
He faced the arrows and died in front of his church.

But winding into the greater artery
Of thought that bore upon the coming passion

Were little tributaries of wayward wish
And reminiscence. Paris with its vespers
Was folded in the mind of Lalemant,
And the soft Gothic lights and traceries
Were shading down the ridges of his vows.   1990
But two years past at Bourges he had walked the
        cloisters,
Companioned by Saint Augustine and Francis,
And wrapped in quiet holy mists. Brébeuf,
His mind a moment throwing back the curtain
Of eighteen years, could see the orchard lands,
The *cidreries*, the peasants at the Fairs,
The undulating miles of wheat and barley,
Gardens and pastures rolling like a sea
From Lisieux to Le Havre. Just now the surf
Was pounding on the limestone Norman beaches   2000
And on the reefs of Calvados. Had dawn
This very day not flung her surplices
Around the headlands and with golden fire
Consumed the silken argosies that made
For Rouen from the estuary of the Seine?
A moment only for that veil to lift –
A moment only for those bells to die
That rang their matins at Condé-sur-Vire.

By noon St. Ignace! The arrival there
The signal for the battle-cries of triumph,   2010
The gauntlet of the clubs. The stakes were set
And the ordeal of Jogues was re-enacted
Upon the priests – even with wilder fury,
For here at last was trapped their greatest victim,
Echon. The Iroquois had waited long
For this event. Their hatred for the Hurons
Fused with their hatred for the French and priests
Was to be vented on this sacrifice,
And to that camp had come apostate Hurons,
United with their foes in common hate   2020
To settle up their reckoning with *Echon*.

*

Now three o'clock, and capping the height of the passion,
Confusing the sacraments under the pines of the forest,
Under the incense of balsam, under the smoke
Of the pitch, was offered the rite of the font. On the head,
The breast, the loins and the legs, the boiling water!
While the mocking paraphrase of the symbols was
        hurled
At their faces like shards of flint from the arrow heads –
'We baptize thee with water ...
                                That thou mayest be led
To Heaven ...   2030
                To that end we do anoint thee.
We treat thee as a friend: we are the cause
Of thy happiness; we are thy priests; the more
Thou sufferest, the more thy God will reward thee,
So give us thanks for our kind offices.'

The fury of taunt was followed by fury of blow.
Why did not the flesh of Brébeuf cringe to the scourge,
Respond to the heat, for rarely the Iroquois found
A victim that would not cry out in such pain – yet here
The fire was on the wrong fuel. Whenever he spoke,
It was to rally the soul of his friend whose turn   2040
Was to come through the night while the eyes were
        uplifted in prayer,
Imploring the Lady of Sorrows, the mother of Christ,
As pain brimmed over the cup and the will was called
To stand the test of the coals. And sometimes the speech
Of Brébeuf struck out, thundering reproof to his foes,
Half-rebuke, half-defiance, giving them roar for roar.
Was it because the chancel became the arena,
Brébeuf a lion at bay, not a lamb on the altar,
As if the might of a Roman were joined to the cause
Of Judaea? Speech they could stop for they girdled   2050
        his lips,
But never a moan could they get. Where was the source

Of his strength, the home of his courage that topped the
     best
Of their braves and even out-fabled the lore of their
     legends?
In the bunch of his shoulders which often had carried a
     load
Extorting the envy of guides at an Ottawa portage?
The heat of the hatchets was finding a path to that source.
In the thews of his thighs which had mastered the trails
     of the Neutrals?
They would gash and beribbon those muscles. Was
          it the blood?
They would draw it fresh from its fountain. Was it the
     heart?
They dug for it, fought for the scraps in the way of the   2060
     wolves.
But not in these was the valour or stamina lodged;
Nor in the symbol of Richelieu's robes or the seals
Of Mazarin's charters, nor in the stir of the *lilies*
Upon the Imperial folds; nor yet in the words
Loyola wrote on a table of lava-stone
In the cave of Manresa – not in these the source –
But in the sound of invisible trumpets blowing
Around two slabs of board, right-angled, hammered
By Roman nails and hung on a Jewish hill.

The wheel had come full circle with the visions   2070
In France of Brébeuf poured through the mould of
     St. Ignace.
Lalemant died in the morning at nine, in the flame
Of the pitch belts. Flushed with the sight of the bodies,
     the foes
Gathered their clans and moved back to the north and
     west
To join in the fight against the tribes of the Petuns.
There was nothing now that could stem the Iroquois
     blast.

However undaunted the souls of the priests who were
  left,
However fierce the sporadic counter attacks
Of the Hurons striking in roving bands from the ambush,
Or smashing out at their foes in garrison raids,   2080
The villages fell before a blizzard of axes
And arrows and spears, and then were put to the torch.

The days were dark at the fort and heavier grew
The burdens on Ragueneau's shoulders. Decision was his.
No word from the east could arrive in time to shape
The step he must take. To and fro – from altar to hill,
From hill to altar, he walked and prayed and watched.
As governing priest of the Mission he felt the pride
Of his Order whipping his pulse, for was not St. Ignace
The highest test of the Faith? And all that torture   2090
And death could do to the body was done. The Will
And the Cause in their triumph survived. Loyola's
  mountains,
Sublime at their summits, were scaled to the uttermost
  peak.
Ragueneau, the Shepherd, now looked on a battered fold.
In a whirlwind of fire St. Jean, like St. Joseph, crashed
Under the Iroquois impact. Firm at his post,
Garnier suffered the fate of Daniel. And now
Chabanel, last in the roll of the martyrs, entrapped
On his knees in the woods met death at apostate hands.

The drama was drawing close to its end. It fell   2100
To Ragueneau's lot to perform a final rite –
To offer the fort in sacrificial fire!
He applied the torch himself. 'Inside an hour,'
He wrote, 'we saw the fruit of ten years' labour
Ascend in smoke, – then looked our last at the fields,
Put altar-vessels and food on a raft of logs,
And made our way to the island of St. Joseph.'
But even from there was the old tale retold –

Of hunger and the search for roots and acorns;
Of cold and persecution unto death   2110
By the Iroquois; of Jesuit will and courage
As the shepherd-priest with Chaumonot led back
The remnant of a nation to Quebec.

THE MARTYRS' SHRINE

Three hundred years have passed, and the winds of God
Which blew over France are blowing once more
              through the pines
That bulwark the shores of the great Fresh Water Sea.
Over the wastes abandoned by human tread,
Where only the bittern's cry was heard at dusk;
Over the lakes where the wild ducks built their nests,
The skies that had banked their fires are shining again   2120
With the stars that guided the feet of Jogues and Brébeuf.
The years as they turned have ripened the martyrs' seed,
And the ashes of St. Ignace are glowing afresh.
The trails, having frayed the threads of the cassocks, sank
Under the mould of the centuries, under fern
And brier and fungus – there in due time to blossom
Into the highways that lead to the crest of the hill
Which havened both shepherd and flock in the days
      of their trial.
For out of the torch of Ragueneau's ruins the candles
Are burning today in the chancel of Sainte Marie.   2130
The Mission sites have returned to the fold of the Order.
Near to the ground where the cross broke under the
      hatchet,
And went with it into the soil to come back at the turn
Of the spade with the carbon and calcium char of the
      bodies,
The shrines and altars are built anew; the *Aves*
And prayers ascend, and the Holy Bread is broken.

COME AWAY, DEATH

Willy-nilly, he comes or goes, with the clown's logic,
Comic in epitaph, tragic in epithalamium,
And unseduced by any mused rhyme.
However blow the winds over the pollen,
Whatever the course of the garden variables,
He remains the constant,
Ever flowering from the poppy seeds.

There was a time he came in formal dress,
Announced by Silence tapping at the panels
In deep apology.   10
A touch of chivalry in his approach,
He offered sacramental wine,
And with acanthus leaf
And petals of the hyacinth
He took the fever from the temples
And closed the eyelids,
Then led the way to his cool longitudes
In the dignity of the candles.

His mediaeval grace is gone –
Gone with the flame of the capitals   20
And the leisured turn of the thumb
Leafing the manuscripts,
Gone with the marbles
And the Venetian mosaics,
With the bend of the knee
Before the rose-strewn feet of the Virgin.
The *paternosters* of his priests,
Committing clay to clay,
Have rattled in their throats
Under the gride of his traction tread.   30

One night we heard his footfall – one September night –
In the outskirts of a village near the sea.
There was a moment when the storm
Delayed its fist, when the surf fell
Like velvet on the rocks – a moment only;
The strangest lull we ever knew!
A sudden truce among the oaks
Released their fratricidal arms;
The poplars straightened to attention
As the winds stopped to listen   40
To the sound of a motor drone –
And then the drone was still.
We heard the tick-tock on the shelf,
And the leak of valves in our hearts.
A calm condensed and lidded
As at the core of a cyclone ended breathing.
This was the monologue of Silence
Grave and unequivocal.

What followed was a bolt
Outside the range and target of the thunder,   50
And human speech curved back upon itself
Through Druid runways and the Piltdown scarps,
Beyond the stammers of the Java caves,
To find its origins in hieroglyphs
On mouths and eyes and cheeks
Etched by a foreign stylus never used
On the outmoded page of the Apocalypse.

THE TRUANT

'What have you there?' the great Panjandrum said
To the Master of the Revels who had led
A bucking truant with a stiff backbone
Close to the foot of the Almighty's throne.

'Right Reverend, most adored,
And forcibly acknowledged Lord
By the keen logic of your two-edged sword!
This creature has presumed to classify
Himself – a biped, rational, six feet high
And two feet wide; weighs fourteen stone;   10
Is guilty of a multitude of sins.
He has abjured his choric origins,
And like an undomesticated slattern,
Walks with tangential step unknown
Within the weave of the atomic pattern.
He has developed concepts, grins
Obscenely at your Royal bulletins,
Possesses what he calls a will
Which challenges your power to kill.'

'What is his pedigree?'   20

'The base is guaranteed, your Majesty –
Calcium, carbon, phosphorus, vapour
And other fundamentals spun
From the umbilicus of the sun,
And yet he says he will not caper
Around your throne, nor toe the rules
For the ballet of the fiery molecules.'

'His concepts and denials – scrap them, burn them –
To the chemists with them promptly.'

                                        'Sire,
The stuff is not amenable to fire.   30
Nothing but their own kind can overturn them.
The chemists have sent back the same old story –
"With our extreme gelatinous apology,
We beg to inform your Imperial Majesty,
Unto whom be dominion and power and glory,
There still remains that strange precipitate
Which has the quality to resist
Our oldest and most trusted catalyst.

It is a substance we cannot cremate
By temperatures known to our Laboratory."'   40

And the great Panjandrum's face grew dark –
'I'll put those chemists to their annual purge,
And I myself shall be the thaumaturge
To find the nature of this fellow's spark.
Come, bring him nearer by yon halter rope:
I'll analyse him with the cosmoscope.'

Pulled forward with his neck awry,
The little fellow six feet short,
Aware he was about to die,
Committed grave contempt of court   50
By answering with a flinchless stare
The Awful Presence seated there.

The ALL HIGH swore until his face was black.
He called him a coprophagite,
A genus *homo*, egomaniac,
Third cousin to the family of worms,
A sporozoan from the ooze of night,
Spawn of a spavined troglodyte:
He swore by all the catalogue of terms
Known since the slang of carboniferous Time.   60
He said that he could trace him back
To pollywogs and earwigs in the slime.
And in his shrillest tenor he began
Reciting his indictment of the man,
Until he closed upon this capital crime –
'You are accused of singing out of key,
(A foul unmitigated dissonance)
Of shuffling in the measures of the dance,
Then walking out with that defiant, free
Toss of your head, banging the doors,   70
Leaving a stench upon the jacinth floors.
You have fallen like a curse
On the mechanics of my Universe.

'Herewith I measure out your penalty –
Hearken while you hear, look while you see:
I send you now upon your homeward route
Where you shall find
Humiliation for your pride of mind.
I shall make deaf the ear, and dim the eye,
Put palsy in your touch, make mute   80
Your speech, intoxicate your cells and dry
Your blood and marrow, shoot
Arthritic needles through your cartilage,
And having parched you with old age,
I'll pass you wormwise through the mire;
And when your rebel will
Is mouldered, all desire
Shrivelled, all your concepts broken,
Backward in dust I'll blow you till
You join my spiral festival of fire.   90
Go, Master of the Revels – I have spoken.'

And the little genus *homo*, six feet high,
Standing erect, countered with this reply –
'You dumb insouciant invertebrate,
You rule a lower than a feudal state –
A realm of flunkey decimals that run,
Return; return and run; again return,
Each group around its little sun,
And every sun a satellite.
There they go by day and night,   100
Nothing to do but run and burn,
Taking turn and turn about,
Light-year in and light-year out,
Dancing, dancing in quadrillions,
Never leaving their pavilions.

'Your astronomical conceit
Of bulk and power is anserine.
Your ignorance so thick,

You did not know your own arithmetic.
We flung the graphs about your flying feet;   110
We measured your diameter –
Merely a line
Of zeros prefaced by an integer.
Before we came
You had no name.
You did not know direction or your pace;
We taught you all you ever knew
Of motion, time and space.
We healed you of your vertigo
And put you in our kindergarten show,   120
Perambulated you through prisms, drew
Your mileage through the Milky Way,
Lassoed your comets when they ran astray,
Yoked Leo, Taurus, and your team of Bears
To pull our kiddy cars of inverse squares.

'Boast not about your harmony,
Your perfect curves, your rings
Of *pure and endless light* – 'Twas we
Who pinned upon your Seraphim their wings,
And when your brassy heavens rang   130
With joy that morning while the planets sang
Their choruses of archangelic lore,
'Twas we who ordered the notes upon their score
Out of our winds and strings.
Yes! all your shapely forms
Are ours – parabolas of silver light,
Those blueprints of your spiral stairs
From nadir depth to zenith height,
Coronas, rainbows after storms,
Auroras on your eastern tapestries   140
And constellations over western seas.

'And when, one day, grown conscious of your age,
While pondering an eolith,
We turned a human page

And blotted out a cosmic myth
With all its baby symbols to explain
The sunlight in Apollo's eyes,
Our rising pulses and the birth of pain,
Fear, and that fern-and-fungus breath
Stalking our nostrils to our caves of death –   150
That day we learned how to anatomize
Your body, calibrate your size
And set a mirror up before your face
To show you what you really were – a rain
Of dull Lucretian atoms crowding space,
A series of concentric waves which any fool
Might make by dropping stones within a pool,
Or an exploding bomb forever in flight
Bursting like hell through Chaos and Old Night.

'You oldest of the hierarchs   160
Composed of electronic sparks,
We grant you speed,
We grant you power, and fire
That ends in ash, but we concede
To you no pain nor joy nor love nor hate,
No final tableau of desire,
No causes won or lost, no free
Adventure at the outposts – only
The degradation of your energy
When at some late   170
Slow number of your dance your sergeant-major Fate
Will catch you blind and groping and will send
You reeling on that long and lonely
Lockstep of your wave-lengths towards your end.

'We who have met
With stubborn calm the dawn's hot fusillades;
Who have seen the forehead sweat
Under the tug of pulleys on the joints,
Under the liquidating tally
Of the cat-and-truncheon bastinades;   180

Who have taught our souls to rally
To mountain horns and the sea's rockets
When the needle ran demented through the points;
We who have learned to clench
Our fists and raise our lightless sockets
To morning skies after the midnight raids,
Yet cocked our ears to bugles on the barricades,
And in cathedral rubble found a way to quench
A dying thirst within a Galilean valley –
No! by the Rood, we will not join your ballet.'   190

THE GOOD EARTH

Let the mind rest awhile, lower the eyes,
Relieve the spirit of its Faustian clamour:
An atom holds more secrets than the skies;
Be patient with the earth and do not cram her

With seed beyond the wisdom of her soil.
She knows the foot and hoof of man and ox,
She learned the variations of their toil –
The ploughshare's sensitivity to rocks.

Gather the stones for field and garden walls,
Build cellars for your vegetable stores,   10
Forgo the architecture of your halls,
Until your hands have fashioned stable doors.

She likes the smell of nitrates from the stalls,
She hates a disciplined tread, the scorching roar
At the grain's roots: she is nervous at the calls
Of men in panic at a strike of ore.

Patient she is in her flesh servitude,
Tolerant to curry ticklings of the harrow,

But do not scratch past her agrarian mood
To cut the calcium in her bone and marrow.   20

Hold that synthetic seed, for underneath
Deep down she'll answer to your horticulture:
She has a way of germinating teeth
And yielding crops of carrion for the vulture.

TOWARDS THE LAST SPIKE

It was the same world then as now – the same,
Except for little differences of speed
And power, and means to treat myopia
To show an axe-blade infinitely sharp
Splitting things infinitely small, or else
Provide the telescopic sight to roam
Through curved dominions never found in fables.
The same, but for new particles of speech –
Those algebraic substitutes for nouns
That sky cartographers would hang like signboards   10
Along the trespass of our thoughts to stop
The stutters of our tongues with their equations.

As now, so then, blood kept its ancient colour,
And smoothly, roughly, paced its banks; in calm
Preserving them, in riot rupturing them.
Wounds needed bandages and stomachs food:
The hands outstretched had joined the lips in prayer –
'Give us our daily bread, give us our pay.'
The past flushed in the present and tomorrow
Would dawn upon today: only the rate   20
To sensitize or numb a nerve would change;
Only the quickening of a measuring skill
To gauge the onset of a birth or death
With the precision of micrometers.

Men spoke of acres then and miles and masses,
Velocity and steam, cables that moored
Not ships but continents, world granaries,
The east-west cousinship, a nation's rise,
Hail of identity, a world expanding,
If not the universe: the feel of it   30
Was in the air – 'Union required the Line.'
The theme was current at the banquet tables,
And arguments profane and sacred rent
God-fearing families into partisans.
Pulpit, platform and floor were sounding-boards;
Cushions beneath the pounding fists assumed
The hues of western sunsets; nostrils sniffed
The prairie tang; the tongue rolled over texts:
Even St. Paul was being invoked to wring
The neck of Thomas in this war of faith   40
With unbelief. Was ever an adventure
Without its cost? Analogies were found
On every page of history or science.
A nation, like the world, could not stand still.
What was the use of records but to break them?
The tougher armour followed the new shell;
The newer shell the armour; lighthouse rockets
Sprinkled their stars over the wake of wrecks.
Were not the engineers at work to close
The lag between the pressures and the valves?   50
The same world then as now thirsting for power
To crack those records open, extra pounds
Upon the inches, extra miles per hour.
The mildewed static schedules which before
Had like asbestos been immune to wood
Now curled and blackened in the furnace coal.
This power lay in the custody of men
From down-and-outers needing roofs, whose hands
Were moulded by their fists, whose skins could feel
At home incorporate with dolomite,   60
To men who with the marshal instincts in them,

Deriving their authority from wallets,
Directed their battalions from the trestles.

THE GATHERING

(*'Oats – a grain which in England is generally given to
horses, but in Scotland supports the people.' – Dr. Samuel
Johnson. 'True, but where will you find such horses, where
such men?' – Lord Elibank's reply as recorded by Sir Walter
Scott.*)

Oatmeal was in their blood and in their names.
Thrift was the title of their catechism.
It governed all things but their mess of porridge
Which, when it struck the hydrochloric acid
With treacle and skim-milk, became a mash.
Entering the duodenum, it broke up
Into amino acids: then the liver   70
Took on its natural job as carpenter:
Foreheads grew into cliffs, jaws into juts.
The meal, so changed, engaged the follicles:
Eyebrows came out as gorse, the beards as thistles,
And the chest-hair the fell of Grampian rams.
It stretched and vulcanized the human span:
Nonagenarians worked and thrived upon it.
Out of such chemistry run through by genes,
The food released its fearsome racial products: –
The power to strike a bargain like a foe,   80
To win an argument upon a burr,
Invest the language with a Bannockburn,
Culloden or the warnings of Lochiel,
Weave loyalties and rivalries in tartans,
Present for the amazement of the world
Kilts and the civilized barbaric Fling,
And pipes which, when they acted on the mash,
Fermented lullabies to *Scots wha hae*.

Their names were like a battle-muster – Angus
(He of the Shops) and Fleming (of the Transit),   90
Hector (of the *Kicking Horse*), Dawson,
'Cromarty' Ross, and Beatty (Ulster Scot),
Bruce, Allan, Galt and Douglas, and the 'twa' –
Stephen (Craigellachie)* and Smith (Strathcona) –
Who would one day climb from their Gaelic hide-outs,
Take off their plaids and wrap them round the mountains.
And then the everlasting tread of the Macs,
Vanguard, centre and rear, their roving eyes
On summits, rivers, contracts, beaver, ledgers;
Their ears cocked to the skirl of Sir John A.,   100
The general of the patronymic march.

(*Sir John revolving round the Terms of Union with British
Columbia. Time, late at night.*)

Insomnia had ripped the bed-sheets from him
Night after night. How long was this to last?
Confederation had not played this kind
Of trickery on him. That was rough indeed,
So gravelled, that a man might call for rest
And take it for a life accomplishment.
It was his laurel though some of the leaves
Had dried. But this would be a longer tug
Of war which needed for his team thick wrists   110
And calloused fingers, heavy heels to dig
Into the earth and hold – men with bull's beef
Upon their ribs. Had he himself the wind,
The anchor-waist to peg at the rope's end?
'Twas bad enough to have these questions hit
The waking mind: 'twas much worse when he dozed;
For goblins had a way of pinching him,

*'Stand Fast, Craigellachie,' the war-cry of the Clan Grant, named after a rock in
the Spey Valley, and used as a cable message from Stephen in London to the
Directors in Montreal.

Slapping a nightmare on to dwindling snoozes.
They put him and his team into a tug
More real than life. He heard a judge call out –   120
'Teams settle on the rope and take the strain!'
And with the coaches' *heave*, the running welts
Reddened his palms, and then the gruelling *backlock*
Inscribed its indentations on his shoulders.
This kind of burn he knew he had to stand;
It was the game's routine; the other fire
Was what he feared the most for it could bake him –
That white dividing rag tied to the rope
Above the centre pole had with each heave
Wavered with chances equal. With the backlock,   130
Despite the legs of Tupper and Cartier,
The western anchor dragged; the other side
Remorselessly was gaining, holding, gaining.
No sleep could stand this strain and, with the nightmare
Delivered of its colt, Macdonald woke.

Tired with the midnight toss, lock-jawed with yawns,
He left the bed and, shuffling to the window,
He opened it. The air would cool him off
And soothe his shoulder burns. He felt his ribs:
Strange, nothing broken – how those crazy drowses   140
Had made the fictions tangle with the facts!
He must unscramble them with steady hands.
Those Ranges pirouetting in his dreams
Had their own knack of standing still in light,
Revealing peaks whose known triangulation
Had to be read in prose severity.
Seizing a telescope, he swept the skies,
The north-south drift, a self-illumined chart.
Under Polaris was the Arctic Sea
And the sub-Arctic gates well stocked with names: 150
Hudson, Davis, Baffin, Frobisher;
And in his own day Franklin, Ross and Parry
Of the Canadian Archipelago;

Kellett, McClure, McClintock, of *The Search*.
Those straits and bays had long been kicked by keels,
And flags had fluttered on the Capes that fired
His youth, making familiar the unknown.
What though the odds were nine to one against,
And the Dead March was undertoning trumpets,
There was enough of strychnine in the names   160
To make him flip a penny for the risk,
Though he had palmed the coin reflectively
Before he threw and watched it come down *heads*.
That stellar path looked too much like a road map
Upon his wall – the roads all led to market –
The north-south route. He lit a candle, held
It to a second map full of blank spaces
And arrows pointing west. Disturbed, he turned
The lens up to the zenith, followed the course
Tracked by a cloud of stars that would not keep   170
Their posts – Capella, Perseus, were reeling;
Low in the north-west, Cassiopeia
Was qualmish, leaning on her starboard arm-rest,
And Aries was chasing, butting Cygnus,
Just diving. Doubts and hopes struck at each other.
Why did those constellations look so much
Like blizzards? And what lay beyond the blizzards?

'Twas chilly at the window. He returned
To bed and savoured soporific terms:
Superior, the *Red River, Selkirk, Prairie*,   180
Port Moody and *Pacific*. Chewing them,
He spat out *Rocky* grit before he swallowed.
Selkirk! This had the sweetest taste. Ten years
Before, the Highland crofters had subscribed
Their names in a memorial for the Rails.
Sir John reviewed the story of the struggle,
That four months' journey from their native land –
The Atlantic through the Straits to Hudson Bay,
Then the Hayes River to Lake Winnipeg

Up to the Forks of the Assiniboine.   190
He could make use of that – just what he needed,
A Western version of the Arctic daring,
Romance and realism, double dose.
How long ago? Why, this is '71.
Those fellows came the time Napoleon
Was on the steppes. For sixty years they fought
The seasons, 'hoppers, drought, hail, wind and snow;
Survived the massacre at Seven Oaks,
The 'Pemmican War' and the Red River floods.
They wanted now the Road – those pioneers   200
Who lived by spades instead of beaver traps.
Most excellent word that, pioneers! Sir John
Snuggled himself into his sheets, rolling
The word around his tongue, a theme for song,
Or for a peroration to a speech.

THE HANGOVER AT DAWN

He knew the points that had their own appeal.
These did not bother him: the patriot touch,
The Flag, the magnetism of explorers,
The national unity. These could burn up
The phlegm in most of the provincial throats.   210
But there was one tale central to his plan
(The focus of his headache at this moment),
Which would demand the limit of his art –
The ballad of his courtship in the West:
Better reveal it soon without reserve.

THE LADY OF BRITISH COLUMBIA

Port Moody and Pacific! He had pledged
His word the Line should run from sea to sea.
'From sea to sea,' a hallowed phrase. Music
Was in that text if the right key were struck,

And he must strike it first, for, as he fingered   220
The clauses of the pledge, rough notes were rasping –
'No Road, No Union,' and the converse true.
East-west against the north-south run of trade,
For California like a sailor-lover
Was wooing over-time. He knew the ports.
His speech was as persuasive as his arms,
As sinuous as Spanish arias –
Tamales, Cazadero, Mendecino,
Curling their baritones around the Lady.
Then Santa Rosa, Santa Monica,   230
Held absolution in their syllables.
But when he saw her stock of British temper
Starch at ironic sainthood in the whispers –
'Rio de nuestra señora de buena guia,'*
He had the tact to gutturalize the liquids,
Steeping the tunes to drinking songs, then take
Her on a holiday where she could watch
A roving sea-born Californian pound
A downy chest and swear by San Diego.

Sir John, wise to the tricks, was studying hard   240
A fresh proposal for a marriage contract.
He knew a game was in the ceremony.
That southern fellow had a healthy bronze
Complexion, had a vast estate, was slick
Of manner. In his ardour he could tether
Sea-roses to the blossoms of his orchards,
And for his confidence he had the prime
Advantage of his rival – *he was there.*

THE LONG-DISTANCE PROPOSAL

A game it was, and the Pacific lass
Had poker wisdom on her face. Her name   250

*'River of Our Lady of Safe Conduct.'

Was rich in values – *British*; this alone
Could raise Macdonald's temperature: so could
Columbia with a different kind of fever,
And in between the two, *Victoria*.
So the *Pacific* with its wash of letters
Could push the Fahrenheit another notch.
She watched for bluff on those Disraeli features,
Impassive but for arrowy chipmunk eyes,
Engaged in fathoming a contract time.
With such a dowry she could well afford   260
To take the risk of tightening the terms –
'Begin the Road in two years, end in ten' –
Sir John, a moment letting down his guard,
Frowned at the Rocky skyline, but agreed.

(*The Terms ratified by Parliament, British Columbia enters
Confederation July, 1871, Sandford Fleming being
appointed engineer-in-chief of the proposed Railway,
Walter Moberly to co-operate with him in the location of
routes. 'Of course, I don't know how many millions you
have, but it is going to cost you money to get through
those canyons.' – Moberly to Macdonald.*)

THE PACIFIC SCANDAL

(*Huntingdon's charges of political corruption based on cor-
respondence and telegrams rifled from the offices of the
solicitor of Sir Hugh Allan, Head of the Canada Pacific
Company; Sir John's defence; and the appearance of the
Honourable Edward Blake who rises to reply to Sir John at
2 a.m.*)

BLAKE IN MOOD

Of all the subjects for debate here was
His element. His soul as clean as surf,

No one could equal him in probing cupboards
Or sweeping floors and dusting shelves, finding
A skeleton inside an overcoat;
Or shaking golden eagles from a pocket   270
To show the copper plugs within the coins.
Rumours he heard had gangrened into facts –
Gifts nuzzling at two-hundred-thousand dollars,
Elections on, and with a contract pending.
The odour of the bills had blown his gorge.
His appetite, edged by a moral hone,
Could surfeit only on the Verities.

NOVEMBER 3, 1873

A Fury rode him to the House. He took
His seat, and with a stoic gloom he heard
The Chieftain's great defence and noted well   280
The punctuation of the cheers. He needed all
The balance of his mind to counterpoise
The movements of Macdonald as he flung
Himself upon the House, upon the Country,
Upon posterity, upon his conscience.
That plunging played the devil with Blake's tiller,
Threatened the set of his sail. To save the course,
To save himself, in that five hours of gale,
He had to jettison his meditation,
His brooding on the follies of mankind,   290
Clean out the wadding from his tortured ears:
That roaring mob before him could be quelled
Only by action; so when the last round
Of the applause following the peroration
Was over, slowly, weightily, Blake rose.

A statesman-chancellor now held the Floor.
He told the sniffing Commons that a sense

Keener than smell or taste must be invoked
To get the odour. Leading them from facts
Like telegrams and stolen private letters,   300
He soared into the realm of principles
To find his scourge; and then the men involved,
Robed like the Knights of Malta, Blake undressed,
Their cloaks inverted to reveal the shoddy,
The tattered lining and bare-threaded seams.
He ripped the last stitch from them – by the time
Recess was called, he had them in the dock
As brigands in the Ministry of Smells,
Naked before the majesty of Heaven.

For Blake recesses were but sandwiches   310
Provided merely for cerebral luncheons –
No time to spread the legs under the table,
To chat and chaff a while, to let the mind
Roam, like a goblet up before the light
To bask in natural colour, or by whim
Of its own choice to sway luxuriously
In tantalizing arcs before the nostrils.
A meal was meant by Nature for nutrition –
A sorry farinaceous business scaled
Exactly to caloric grains and grams   320
Designed for intellectual combustion,
For energy directed into words
Towards proof. Abuse was overweight. He saw
No need for it; no need for caricature,
And if a villainous word had to be used,
'Twas for a villain – keen upon the target.
Irrelevance was like a moral lesion
No less within a speech than in a statute.
What mattered it who opened up the files,
Sold for a bid the damning correspondence –   330
That Montreal-Chicago understanding?
A dirty dodge, so let it be conceded.
But *here* the method was irrelevant.

Whether by legal process or by theft,
The evidence was there unalterable.
So with the House assembled, he resumed
Imperial indictment of the bandits.
The logic left no loopholes in the facts.
Figures that ran into the hundred-thousands
Were counted up in pennies, each one shown   340
To bear the superscription of debasement.

Again recess, again the sandwiches,
Again the invocation of the gods:
Each word, each phrase, each clause went to position,
Each sentence regimented like a lockstep.
The only thing that would not pace was time;
The hours dragged by until the thrushes woke –
Two days, two nights – someone opened a window,
And members of the House who still were conscious
Uncreaked their necks to note that even Sir John   350
Himself had put his fingers to his nose.

(*The appeal to the country: Macdonald defeated: Macken-
zie assumes power, 1874.*)

A change of air, a drop in temperature!
The House had rarely known sobriety
Like this. No longer clanged the 'Westward Ho!'
And quiet were the horns upon the hills.
Hard times ahead. The years were rendering up
Their fat. Measured and rationed was the language
Directed to the stringency of pockets.
The eye must be convinced before the *vision*.
'But one step at a time,' exclaimed the feet.   360
It was the story of the hen or egg;
Which came before the other? ''Twas the hen,'
Cried one; 'undoubtedly the hen must lay
The egg, hatch it and mother it.' 'Not so,'
Another shouted, ''Twas the egg or whence

The hen?' For every one who cleared his throat
And called across the House with Scriptural passion –
'The Line is meant to bring the loaves and fishes,'
A voting three had countered with the question –
'Where are the multitudes that thirst and hunger?'   370
Passion became displaced by argument.
Till now the axles justified their grease,
Taught coal a lesson in economy.
All doubts here could be blanketed with facts,
With phrases smooth as actuarial velvet.

For forty years in towns and cities men
Had watched the Lines baptized with charters, seen
Them grow, marry and bring forth children.
Parades and powder had their uses then
For gala days; and bands announced arrivals,   380
Betrothals, weddings and again arrivals.
Champagne brimmed in the font as they were named
With titles drawn from the explorers' routes,
From Saints and Governors, from space and seas
And compass-points – Saints Andrew, Lawrence, Thomas,
Louis and John; Champlain, Simcoe; Grand Trunk,
Intercolonial, the Canadian Southern,
Dominion-Atlantic, the Great Western – names
That caught a continental note and tried
To answer it. Half-gambles though they were,   390
Directors built those Roads and heard them run
To the sweet silver jingle in their minds.

The airs had long been mastered like old songs
The feet could tap to in the galleries.
But would they tap to a new rhapsody,
A harder one to learn and left unfinished?
What ear could be assured of absolute pitch
To catch this kind of music in the West?
The far West? Men had used this flattering name
For East or but encroachment on the West.   400

And was not Lake Superior still the East,
A natural highway which ice-ages left,
An unappropriated legacy?
There was no discord in the piston-throbs
Along this Road. This was old music too.
That northern spine of rock, those western mountains,
Were barriers built of God and cursed of Blake.
Mild in his oaths, Mackenzie would avoid them.
He would let contracts for the south and west,
Push out from settlement to settlement.   410
This was economy, just plain horse-sense.
The Western Lines were there – American.
He would link up with them, could reach the Coast.
The Eagle and the Lion were good friends:
At least the two could meet on sovereign terms
Without a sign of fur and feathers flying.
As yet, but who could tell? So far, so good.
Spikes had been driven at the boundary line,
From Emerson across the Red to Selkirk,
And then to Thunder Bay – to Lake Superior;   420
Across the prairies in God's own good time,
His plodding, patient, planetary time.

Five years' delay: surveys without construction;
Short lines suspended, discord in the Party.
The West defrauded of its glittering peaks,
The public blood was stirring and protesting
At this continuous dusk upon the mountains.
The old conductor off the podium,
The orchestra disbanded at the time
The daring symphony was on the score,   430
The audience cupped their ears to catch a strain:
They heard a plaintive thinning oboe-A
That kept on thinning while slow feeble steps
Approached the stand. Was this the substitute
For what the auditorium once knew –
The maestro who with tread of stallion hoofs

Came forward shaking platforms and the rafters,
And followed up the concert pitch with sound
Of drums and trumpets and the organ blasts
That had the power to toll out apathy   440
And make snow peaks ring like Cathedral steeples?
Besides, accompanying those bars of music,
There was an image men had not forgotten,
The shaggy chieftain standing at his desk,
That last-ditch fight when he was overthrown,
That desperate five hours. At least they knew
His personal pockets were not lined with pelf,
Whatever loot the others grabbed. The words
British, the West instead of South, the Nation,
The all-Canadian route – these terms were singing   450
Fresher than ever while the grating tones
Under the stress of argument had faded
Within the shroud of their monotony.

(*Sir John returns to power in 1878 with a National Policy
of Protective Tariff and the Transcontinental.*)

Two years of tuning up: it needed that
To counterpoint Blake's eloquence or lift
Mackenzie's non-adventurous common sense
To the ignition of an enterprise.
The pace had to be slow at first, a tempo
Cautious, simple to follow. Sections strewn
Like amputated limbs along the route   460
Were sutured. This appealed to sanity.
No argument could work itself to sweat
Against a prudent case, for the terrain
Looked easy from the Lake to the Red River.
To stop with those suspensions was a waste
Of cash and time. But the huge task announced
Ten years before had now to start afresh –
The moulding of men's minds was harder far
Than moulding of the steel and prior to it.

It was the battle of ideas and words   470
And kindred images called by the same name,
Like brothers who with temperamental blood
Went to it with their fists. Canyons and cliffs
Were precipices down which men were hurled,
Or something to be bridged and sheared and scaled.
Likewise the Pass had its ambiguous meaning.
The leaders of the factions in the House
And through the country spelled the word the same:
The way they got their tongue around the word
Was different, for some could make it hiss   480
With sound of blizzards screaming over ramparts:
The Pass – the Yellowhead, the Kicking Horse –
Or jam it with *coureur-de-bois* romance,
Or join it to the empyrean. Eagles,
In flight banking their wings above a fish-stream,
Had guided the explorers to a route
And given the Pass the title of their wings.
The stories lured men's minds up to the mountains
And down along the sandbars of the rivers.
Rivalling the 'brown and barren' on the maps,   490
Officially 'not fit for human life,'
Were vivid yellows flashing in the news –
'Gold in the Cariboo,' 'Gold in the Fraser.'
The swish of gravel in the placer-cradles
Would soon be followed by the spluttering fuses,
By thunder echoing thunder; for one month
After Blake's Ottawa roar would Onderdonk
Roar back from Yale by ripping canyon walls
To crash the tons by millions in the gorges.

The farther off, as by a paradox   500
Of magnets, was the golden lure the stronger:
Two thousand miles away, imagined peaks
Had the vacation pull of mountaineering,
But with the closer vision would the legs
Follow the mind? 'Twas Blake who raised the question

And answered it. Though with his natural eyes
Up to this time he had not sighted mountains,
He was an expert with the telescope.

THE ATTACK

Sir John was worried. The first hour of Blake
Was dangerous, granted the theme. Eight years   510
Before, he had the theme combined with language.
Impeachment – word with an historic ring,
Reserved for the High Courts of Parliament,
Uttered only when men were breathing hard
And when the vertebrae were musket-stiff:
High ground was that for his artillery,
And *there*, despite the hours the salvos lasted.

But *here* this was a theme less vulnerable
To fire, Macdonald thought, to Blake's gunfire,
And yet he wondered what the orator   520
Might spring in that first hour, what strategy
Was on the Bench. He did not mind the close
Mosaic of the words – too intricate,
Too massive in design. Men might admire
The speech and talk about it, then forget it.
But few possessed the patience or the mind
To tread the mazes of the labyrinth.
Once in a while, however, would Blake's logic
Stumble upon stray figures that would leap
Over the walls of other folds and catch   530
The herdsmen in their growing somnolence.
The waking sound was not – 'It can't be done';
That was a dogma, anyone might say it.
It was the following burning corollary:
'To build a Road over that sea of mountains.'
This carried more than argument. It was
A flash of fire which might with proper kindling

Consume its way into the public mind.
The House clicked to the ready and Sir John,
Burying his finger-nails into his palms,   540
Muttered – 'God send us no more metaphors
Like that – except from Tory factories.'

Had Blake the lift of Chatham as he had
Burke's wind and almost that sierra span
Of mind, he might have carried the whole House
With him and posted it upon that sea
Of mountains with sub-zeros on their scalps,
Their glacial ribs waiting for warmth of season
To spring an avalanche. Such similes
Might easily glue the members to their seats   550
With frost in preparation for their ride.
Sir John's 'from sea to sea' was Biblical;
It had the stamp of reverent approval;
But Blake's was pagan, frightening, congealing.
The chieftain's lips continued as in prayer,
A fiercely secular and torrid prayer –
'May Heaven intervene to stop the flow
Of such unnatural images and send
The rhetorician back to decimals,
Back to his tessellated subtleties.'   560
The prayer was answered for High Heaven did it.
The second hour entered and passed by,
A third, a fourth. Sir John looked round the House,
Noticed the growing shuffle of the feet,
The agony of legs, the yawn's contagion.
Was that a snore? Who was it that went out?
He glanced at the Press Gallery. The pens
Were scratching through the languor of the ink
To match the words with shorthand and were failing.
He hoped the speech would last another hour,   570
And still another. Well within the law,
This homicidal master of the opiates
Loosened the hinges of the Opposition:

The minds went first; the bodies sagged; the necks
Curved on the benches and the legs sprawled out.
And when the Fundy Tide had ebbed, Sir John,
Smiling, watched the debris upon the banks,
For what were yesterday grey human brains
Had with decomposition taken on
The texture and complexion of red clay.   580

(*In 1880 Tupper lets contract to Onderdonk for survey and
construction through the Pacific Section of the mountains.
Sir John, Tupper, Pope, and McIntyre go to London to
interest capital but return without a penny.*)

Failing to make a dent in London dams,
Sir John set out to plumb a reservoir
Closer in reach. He knew its area,
Its ownership, the thickness of its banks,
Its conduits – if he could get his hands
Upon the local stopcocks, could he turn them?
The reservoir was deep. Two centuries
Ago it started filling when a king
Had in a furry moment scratched a quill
Across the bottom of His Royal Charter –   590
'Granting the Governor and His Company
Of Gentlemen Adventurers the right
Exclusive to one-third a continent.'
Was it so easy then? A scratch, a seal,
A pinch of snuff tickling the sacred nostrils,
A puff of powder and the ink was dry.
Sir John twisted his lips: he thought of London.
Empire and wealth were in that signature
For royal, princely, ducal absentees,
For courtiers to whom the parallels   600
Were nothing but chalk scratches on a slate.
For them wild animals were held in game
Preserves, foxes as quarry in a chase,
And hills were hedges, river banks were fences,

And cataracts but fountains in a garden
Tumbling their bubbles into marble basins.
Where was this place called Hudson Bay? Some place
In the Antipodes? Explorers, traders,
Would bring their revenues over that signet.
Two centuries – the new empire advanced,   610
Was broken, reunited, torn again.
The *fleur-de-lis* went to half-mast, the *Jack*
To the mast-head, but fresher rivalries
Broke out – Nor'-Westers at the Hudson's throat
Over the pelts, over the pemmican;
No matter what – the dividends flowed in
As rum flowed out like the Saskatchewan.

The twist left Sir John's lips and he was smiling.
Though English in ambition and design,
This reservoir, he saw there in control   620
Upon the floodgates not a Londoner
In riding breeches but, red-flannel-shirted,
Trousered in homespun, streaked and blobbed with
        seal-oil,
A Scot with smoke of peat fire on his breath –
Smith? Yes: but christened Donald Alexander
And joined through issue from the Grants and Stuarts.

To smite the rock and bring forth living water,
Take lead or tin and transmute both to silver,
Copper to gold, betray a piece of glass
To diamonds, fabulize a continent,   630
Were wonders once believed, scrapped and revived;
For Moses, Marco Polo, Paracelsus,
Fell in the same retort and came out *Smith*.
A miracle on legs, the lad had left
Forres and Aberdeen, gone to Lachine –
'Tell Mr. Smith to count and sort the rat-skins.'
Thence Tadoussac and Posts off Anticosti;
From there to Rigolet in Labrador,

A thousand miles by foot, snowshoe and dog-sled.
He fought the climate like a weathered yak,   640
And conquered it, ripping the stalactites
From his red beard, thawing his feet, and wringing
Salt water from his mitts; but most of all
He learned the art of making change. Blankets,
Ribbons and beads, tobacco, guns and knives,
Were swapped for muskrat, marten, fox and beaver.
And when the fur trade thinned, he trapped the salmon,
Canned it; hunted the seal, traded its oil
And fertilized the gardens with the carcass.
Even the melons grew in Labrador.   650
What could resist this touch? Water from rock!
Why not? No more a myth than pelts should be
Thus fabricated into bricks of gold.

If rat-skins, why not tweeds? If looms could take
Raw wool and twill it into selling shape,
They could under the draper's weaving mind
Be patterning gold braid:
                          So thought George Stephen.

His legs less sturdy than his cousin Donald's,
His eyes were just as furiously alert.
His line of vision ran from the north-west   660
To the Dutch-held St. Paul-Pacific Railway.
Allied with Smith, Kitson and Kennedy,
Angus, Jim Hill and Duncan McIntyre,
Could he buy up this semi-bankrupt Road
And turn the northern traffic into it?
Chief bricklayer of all the Scotian clans,
And foremost as a banking metallurgist,
He took the parchments at their lowest level
And mineralized them, roasted them to shape,
Then mortared them into the pyramid,   670
Till with the trowel-stretching exercise
He grew so Atlas-strong that he could carry
A mountain like a namesake on his shoulders.

(The Charter granted to The Canadian Pacific Railway,
February 17, 1881, with George Stephen as first President
... One William Cornelius Van Horne arrives in Win-
nipeg, December 31, 1881, and there late at night, forty
below zero, gives vent to a soliloquy.)

Stephen had laid his raw hands on Van Horne,
Pulled him across the border, sent him up
To get the feel of northern temperatures.
He knew through Hill the story of his life
And found him made to order. Nothing less
Than geologic space his field of work,
He had in Illinois explored the creeks   680
And valleys, brooded on the rocks and quarries.
Using slate fragments, he became a draughtsman,
Bringing to life a landscape or a cloud,
Turning a tree into a beard, a cliff
Into a jaw, a creek into a mouth
With banks for lips. He loved to work on shadows.
Just now the man was forcing the boy's stature,
The while the youth tickled the man within.
Companioned by the shade of Agassiz,
He would come home, his pockets stuffed with fossils –   690
Crinoids and fish-teeth – and his tongue jabbering
Of the earth's crust before the birth of life,
Prophetic of the days when he would dig
Into Laurentian rock. The Morse-key tick
And tape were things mesmeric – space and time
Had found a junction. Electricity
And rock, one novel to the coiling hand,
The other frozen in the lap of age,
Were playthings for the boy, work for the man.
As man he was the State's first operator;   700
As boy he played a trick upon his boss
Who, cramped with current, fired him on the instant;
As man at school, escaping Latin grammar,
He tore the fly-leaf from the text to draw

The contour of a hill; as boy he sketched
The principal, gave him flapdoodle ears,
Bristled his hair, turned eyebrows into quills,
His whiskers into flying buttresses,
His eye-tusks into rusted railroad spikes,
And made a truss between his nose and chin.   710
Expelled again, he went back to the keys,
To bush and rock and found companionship
With quarry-men, stokers and station-masters,
Switchmen and locomotive engineers.

Now he was transferred to Winnipeg.
Of all the places in an unknown land
Chosen by Stephen for Van Horne, this was
The pivot on which he could turn his mind.
Here he could clap the future on the shoulder
And order Fate about as his lieutenant,   720
For he would take no nonsense from a thing
Called Destiny – the stars had to be with him.
He spent the first night in soliloquy,
Like Sir John A. but with a difference.
Sir John wanted to sleep but couldn't do it:
Van Horne could sleep but never wanted to.
It was a waste of time, his bed a place
Only to think or dream with eyes awake.
Opening a jack-knife, he went to the window,
Scraped off the frost. Great treks ran through his mind,   730
East-west. Two centuries and a half gone by,
One trek had started from the Zuyder Zee
To the new Amsterdam. 'Twas smooth by now,
Too smooth. His line of grandsires and their cousins
Had built a city from Manhattan dirt.
Another trek to Illinois; it too
Was smooth, but this new one it was his job
To lead, then build a highway which men claimed
Could not be built. Statesmen and engineers
Had blown their faces blue with their denials: 740

The men who thought so were asylum cases
Whose monomanias harmless up to now
Had not swept into cells. His bearded chin
Pressed to the pane, his eyes roved through the west.
He saw the illusion at its worst – the frost,
The steel precision of the studded heavens,
Relentless mirror of a covered earth.
His breath froze on the scrape: he cut again
And glanced at the direction west-by-south.
That westward trek was the American,   750
Union-Pacific – easy so he thought,
Their forty million stacked against his four.
Lonely and desolate this. He stocked his mind
With items of his task: the simplest first,
Though hard enough, the Prairies, then the Shore
North of the Lake – a quantity half-guessed.
Mackenzie like a balky horse had shied
And stopped at this. Van Horne knew well the reason,
But it was vital for the all-land route.
He peered through at the South. Down there Jim Hill 760
Was whipping up his horses on a road
Already paved. The stations offered rest
With food and warmth, and their well-rounded names
Were tossed like apples to the public taste.

He made a mental note of his three items.
He underlined the Prairies, double-lined
The Shore and triple-lined *Beyond the Prairies*,
Began counting the Ranges – first the Rockies;
The Kicking Horse ran through them, this he knew;
The Selkirks? Not so sure. Some years before 770
Had Moberly and Perry tagged a route
Across the lariat loop of the Columbia.
Now Rogers was traversing it on foot,
Reading an aneroid and compass, chewing
Sea-biscuit and tobacco. Would the steel
Follow this trail? Van Horne looked farther west.

There was the Gold Range, there the Coastal Mountains.
He stopped, putting a period to the note,
As rivers troubled nocturnes in his ears.
His plans must not seep into introspection –   780
Call it a night, for morning was at hand,
And every hour of daylight was for work.

(*Van Horne goes to Montreal to meet the Directors.*)

He had agenda staggering enough
To bring the sweat even from Stephen's face.
As daring as his plans, so daring were
His promises. To build five hundred miles
Upon the prairies in one season: this
Was but a cushion for the jars ahead.
The Shore – he had to argue, stamp and fight
For this. The watercourses had been favoured,   790
The nation schooled to that economy.
He saw that Stephen, after wiping beads
From face and forehead, had put both his hands
Deep in his pockets – just a habit merely
Of fingering change – but still Van Horne went on
To clinch his case: the north shore could avoid
The over-border route – a national point
If ever there was one. He promised this
As soon as he was through with buffalo-grass.
And then the little matter of the Rockies: 800
This must be swallowed without argument,
As obvious as space, clear as a charter.
But why the change in Fleming's survey? Why
The Kicking Horse and not the Yellowhead?
The national point again. The Kicking Horse
Was shorter, closer to the boundary line;
No rival road would build between the two.
He did not dwell upon the other Passes.
He promised all with surety of schedule,
And with a self-imposed serenity   810
That dried the sweat upon the Board Room faces.

NUMBER ONE

Oak Lake to Calgary. Van Horne took off
His coat. The North must wait, for that would mean
His shirt as well. First and immediate
This prairie pledge – five hundred miles, and it
Was winter. Failure of this trial promise
Would mean – no, it must not be there for meaning.
An order from him carried no repeal:
It was as final as an execution.
A cable started rolling mills in Europe: 820
A tap of Morse sent hundreds to the bush,
Where axes swung on spruce and the saws sang,
Changing the timber into pyramids
Of poles and sleepers. Clicks, despatches, words,
Like lanterns in a night conductor's hands,
Signalled the wheels: a nod put Shaughnessy
In Montreal: supplies moved on the minute.
Thousands of men and mules and horses slipped
Into their togs and harness night and day.
The grass that fed the buffalo was turned over,   830
The black alluvial mould laid bare, the bed
Levelled and scraped. As individuals
The men lost their identity; as groups,
As gangs, they massed, divided, subdivided,
Like numerals only – sub-contractors, gangs
Of engineers, and shovel gangs for bridges,
Culverts, gangs of mechanics stringing wires,
Loading, unloading and reloading gangs,
Gangs for the fish-plates and the spiking gangs,
Putting a silver polish on the nails.   840
But neither men nor horses ganged like mules:
Wiser than both they learned to unionize.
Some instinct in their racial nether regions

Had taught them how to sniff the five-hour stretch
Down to the fine arithmetic of seconds.
They tired out their rivals and they knew it.
They'd stand for overwork, not overtime.
Faster than workmen could fling down their shovels,
They could unhinge their joints, unhitch their tendons;
Jumping the foreman's call, they brayed 'Unhook'   850
With a defiant, corporate instancy.
The promise which looked first without redemption
Was being redeemed. From three to seven miles
A day the parallels were being laid,
Though Eastern throats were hoarse with the old
        question –
Where are the settlements? And whence the gift
Of tongues which could pronounce place-names that
        purred
Like cats in relaxation after kittens?
Was it a part of the same pledge to turn
A shack into a bank for notes renewed;   860
To call a site a city when men saw
Only a water-tank? This was an act
Of faith indeed – substance of things unseen –
Which would convert preachers to miracles,
Lure teachers into lean-to's for their classes.
And yet it happened that while labourers
Were swearing at their blisters in the evening
And straightening out their spinal kinks at dawn,
The tracks joined up Oak Lake to Calgary.

NUMBER TWO

On the North Shore a reptile lay asleep –   870
A hybrid that the myths might have conceived,
But not delivered, as progenitor
Of crawling, gliding things upon the earth.
She lay snug in the folds of a huge boa

Whose tail had covered Labrador and swished
Atlantic tides, whose body coiled itself
Around the Hudson Bay, then curled up north
Through Manitoba and Saskatchewan
To Great Slave Lake. In continental reach
The neck went past the Great Bear Lake until   880
Its head was hidden in the Arctic Seas.
This folded reptile was asleep or dead:
So motionless, she seemed stone dead – just seemed:
She was too old for death, too old for life, .
For as if jealous of all living forms
She had lain there before bivalves began
To catacomb their shells on western mountains.
Somewhere within this life-death zone she sprawled,
Torpid upon a rock-and-mineral mattress.
Ice-ages had passed by and over her,   890
But these, for all their motion, had but sheared
Her spotty carboniferous hair or made
Her ridges stand out like the spikes of molochs.
Her back grown stronger every million years,
She had shed water by the longer rivers
To Hudson Bay and by the shorter streams
To the great basins to the south, had filled
Them up, would keep them filled until the end
Of Time.

          Was this the thing Van Horne set out
To conquer? When Superior lay there   900
With its inviting levels? Blake, Mackenzie,
Offered this water like a postulate.
'Why those twelve thousand men sent to the North?
Nonsense and waste with utter bankruptcy.'
And the Laurentian monster at the first
Was undisturbed, presenting but her bulk
To the invasion. All she had to do
Was lie there neither yielding nor resisting.
Top-heavy with accumulated power

And overgrown survival without function,   910
She changed her spots as though brute rudiments
Of feeling foreign to her native hour
Surprised her with a sense of violation
From an existence other than her own –
Or why take notice of this unknown breed,
This horde of bipeds that could toil like ants,
Could wake her up and keep her irritated?
They tickled her with shovels, dug pickaxes
Into her scales and got under her skin,
And potted holes in her with drills and filled   920
Them up with what looked like fine grains of sand,
Black sand. It wasn't noise that bothered her,
For thunder she was used to from her cradle –
The head-push and nose-blowing of the ice,
The height and pressure of its body: these
Like winds native to clime and habitat
Had served only to lull her drowsing coils.
It was not size or numbers that concerned her.
It was their foreign build, their gait of movement.
They did not crawl – nor were they born with wings.   930
They stood upright and walked, shouted and sang;
They needed air – that much was true – their mouths
Were open but the tongue was alien.
The sounds were not the voice of winds and waters,
Nor that of any beasts upon the earth.
She took them first with lethargy, suffered
The rubbing of her back – those little jabs
Of steel were like the burrowing of ticks
In an elk's hide needing an antler point,
Or else left in a numb monotony.   940
These she could stand but when the breed
Advanced west on her higher vertebrae,
Kicking most insolently at her ribs,
Pouring black powder in her cavities,
And making not the clouds but her insides
The home of fire and thunder, then she gave

Them trial of her strength: the trestles tottered;
Abutments, bridges broke; her rivers flooded:
She summoned snow and ice, and then fell back
On the last weapon in her armoury –   950
The first and last – her passive corporal bulk,
To stay or wreck the schedule of Van Horne.

NUMBER THREE

The big one was the mountains – seas indeed!
With crests whiter than foam: they poured like seas,
Fluting the green banks of the pines and spruces.
An eagle-flight above they hid themselves
In clouds. They carried space upon their ledges.
Could these be overridden frontally,
Or like typhoons outsmarted on the flanks?
And what were on the flanks? The troughs and canyons,   960
Passes more dangerous to the navigator
Than to Magellan when he tried to read
The barbarous language of his Strait by calling
For echoes from the rocky hieroglyphs
Playing their pranks of hide-and-seek in fog:
As stubborn too as the old North-West Passage,
More difficult, for ice-packs could break up;
And as for bergs, what polar architect
Could stretch his compass points to draught such peaks
As kept on rising there beyond the foothills?   970
And should the bastions of the Rockies yield
To this new human and unnatural foe,
Would not the Selkirks stand? This was a range
That looked like some strange dread outside a door
Which gave its name but would not show its features,
Leaving them to the mind to guess at. This
Meant tunnels – would there be no end to boring?
There must be some day. Fleming and his men
Had nosed their paths like hounds; but paths and
        trails,

Measured in every inch by chain and transit, 980
Looked easy and seductive on a chart.
The rivers out there did not flow: they tumbled.
The cataracts were fed by glaciers;
Eddies were thought as whirlpools in the Gorges,
And gradients had paws that tore up tracks.

Terror and beauty like twin signal flags
Flew on the peaks for men to keep their distance.
The two combined as in a storm at sea –
'Stay on the shore and take your fill of breathing,
But come not to the decks and climb the rigging.' 990
The Ranges could put cramps in hands and feet
Merely by the suggestion of the venture.
They needed miles to render up their beauty,
As if the gods in high aesthetic moments,
Resenting the profanity of touch,
Chiselled this sculpture for the eye alone.

(*Van Horne in momentary meditation at the Foothills.*)

His name was now a legend. The North Shore,
Though not yet conquered, yet had proved that he
Could straighten crooked roads by pulling at them,
Shear down a hill and drain a bog or fill 1000
A valley overnight. Fast as a bobcat,
He'd climb and run across the shakiest trestle
Or, with a locomotive short of coal,
He could supply the head of steam himself.
He breakfasted on bridges, lunched on ties;
Drinking from gallon pails, he dined on moose.
He could tire out the lumberjacks; beat hell
From workers but no more than from himself.
Only the devil or Paul Bunyan shared
With him the secret of perpetual motion, 1010
And when he moved among his men they looked
For shoulder sprouts upon the Flying Dutchman.

But would his legend crack upon the mountains?
There must be no retreat: his bugles knew
Only one call – the summons to advance
Against two fortresses: the mind, the rock.
To prove the first defence was vulnerable,
To tap the treasury at home and then
Untie the purse-strings of the Londoners,
As hard to loosen as salt-water knots –   1020
That job was Stephen's, Smith's, Tupper's, Macdonald's.
He knew its weight: had heard, as well as they,
Blake pumping at his pulmonary bellows,
And if the speeches made the House shock-proof
Before they ended, they could still peal forth
From print more durable than spoken tones.
Blake had returned to the attack and given
Sir John the ague with another phrase
As round and as melodious as the first:
'The Country's wealth, its millions after millions   1030
Squandered – *lost in the gorges of the Fraser*':
A beautiful but ruinous piece of music
That could only be drowned with drums and fifes.
Tupper, fighting with fists and nails and toes,
Had taken the word *scandal* which had cut
His master's ballots, and had turned the edge
With his word *slander*, but Blake's *sea*, how turn
That edge? Now this last devastating phrase!
But let Sir John and Stephen answer this
Their way. Van Horne must answer it in his.   1040

INTERNECINE STRIFE

The men were fighting foes which had themselves
Waged elemental civil wars and still
Were hammering one another at this moment.
The peaks and ranges flung from ocean beds
Had wakened up one geologic morning

To find their scalps raked off, their lips punched in,
The colour of their skins charged with new dyes.
Some of them did not wake or but half-woke;
Prone or recumbent with the eerie shapes
Of creatures that would follow them. Weather   1050
Had acted on their spines and frozen them
To stegosaurs or, taking longer cycles,
Divining human features, had blown back
Their hair and, pressing on their cheeks and temples,
Bestowed on them the gravity of mummies.
But there was life and power which belied
The tombs. Guerrilla evergreens were climbing
In military order: at the base
The *ponderosa* pine; the fir backed up
The spruce; and it the Stoney Indian lodge-poles;   1060
And these the white-barks; then, deciduous,
The outpost suicidal Lyell larches
Aiming at summits, digging scraggy roots
Around the boulders in the thinning soil,
Till they were stopped dead at the timber limit –
Rock *versus* forest with the rock prevailing.
Or with the summer warmth it was the ice,
In treaty with the rock to hold a line
As stubborn as a Balkan boundary,
That left its caves to score the Douglases,   1070
And smother them with half a mile of dirt,
And making snow-sheds, covering the camps,
Futile as parasols in polar storms.
One enemy alone had battled rock
And triumphed: searching levels like lost broods,
Keen on their ocean scent, the rivers cut
The quartzite, licked the slate and softened it,
Till mud solidified was mud again,
And then, digesting it like earthworms, squirmed
Along the furrows with one steering urge –   1080
To navigate the mountains in due time
Back to their home in worm-casts on the tides.

Into this scrimmage came the fighting men,
And all but rivers were their enemies.
Whether alive or dead the bush resisted:
Alive, it must be slain with axe and saw,
If dead, it was in tangle at their feet.
The ice could hit men as it hit the spruces.
Even the rivers had betraying tricks,
Watched like professed allies across a border.   1090
They smiled from fertile plains and easy runs
Of valley gradients: their eyes got narrow,
Full of suspicion at the gorges where
They leaped and put the rickets in the trestles.
Though natively in conflict with the rock,
Both leagued against invasion. At Hell's Gate
A mountain laboured and brought forth a bull
Which, stranded in mid-stream, was fighting back
The river, and the fight turned on the men,
Demanding from this route their bread and steel.   1100
And there below the Gate was the Black Canyon
With twenty-miles-an-hour burst of speed.

(*Onderdonk builds the* Skuzzy *to force the passage.*)

'Twas more than navigation: only eagles
Might follow up this run; the spawning salmon
Gulled by the mill-race had returned to rot
Their upturned bellies in the canyon eddies.
Two engines at the stern, a forrard winch,
Steam-powered, failed to stem the cataract.
The last resource was shoulders, arms and hands.
Fifteen men at the capstan, creaking hawsers,   1110
Two hundred Chinese tugging at shore ropes
To keep her bow-on from the broadside drift,
The *Skuzzy* under steam and muscle took
The shoals and rapids, and warped through the Gate,
Until she reached the navigable water –
The adventure was not sailing: it was climbing.

As hard a challenge were the precipices
Worn water-smooth and sheer a thousand feet.
Surveyors from the edges looked for footholds,
But, finding none, they tried marine manoeuvres.   1120
Out of a hundred men they drafted sailors
Whose toes as supple as their fingers knew
The wash of reeling decks, whose knees were hardened
Through tying gaskets at the royal yards:
They lowered them with knotted ropes and drew them
Along the face until the lines were strung
Between the juts. Barefooted, dynamite
Strapped to their waists, the sappers followed, treading
The spider films and chipping holes for blasts,
Until the cliffs delivered up their features   1130
Under the civil discipline of roads.

RING, RING THE BELLS

Ring, ring the bells, but not the engine bells:
Today only the ritual of the steeple
Chanted to the dull tempo of the toll.
Sorrow is stalking through the camps, speaking
A common mother-tongue. 'Twill leave tomorrow
To turn that language on a Blackfoot tepee,
Then take its leisurely Pacific time
To tap its fingers on a coolie's door.
Ring, ring the bells but not the engine bells: 1140
Today only that universal toll,
For granite, mixing dust with human lime,
Had so compounded bodies into boulders
As to untype the blood, and, then, the Fraser,
Catching the fragments from the dynamite,
Had bleached all birthmarks from her swirling dead.

Tomorrow and the engine bells again!

THE LAKE OF MONEY

(The appeal to the Government for a loan of twenty-two-
and-a-half million, 1883.)

Sir John began to muse on his excuses.
Was there no bottom to this lake? One mile
Along that northern strip had cost – how much?   1150
Eleven dollars to the inch. The Road
In all would measure up to ninety millions,
And diverse hands were plucking at his elbow.
The Irish and the Dutch he could outface,
Outquip. He knew Van Horne and Shaughnessy
Had little time for speeches – one was busy
In grinding out two thousand miles; the other
Was working wizardry on creditors,
Pulling rabbits from hats, gold coins from sleeves
In Montreal. As for his foes like Blake,   1160
He thanked his household gods the Irishman
Could claim only a viscous brand of humour,
Heavy, impenetrable till the hour
To laugh had taken on a chestnut colour.
But Stephen was his friend, hard to resist.
And there was Smith. He knew that both had pledged
Their private fortunes as security
For the construction of the Road. But that
Was not enough. Sir John had yet to dip
And scrape farther into the public pocket,   1170
Explore its linings: his, the greater task;
His, to commit a nation to the risk.
How could he face the House with pauper hands?
He had to deal with Stephen first – a man
Laconic, nailing points and clinching them.
Oratory, the weapon of the massed assemblies
Was not the weapon here – Scot meeting Scot.
The burr was hard to take; and Stephen had
A Banffshire-cradled *r*. Drilling the ear,

It paralysed the nerves, hit the red cells.   1180
The logic in the sound, escaping print,
Would seep through channels and befog the cortex.

Sir John counted the exits of discretion:
Disguise himself? A tailor might do much;
A barber might trim down his mane, brush back
The forelock, but no artist of massage,
Kneading that face from brow to nasal tip,
Could change a chunk of granite into talc.
His rheumatism? Yet he still could walk.
Neuralgia did not interfere with speech.   1190
The bronchial tubing needed softer air?
Vacations could not cancel all appointments.
Men saw him in the flesh at Ottawa.
He had to speak this week, wheedling committees,
Much easier than to face a draper's clerk,
Tongue-trained on Aberdonian bargain-counters.
He raised his closed left hand to straighten out
His fingers one by one – four million people.
He had to pull a trifle on that fourth,
Not so resilient as the other three.   1200
Only a wrench could stir the little finger
Which answered with a vicious backward jerk.

The dollar fringes of one hundred million
Were smirching up the blackboard of his mind.
But curving round and through them was the thought
He could not sponge away. Had he not fathered
The Union? Prodigy indeed it was
From Coast to Coast. Was not the Line essential?
What was this fungus sprouting from his rind
That left him at the root less clear a growth   1210
Than this Dutch immigrant, William Van Horne?
The name suggested artificial land
Rescued from swamp by bulging dikes and ditches;
And added now to that were bogs and sloughs

And that most cursèd diabase which God
Had left from the explosions of his wrath.
And yet this man was challenging his pride.
North-Sea ancestral moisture on his beard,
Van Horne was now the spokesman for the West,
The champion of an all-Canadian route,   1220
The Yankee who had come straight over, linked
His name and life with the Canadian nation.
Besides, he had infected the whole camp.
Whether acquired or natural, the stamp
Of faith had never left his face. Was it
The artist's instinct which had made the Rockies
And thence the Selkirks, scenes of tourist lure,
As easy for the passage of an engine
As for the flight of eagles? Miracles
Became his thought: the others took their cue   1230
From him. They read the lines upon his lips.
But miracles did not spring out of air.
Under the driving will and sweltering flesh
They came from pay-cars loaded with the cash.
So that was why Stephen had called so often –
Money – that lake of money, bonds, more bonds.

(*The Bill authorizing the loan stubbornly carries the House.*)

DYNAMITE ON THE NORTH SHORE

The lizard was in sanguinary mood.
She had been waked again: she felt her sleep
Had lasted a few seconds of her time.
The insects had come back – the ants, if ants   1240
They were – dragging *those* trees, *those* logs athwart
Her levels, driving in *those* spikes; and how
The long grey snakes unknown within her region
Wormed from the east, unstriped, sunning themselves
Uncoiled upon the logs and then moved on,

Growing each day, ever keeping abreast!
She watched them, waiting for a bloody moment,
Until the borers halted at a spot,
The most invulnerable of her whole column,
Drove in that iron, wrenched it in the holes,   1250
Hitting, digging, twisting. Why that spot?
Not this the former itch. That sharp proboscis
Was out for more than self-sufficing blood
About the cuticle: 'twas out for business
In the deep layers and the arteries.

And this consistent punching at her belly
With fire and thunder slapped her like an insult,
As with the blasts the caches of her broods
Broke – nickel, copper, silver and fool's gold,
Burst from their immemorial dormitories   1260
To sprawl indecent in the light of day.
Another warning – this time different.

Westward above her webs she had a trap –
A thing called muskeg, easy on the eyes
Stung with the dust of gravel. Cotton grass,
Its white spires blending with the orchids,
Peeked through green table-cloths of sphagnum moss.
Carnivorous bladder-wort studded the acres,
Passing the water-fleas through their digestion.
Sweet-gale and sundew edged the dwarf black spruce;   1270
And herds of cariboo had left their hoof-marks,
Betraying visual solidity,
But like the thousands of the pitcher plants,
Their downward-pointing hairs alluring insects,
Deceptive – and the men were moving west!
Now was her time. She took three engines, sank them
With seven tracks down through the hidden lake
To the rock bed, then over them she spread
A counterpane of leather-leaf and slime.
A warning, that was all for now. 'Twas sleep   1280

She wanted, sleep, for drowsing was her pastime
And waiting through eternities of seasons.
As for intruders bred for skeletons –
Some day perhaps when ice began to move,
Or some convulsion ran fires through her tombs,
She might stir in her sleep and far below
The reach of steel and blast of dynamite,
She'd claim their bones as her possessive right
And wrap them cold in her pre-Cambrian folds.

THREATS OF SECESSION

The Lady's face was flushed. Thirteen years now   1290
Since that engagement ring adorned her finger!
Adorned? Betrayed. She often took it off
And flung it angrily upon the dresser,
Then took excursions with her sailor-lover.
Had that man with a throat like Ottawa,
That tailored suitor in a cut-away,
Presumed compliance on her part? High time
To snub him for delay – for was not time
The marrow of agreement? At the mirror
She tried to cream a wrinkle from her forehead,   1300
Toyed with the ring, replaced it and removed it.
Harder, she thought, to get it on and off –
This like the wrinkle meant but one thing, age.
So not too fast; play safe. Perhaps the man
Was not the master of his choice. Someone
Within the family group might well contest
Exotic marriage. Still, her plumes were ruffled
By Blake's two-nights' address before the Commons:
Three lines inside the twenty-thousand words
Had maddened her. She searched for hidden meanings –   1310
'Should she insist on those preposterous terms
And threaten to secede, then let her go,
Better than ruin the country.' 'Let her go,'

And 'ruin' – language this to shake her bodice.
Was this indictment of her character,
Or worse, her charm? Or was it just plain dowry?
For this last one at least she had an answer.
Pay now or separation – this the threat.
Dipping the ring into a soapy lather,
She pushed it to the second knuckle, twirled   1320
It past. Although the diamond was off-colour,
She would await its partner ring of gold –
The finest carat; yes, by San Francisco!

BACK TO THE MOUNTAINS

As grim an enemy as rock was time.
The little men from five-to-six feet high,
From three-to-four score years in lease of breath,
Were flung in double-front against them both
In years a billion strong; so long was it
Since brachiapods in mollusc habitats
Were clamping shells on weed in ocean mud.   1330
Now only yesterday had Fleming's men,
Searching for toeholds on the sides of cliffs,
Five thousand feet above sea-level, set
A tripod's leg upon a trilobite.
And age meant pressure, density. Sullen
With aeons, mountains would not stand aside;
Just block the path – morose but without anger,
No feeling in the menace of their frowns,
Immobile for they had no need of motion;
Their veins possessed no blood – they carried quartzite.   1340
Frontal assault! To go through them direct
Seemed just as inconceivable as ride
Over their peaks. But go through them the men
Were ordered and their weapons were their hands
And backs, pickaxes, shovels, hammers, drills
And dynamite – against the rock and time;

For here the labour must be counted up
In months subject to clauses of a contract
Distinguished from the mortgage-run an age
Conceded to the trickle of the rain   1350
In building river-homes. The men bored in,
The mesozoic rock arguing the inches.

This was a kind of surgery unknown
To mountains or the mothers of the myths.
These had a chloroform in leisured time,
Squeezing a swollen handful of light-seconds,
When water like a wriggling casuist
Had probed and found the areas for incision.
Now time was rushing labour – inches grew
To feet, to yards: the drills – the single jacks,   1360
The double jacks – drove in and down; the holes
Gave way to excavations, these to tunnels,
Till men sodden with mud and roof-drip steamed
From sunlight through the tar-black to the sunlight.

HOLLOW ECHOES FROM THE TREASURY VAULT

Sir John was tired as to the point of death.
His chin was anchored to his chest. Was Blake
Right after all? And was Mackenzie right?
Superior could be travelled on. Besides,
It had a bottom, but those northern bogs
Like quicksands could go down to the earth's core.   1370
Compared with them, quagmires of ancient legend
Were backyard puddles for old ducks. To sink
Those added millions down that wallowing hole!
He thought now through his feet. Many a time
When argument cemented opposition,
And hopeless seemed his case, he could think up
A tale to laugh the benches to accord.
No one knew better, when a point had failed

The brain, how to divert it through the ribs.
But now his stock of stories had run out.   1380
This was exhaustion at its coma level.
Or was he sick? Never had spots like these
Assailed his eyes. He could not rub them out –
Those shifting images – was it the sunset
Refracted through the bevelled window edges?
He shambled over and drew down the blind;
Returned and slumped; it was no use; the spots
Were there. No light could ever shoot this kind
Of orange through a prism, or this blue,
And what a green! The spectrum was ruled out;   1390
Its bands were too inviolate. He rubbed
The lids again – a brilliant gold appeared
Upon a silken backdrop of pure white,
And in the centre, red – a scarlet red,
A dancing, rampant and rebellious red
That like a stain spread outward covering
The vision field. He closed his eyes and listened:
Why, what was that? 'Twas bad enough that light
Should play such pranks upon him, but must sound
Crash the Satanic game, reverberate   1400
A shot fifteen years after it was fired,
And culminate its echoes with the thud
Of marching choruses outside his window:

> 'We'll hang Riel up the Red River,
> And he'll roast in hell forever,
> We'll hang him up the River
> With a yah-yah-yah.'

The noose was for the shot: 'twas blood for blood;
The death of Riel for the death of Scott.
What could not Blake do with that on the Floor,   1410
Or that young, tall, bilingual advocate
Who with the carriage of his syllables
Could bid an audience like an orchestra

Answer his body swaying like a reed?
Colours and sounds made riot of his mind –
White horses in July processional prance,
The blackrobe's swish, the Métis' sullen tread,
And out there in the rear the treaty-wise
Full-breeds with buffalo wallows on their foreheads.

This he could stand no longer, sick indeed: 1420
Send for his doctor, the first thought, then No;
The doctor would advise an oculist,
The oculist return him to the doctor,
The doctor would see-saw him to another –
A specialist on tumours of the brain,
And he might recommend close-guarded rest
In some asylum – Devil take them all,
He had his work to do. He glanced about
And spied his medicine upon the sideboard;
Amber it was, distilled from Highland springs,   1430
That often had translated age to youth
And boiled his blood on a victorious rostrum.
Conviction seized him as he stood, for here
At least he was not cut for compromise,
Nor curried to his nickname Old Tomorrow.
Deliberation in his open stance,
He trenched a deep one, gurgled and sat down.
What were those paltry millions after all?
They stood between completion of the Road
And bankruptcy of both Road and Nation.   1440
Those north-shore gaps must be closed in by steel.
It did not need exhilarated judgment
To see the sense of that. To send the men
Hop-skip-and-jump upon lake ice to board
The flatcars was a revelry for imps.
And all that cutting through the mountain rock,
Four years of it and more, and all for nothing,
Unless those gaps were spanned, bedded and railed.
To quit the Road, to have the Union broken

Was irredeemable. He rose, this time   1450
Invincibility carved on his features,
Hoisted a second, then drew up the blind.
He never saw a sunset just like this.
He lingered in the posture of devotion:
That sun for sure was in the west, or was it?
Soon it would be upholstering the clouds
Upon the Prairies, Rockies and the Coast:
He turned and sailed back under double-reef,
Cabined himself inside an armchair, stretched
His legs to their full length under the table.   1460
Something miraculous had changed the air –
A chemistry that knew how to extract
The iron from the will: the spots had vanished
And in their place an unterrestrial nimbus
Circled his hair: the jerks had left his nerves:
The millions kept on shrinking or were running
From right to left: the fourth arthritic digit
Was straight, and yes, by heaven, the little fifth
Which up to now was just a calcium hook
Was suppling in the Hebridean warmth.   1470
A blessèd peace fell like a dew upon him,
And soon, in trance, drenched in conciliation,
He hiccuped gently – 'Now let S-S-Stephen come!'

(*The Government grants the Directors the right to issue
$35,000,000, guarantees $20,000,000, the rest to be issued
by the Railway Directors. Stephen goes to London, and
Lord Revelstoke, speaking for the House of Baring, takes
over the issue.*)

SUSPENSE IN THE MONTREAL BOARD ROOM

Evening had settled hours before its time
Within the Room and on the face of Angus.
Dejection overlaid his social fur,
Rumpled his side-burns, left moustache untrimmed.

The vision of his Bank, his future Shops,
Was like his outlook for the London visit.
Van Horne was fronting him with a like visage   1480
Except for two spots glowing on his cheeks –
Dismay and anger at those empty pay-cars.
His mutterings were indistinct but final
As though he were reciting to himself
The Athanasian damnatory clauses.
He felt the Receiver's breath upon his neck:
To come so near the end, and then this hurdle!

Only one thing could penetrate that murk –
A cable pledge from London, would it come?
Till now refusal or indifference   1490
Had met the overtures. Would Stephen turn
The trick?
          A door-knock and a telegram
With Stephen's signature! Van Horne ripped it
Apart. Articulation failed his tongue,
But Angus got the meaning from his face
And from a noisy sequence of deductions: –
An inkstand coasted through the office window,
Followed by shredded maps and blotting-pads,
Fluttering like shad-flies in a summer gale;
A bookshelf smitten by a fist collapsed;   1500
Two chairs flew to the ceiling – one retired,
The other roosted on the chandelier.
Some thirty years erased like blackboard chalk,
Van Horne was in a school at Illinois.
Triumphant over his two-hundred weight,
He leaped and turned a cartwheel on the table,
Driving heel sparables into the oak,
Came down to teach his partner a Dutch dance;
And in the presence of the messenger,
Who stared immobilized at what he thought   1510
New colours in the managerial picture,
Van Horne took hold of Angus bodily,

Tore off his tie and collar, mauled his shirt,
And stuffed a Grand Trunk folder down his breeches.

(*The last gap in the mountains – between the Selkirks and
Savona's Ferry – is closed.*)

The Road itself was like a stream that men
Had coaxed and teased or bullied out of Nature.
As if watching for weak spots in her codes,
It sought for levels like the watercourses.
It sinuously took the bends, rejoiced
In plains and easy grades, found gaps, poured through   1520
    them,
But hating steep descents avoided them.
Unlike the rivers which in full rebellion
Against the canyons' hydrophobic slaver
Went to the limit of their argument:
Unlike again, the stream of steel had found
A way to climb, became a mountaineer.
From the Alberta plains it reached the Summit,
And where it could not climb, it cut and curved,
Till from the Rockies to the Coastal Range
It had accomplished what the Rivers had,   1530
Making a hundred clean Caesarian cuts,
And bringing to delivery in their time
Their smoky, lusty-screaming locomotives.

THE SPIKE

Silver or gold? Van Horne had rumbled 'Iron.'
No flags or bands announced this ceremony,
No Morse in circulation through the world,
And though the vital words like Eagle Pass,
Craigellachie, were trembling in their belfries,
No hands were at the ropes. The air was taut
With silences as rigid as the spruces   1540

Forming the background in November mist.
More casual than camera-wise, the men
Could have been properties upon a stage,
Except for road maps furrowing their faces.

Rogers, his both feet planted on a tie,
Stood motionless as ballast. In the rear,
Covering the scene with spirit-level eyes,
Predestination on his chin, was Fleming.
The only one groomed for the ritual
From smooth silk hat and well-cut square-rig beard   1550
Down through his Caledonian longitude,
He was outstaturing others by a foot,
And upright as the mainmast of a brig.
Beside him, barely reaching to his waist,
A water-boy had wormed his way in front
To touch this last rail with his foot, his face
Upturned to see the cheek-bone crags of Rogers.
The other side of Fleming, hands in pockets,
Eyes leaden-lidded under square-crowned hat,
And puncheon-bellied under overcoat,   1560
Unsmiling at the focused lens – Van Horne.
Whatever ecstasy played round that rail
Did not leap to his face. Five years had passed,
Less than five years – so well within the pledge.

The job was done. Was this the slouch of rest?
Not to the men he drove through walls of granite.
The embers from the past were in his soul,
Banked for the moment at the rail and smoking,
Just waiting for the future to be blown.

At last the spike and Donald with the hammer!   1570
His hair like frozen moss from Labrador
Poked out under his hat, ran down his face
To merge with streaks of rust in a white cloud.
What made him fumble the first stroke? Not age:

The snow belied his middle sixties. Was
It lapse of caution or his sense of thrift,
That elemental stuff which through his life
Never pockmarked his daring but had made
The man the canniest trader of his time,
Who never missed a rat-count, never failed   1580
To gauge the size and texture of a pelt?
Now here he was caught by the camera,
Back bent, head bowed, and staring at a sledge,
Outwitted by an idiotic nail.
Though from the crowd no laughter, yet the spike
With its slewed neck was grinning up at Smith.
Wrenched out, it was replaced. This time the hammer
Gave a first tap as with apology,
Another one, another, till the spike
Was safely stationed in the tie and then   1590
The Scot, invoking his ancestral clan,
Using the hammer like a battle-axe,
His eyes bloodshot with memories of Flodden,
Descended on it, rammed it to its home.

*

The stroke released a trigger for a burst
Of sound that stretched the gamut of the air.
The shouts of engineers and dynamiters,
Of locomotive-workers and explorers,
Flanking the rails, were but a tuning-up
For a massed continental chorus. Led   1600
By Moberly (of the Eagles and *this* Pass)
And Rogers (of *his own*), followed by Wilson,
And Ross (charged with the Rocky Mountain Section),
By Egan (general of the Western Lines),
Cambie and Marcus Smith, Harris of Boston,
The roar was deepened by the bass of Fleming,
And heightened by the laryngeal fifes
Of Dug McKenzie and John H. McTavish.
It ended when Van Horne spat out some phlegm

To ratify the tumult with 'Well Done'   1610
Tied in a knot of monosyllables.

Merely the tuning up! For on the morrow
The last blow on the spike would stir the mould
Under the drumming of the prairie wheels,
And make the whistles from the steam out-crow
The Fraser. Like a gavel it would close
Debate, making Macdonald's 'sea to sea'
Pour through two oceanic megaphones –
Three thousand miles of *Hail* from port to port;
And somewhere in the middle of the line   1620
Of steel, even the lizard heard the stroke.
The breed had triumphed after all. To drown
The traffic chorus, she must blend the sound
With those inaugural, narcotic notes
Of storm and thunder which would send her back
Deeper than ever in Laurentian sleep.

NOTES

SELECTED BIBLIOGRAPHY

INDEX OF TITLES

INDEX OF FIRST LINES

Notes

Much more extensive notes (including illustrations and audio-recordings of Pratt reading his works and commenting on them), as well as a detailed timeline of Pratt's life and works, are available on the World Wide Web at www.trentu.ca/pratt/selected.

The following abbreviations are used in the notes:

OHLP   *E.J. Pratt on His Life and Poetry.* Ed. Susan Gingell. University of
       Toronto Press 1983
PUS   *Poems for Upper School.* Macmillan 1963
TSP   *Ten Selected Poems.* Macmillan 1947
VS   *Verses of the Sea.* Macmillan 1930

As well, the following is cited in the notes: *Dictionary of Newfoundland English*, ed. G.M. Story, W.J. Kirwin, and John D.A. Widdowson, 2nd ed. (Toronto: University of Toronto Press 1990).

THE ICE-FLOES

date of composition: probably summer 1921
date of first publication: April 1922
    On 28 March 1898, the SS *Greenland* reached St John's with twenty-five corpses on board. Forty-eight men had been lost on the ice in similar circumstances to those the poem describes. The *Eagle* was a well-known whaling and sealing ship during Pratt's boyhood, but it was not involved in such a tragedy.
1 *Foretop ... Barrel:* 'the barrel at the masthead into which the "look-out" enters
    through a trap-door' [VS, 75]
3 *master-watch:* 'man placed in charge of one of the groups aboard a sealing ves-

sel organized to hunt seals on the ice-floes' [*Dictionary of Newfoundland English*]

7   *slob:* 'water-logged, more penetrable ice' [vs, p. 76]
    growler: 'a heavy, almost submerged fragment of ice so-termed because of the low, crunching sound made when one piece grinds against another – very dangerous to navigation as it often escapes being observed' [vs, p. 76].

10   *white harps:* 'The common seal [is] called the "harp" because of a dark curve upon the back resembling a musical harp ... The hair on [the] young seal is white and soft like wool ...' [vs, pp. 73–4].

25   *bobbing-holes:* 'blow-holes always kept open in the severest weather' [vs, p. 76].

64   *donkey-winch:* 'a type of windlass run by a small engine' [vs, p. 78]

68   *sculped:* 'sealer's term for *skinned*' [vs, p. 78]

69   *pans:* 'A pan is a certain area of ice on which the pelts are heaped; it also means a portion of the ice detached from the main pack' [vs, p. 78].

92   *sirene:* 'local for siren' [vs, p. 78]

120   *heart:* 'When young seals are killed and "sculped," a sealer will attach some of the hearts to his belt, and when hungry will eat them raw' [vs, p. 78].

THE TOLL OF THE BELLS

date of composition: probably summer 1921
date of first publication: 2 April 1923
    See introductory note to 'The Ice-Floes.' For Pratt's account of how he was affected as a boy by the memorial service for the men of the *Greenland*, see OHLP, pp. 60–1.

14   *The tidal triumph of Corinthians:* See 1 Corinthians 15:20ff.

28   *Iliad of Death:* See Homer's *Iliad.*

COME NOT THE SEASONS HERE

date of composition: summer 1922
date of first publication: 2 April 1923
    'a picture of a countryside devastated by war' [OHLP, p. 61]

THE DROWNING

date of composition: summer 1922
date of first publication: 2 April 1923
1   INDENTED] FLUSH LEFT

THE FOG

date of composition: summer 1922
date of first publication: 2 April 1923

THE GROUND SWELL

date of composition: summer 1922
date of first publication: February 1923
'This is a name given to the sound made by the waves suddenly coming up against shallow ground, and spending themselves upon the sand and pebbles of a shore ... It may be the result of a distant sea-storm which has not visited the land, and this sibilant note heard in the dead of night, when there is no wind or noise of any kind, produces an eerie feeling often associated with the thought of disaster' [vs, pp. 78–9].

THE SHARK

date of composition: summer 1922
date of first publication: January 1923

BEFORE AN ALTAR

date of composition: by autumn 1922
date of first publication: 2 April 1923
epigraph *Gueudecourt:* a French village recaptured from the Germans in
    September 1916

NEWFOUNDLAND

date of composition: by autumn 1922
date of first publication: 2 April 1923
26 *gulch-line:* the boundary line of a flow of water

THE WITCHES' BREW

date of composition: summer 1923
date of first publication: late January 1926
    The Witches' Brew was written on the occasion of Pratt's fifth wedding anniversary. For Pratt's comments on the poem and particularly on its function as an

'emotional release' and 'a psychological reaction against [completing his] doctorate,' see OHLP, pp. 33–6, 39–40, 52.

23–4 *Neptune ... Vulcan's union with his daughter:* In some myths, Venus, goddess of love, was the daughter of Neptune, the god of the sea. She was the wife of Vulcan, the Roman god of fire and of metalworking.

29 *sub-aquaceous:* variant of 'subaqueous,' meaning 'under water'

49 *Drake:* Sir Francis Drake (1540?–96), English navigator and admiral, first Englishman to circumnavigate the globe (1577–80); vice admiral in the fleet that defeated the Spanish Armada (1588)

64 *stations:* A station is 'a cove or harbor with space in the foreground for the erection of facilities for the conduct of the fishery in adjacent waters' [*Dictionary of Newfoundland English*].

66 *To serve their god while here below:* a parody of the doxology: 'Praise God from whom all blessings flow – / Praise Him all creatures here below.'

69 *the ivy god:* Bacchus, who wore a band of ivy around his head

71 *Christiania:* alternative name for Oslo, capital of Norway

113 *Laodiceans:* those who are lukewarm or indifferent. See Revelation 3.14–16.

116 *Behring:* (usual spelling 'Bering') strait between Siberia and Alaska

168 *run:* 'a narrow salt-water strait or extended navigable passage between the coast and an island or series of islands; a passage between islands' [*Dictionary of Newfoundland English*]

178 *Baccalieu:* small island at the entrance to Conception Bay, Newfoundland

232 *Salamander:* mythical reptile able to live in fire, or a tailed amphibian

272 *Sadducees:* members of an ancient Jewish sect who opposed the Pharisees, another sect who strictly observed tradition and written law

280 *Deacons good and bad in spots:* probably an allusion to the 'curate's egg' joke in *Punch* (1905), in which a curate who is given a stale egg by his bishop declares that it is 'good in parts'

281 *Wyandots:* a pun on Wyandot, brand-name of a tractor, and Wyandots (usual spelling 'Wyandottes'), a breed of chicken

347/8 *Byron:* George Gordon, Lord Byron (1788–1824), English poet and satirist, notorious for his dissolute way of life. His *The Vision of Judgment* is one of Pratt's models.

353 *Canary:* short for Canary wine, a dry white wine from the Canary Islands off the northwest coast of Africa

353/4 *Wolsey:* Thomas Wolsey (1473?–1530), English cardinal known for his lavish living

355 *Richmond:* Henry Fitzroy, natural son of Henry VIII, named first Duke of Richmond in 1525

Buckingham: Edward Stafford, third Duke of Buckingham (1478–1521), executed in 1521 for high treason after a quarrel with Wolsey

357 *Royal Henry:* Henry VIII (1491–1547)

365/6 *Campeggio:* Lorenzo Campeggio (1474–1539), Italian humanist and cardinal who went to England in 1528 to inquire about Henry VIII's marriage to Catherine of Aragon

366 *Clement:* probably Pope Clement VII (1342–94). Clement VIII (1536–1605) would have been only three years old at Campeggio's death.

369/70 *Pepys:* Samuel Pepys (1633–1703), English diarist. A philanderer, he was familiar with the 'maddening impulse.'

373 *gelatinous Medusa:* jellyfish

373/4 *Paracelsus:* Phillipus Aureolus Paracelsus (1493?–1541), a famous Swiss physician and alchemist

375 *Divinest Luna:* Roman goddess of the moon. 'Luna' is also used to mean the moon itself.

379/80 *Samuel Butler:* 1612–80, author of *Hudibras,* whose mode of epic burlesque Pratt is adapting

383/4 *Samson:* one of the judges of Israel. As a Nazarite dedicated to the Lord, he was required to abstain from alcohol.

385/6 *Saint Patrick:* Christian missionary and patron saint of Ireland (c. 385–461)

387 *Gomorrah:* an ancient city, destroyed with Sodom for wickedness. See Genesis 18.20ff.

398 *myrmidons:* a mythical race of men said to have sprung from ants. In the Trojan War, the myrmidons were led by Achilles.

399/400 *Fabius Maximus:* the Roman general, Quintus Fabius Maximus Verrucosus (d. 203 B.C.), known as *Cunctator,* or 'the Delayer,' because of his ultimately successful tactics against Hannibal, which involved harassment over a number of years rather than direct battle

400/1 *A French General:* Pierre Jean François Bosquet, French army officer at the Battle of Balaklava, 1854, during the Crimean War. The quoted comment ('Magnificent! But it is not war.') was made by Bosquet concerning the charge of the Light Brigade at the battle.

403/4 *Nelson:* Horatio Nelson (1758–1805), British admiral and hero of the Napoleonic Wars. Two of Nelson's great victories were at Trafalgar, 1805, and the Nile, 1798.

405/6 *Carlyle:* Thomas Carlyle (1795–1881), nineteenth-century British writer and thinker, perhaps cited because of his lifelong fascination with heroic men of action

488/9 *Sir Isaac Newton:* English physicist (1642–1727), who formulated the laws of motion and gravitation

492/3 *Blake:* William Blake (1757–1827), English poet, author of 'The Tyger' and 'The Lamb'

496/7 *Bottom:* rustic in Shakespeare's *A Midsummer Night's Dream*

498/9 *Owen Glendower:* rebellious Welshman (1359?–1416?) who led the last seri-
ous attempt to free Wales from English rule. In Shakespeare's *Henry IV, Part 1,*
he says: 'I can call spirits from the vasty deep' (3.1.53).

500/1 *Benjamin Franklin:* American statesman and scientist (1706–90)

502/3 *my kite:* a reference to Franklin's experiment of flying a kite in a thunder-
storm, which proved that lightning is an electrical discharge

504/5 *Aesop:* sixth-century B.C. Greek writer of fables

507 *ignis fatuus:* (Lat., 'foolish fire') will-o'-the-wisp, a phosphorescent light seen
on marshy ground

508/9 *Euclid:* fourth-century B.C. mathematician of Alexandria. He wrote *Ele-
ments of Geometry;* hence the mention of 'circle.'

514/15 *Johnny Walker:* personification of Johnny Walker Scotch Whisky

522/3 *Calvin:* John Calvin (1509–64), French Protestant theologian and founder
of Calvinism; author of *The Institutes of the Christian Religion* (1536), in which
he asserts that God has predestined 'before the world began' the salvation of
certain souls and the damnation of others

572 *Acheron:* (Gk., 'Sorrowful') a river in Hades, or Hades itself

SEA-GULLS

date of composition: probably August 1925
date of first publication: December 1930
4 horizon blue,] horizon blue.

THE SEA-CATHEDRAL

date of composition: probably August 1926
date of first publication: December 1926

THE IRON DOOR

date of composition: from early April to mid-July 1927
date of first publication: 23 September 1927
111 he had heard,] he had heard

Pratt commented on *The Iron Door* in a letter of 27 August 1927 to William A.
Deacon:

The theme came to me at the time of my mother's death last December. It
originated in a dream where my mother ... was standing before a colossal
door – the door of Death – and expecting without any fear of denial what-
soever instant and full admission into the future state where she believed

other members of her family had already entered ... From there I elaborated it into a general conception of the problem of immortality, starting with the feeling of despair and apparent inevitability which faces one at a grave-side ... In front of the door are gathered a vast multitude and a number of individuals emerge who present their cases to the Unseen Warders, or God or the Governor of the Universe whoever he may be, demanding some information of what is going on, on the other side. All but one – the last – are drawn from persons I had known in life. The last one, to my mind, sums up the problem, partly biological, partly environmental, of injustice and irregularity in the moral order, and she presents it in its glaring enigma.

The first case is that of the naive simplicity of a child who relies upon a father to unravel the knots. The second is that of a rugged seaman who with a stark sense of justice asks the 'unknown admiral' if the great traditions of the service might be fairly assumed to prevail on the wastes of the hinder sea, if such a sea might be assumed to exist ... The third – that of my own mother – represents a large number of people who believe implicitly in the essential soundness of the heart of the Universe and who impute to God only the same fair principles which they realise in their own honest natures. The next is a young man who gave up health and prime of life in a futile attempt to save an unknown life when there was not a human eye to stimulate or encourage the sacrifice. Then two more speak, one a searcher after beauty in all its forms in this life who is puzzled that Death should apparently negate the value of the quest; and another a searcher after truth ... who meets with disillusion at the end, yet exhibits a noble stoicism when faced with what looks like extinction. Then comes the last with the most poignant and tragic appeal.

In order to make the psychological contrast as sharp as possible I put in a stanza or rather section describing the desolation of the world at this point ... The only demand I make is that there shall be life and light with continued life effort on the other side. Hence I never see inside the door. I only judge by the reflection on the faces of human beings and by certain sounds which intermittently break through that there are vast stretches beyond ...

47 *frore:* 'frozen solid' [*Dictionary of Newfoundland English*]

148 *Life for a life:* See Exodus 21.23; Deuteronomy 19.21.

169 *clench:* (or 'clinch') conclusive settlement

175 *miserere:* prayer for mercy, from the first word of Psalm 50 in the Vulgate, meaning 'have pity'

211 *Theban mockery of the crest:* The meaning of this phrase is uncertain. When Oedipus abdicated as King of Thebes, his two sons, Eteocles and Polynices, agreed to reign in alternate years, but Eteocles, the elder brother, refused to

give up the kingship after his year. In the resulting civil war, the two brothers killed each other. Thus the death's head might perhaps be seen as the crest of Thebes.

EROSION

date of composition: between summer 1930 and winter 1931
date of first publication: June 1931

THE HIGHWAY

date of composition: between mid-June and November 1931
date of first publication: October/November 1931
2 *seneschal:* officer in charge of a household
6 *Aldebaran:* brightest star in the constellation Taurus. The name is from the Arabic meaning 'follower (of the Pleiades).'

THE MAN AND THE MACHINE

date of composition: between late winter and early spring 1932
date of first publication: 30 November 1932

FROM STONE TO STEEL

date of composition: by October 1932
date of first publication: September–October 1932
4 *Java:* Java man, *Pithecanthropus,* a genus known from skulls discovered in Java in 1891; considered one of the links between the apes and man
   Geneva: Geneva, Switzerland, home of the League of Nations and also associated with John Calvin and Protestantism. As such, the city can typify Western Christian civilization. It is likely that the poem reflects both the Geneva Convention of 1929, which stipulated conditions governing treatment of prisoners of war, and the Geneva Disarmament Conference of 1932.
20 *Gethsemane:* the scene of Christ's meditation and betrayal. See Matthew 26.36 and Mark 14.32ff.

THE PRIZE CAT

date of composition: by autumn 1933
date of first publication: February 1935
20 whitethroat's scream.] whitethroat's scream

'... refers to Mussolini's attack on Ethiopia just before the Second World War. I had been pondering over the illusion that, with the growth of civilization and culture, human savagery was disappearing' [*OHLP*, p. 95]. Although Mussolini's primary attack on Ethiopia did not take place until five months after this poem was published, there was an earlier widely reported skirmish between Italy and Ethiopia on 5 December 1934 at Walwal, where the spears of the Ethiopian tribesmen were ranged against the guns and tanks of an Italian force. However, D.G. Pitt, in *The Master Years*, suggests that the poem was submitted to *Queen's Quarterly* in October 1934. It is unclear whether Pratt inserted a reference to Abyssinia after the first draft of the poem or whether, as Pitt argues, the incident provided the poet with an opportunity to make a retrospective statement about human savagery.

5 *gads:* in this context, claws; derived from gadlings, spurs on armour gauntlets

SILENCES

date of composition: autumn 1933
date of first publication: March 1936

FIRE

date of composition: by December 1934
date of first publication: December 1934

THE TITANIC

date of composition: from August 1934 to summer 1935
date of first publication: 16 November 1935
396 *Avocado pear!*] *Avocado pear;*
486 A SPEECH HEADING IS CLEARLY NECESSARY BEFORE 'A Minnesota guy BUT IT IS MISSING IN ALL VERSIONS.
515 said of the Sphinx] said to the Sphinx
571 *double watch installed*] *Double watch installed*
1016 orders – ceased] orders, ceased

The *Titanic*, the largest and most luxurious ocean liner of its time, struck an iceberg on its maiden voyage, on 14 April 1912, and sank with the loss of 1,522 lives, despite its reputation for being unsinkable. Pratt commented on the story of the *Titanic* [*OHLP*, pp. 96, 99–100]:

... I do not suppose that there is in this century a single event narrowly circumscribed in place and time which has given rise to more discussion and heartburnings than the loss of the *Titanic*. Any individual episode of the Great War, as horrible as it may be, is subdued by the general background, just as the destruction of a house would be by the conflagration of a town. Such an incident as the sinking of the *Lusitania* came as the climax of a series of provocations to determine the war-mind of the United States, and in that sense [was] tremendously significant, but at least the sinking was credible and in many quarters expected as a chance of war, but the foundering of the *Titanic*, removed as it was from the bounds of belief, made the disaster the most grotesque event in the history of the sea. The appeal of the story is akin to that which holds our minds when we read about a perfect plot, where every contingency is supposed to be safeguarded, and where the defence has repaired the vulnerable spot in the heel.

...

Was there ever an event outside of the realm of technical drama where so many factors combined to close all the gates of escape, as if some power with intelligence and resource had organized and directed a conspiracy? Apart from such safeguards as constituted her normal protection – like her immense size and flotation, her numerous watertight compartments, her steel bulkheads, her powerful engines and pumps – there were all around her within wireless touch eight ships, some of these, like the *Olympic* and the *Baltic*, the biggest on the sea, talking to her, congratulating her on her maiden voyage as she sped along and warning her of the presence of ice. The whys and the ifs came thick and fast after the event. Why should the belief in her invulnerability stimulated by advertisement have [caused neglect of] the ordinary lifeboat provision – one-third only of her capacity? Why should the iceberg that struck her have arrived at that precise moment in that precise locality? There was only one part of the ship which was not immune to attack. The iceberg sought that line for its thrust. Why should the *Titanic* in endeavouring to avoid head-on collision, a natural impulse, find a greater peril in the glancing blow? In the words of the Washington commissioner, she turned aside the brow only to take it on the temple. Why should the wireless operator on the *Californian* just fifteen miles off have taken off the phones from his ears a minute or so before the distress signal from the stricken ship? And why were the rockets which were actually seen by the *Californian* misunderstood?

For further comments by Pratt on the story of the *Titanic*, see OHLP, pp. 95–107.

11 *air shots:* a reference to the pneumatic hammers used to set rivets

27 *telegraphs:* The telegraph is 'the clock in the engine-room' [PUS, 60].

35 *folders:* 'the advertising booklets' [PUS, p. 58]

50 *hubris:* 'the outstanding sin of pride which in the Greek myths would attempt the most daring ventures such as the slaying of the cattle on the Isle of Helios by the crew of Ulysses [*Odyssey* 12], or the theft of fire [by Prometheus] from Zeus' [PUS, p. 58]

56 *Lloyds:* London insurance underwriting corporation that deals mainly with maritime insurance

57 *Godhaven:* 'a Danish settlement on the west coast of Greenland' [*PUS*, p. 58]

60 *Behring:* (usual spelling 'Bering') strait between Siberia and Alaska

93 *plantigrade:* 'from "sole" and "to walk," applied to animals like bears' [*PUS*, p. 58]

100 *Corundum:* aluminum oxide, noted for its flint-like hardness

130 *sun-hounds:* 'clouds ... following the sun' [*PUS*, p. 58]

135 *Mother Carey eyes:* 'full of foreboding: stormy petrels are sometimes called Mother Carey's chickens. The phrase is a sailor's adaptation of *mater cara*, an epithet of the Virgin Mary' [*PUS*, pp. 58–9].

150 *Blue-Points:* (not usually capitalized) small, edible oysters harvested at Blue Point on Long Island, New York

152 *lobster coral:* lobster roe
    Béchamel: 'a sauce named after Louis de Béchamel, steward of Louis XIV' [*PUS*, p. 59]

176 *Falstaffian:* Sir John Falstaff, the most famous of all Shakespeare's comic characters, had a huge appetite for food and drink.

179 *Savoy chasers:* biscuit covered in sugar served at the end of a meal

196 *Regency:* of the type of furniture made during the Regency in Britain (1811–20), when George, Prince of Wales, was regent

209 *Frank Gotch:* 1878–1917, catch-as-catch-can professional wrestling champion (1905–13)

212 *Jeffries:* Jim Jeffries (1875–1953), world heavyweight boxing champion, 1899–1905; defeated by Jack Johnson in Reno

241 *trolling spoon:* a kind of artificial bait having the form of the bowl of a spoon, used in trolling
    log rotator: cylinder of metal with a propeller at one end; dragged behind the ship to record the distance travelled

246 *cat's paw:* a light breeze that ruffles a small stretch of water

253 *beam:* 'the widest part of a ship' [*PUS*, p. 59]

268 *field ice:* ice that floats in large tracts

269 *growlers:* See note to "The Ice-Floes," 7 [p. 208].

272 *solid pack:* refers to pack ice, an area of ice pieces driven together

280 *Banks:* the Grand Banks, 'large area of shoal water southeast of Newfoundland forming a rich fishing-ground' [*Dictionary of Newfoundland English*]

291 *Smith:* Captain Edward J. Smith

301 *Board:* Maritime Board of Trade

320 *Valley of the Kings:* on the west side of the Nile south of Thebes, where archaeologists found the tombs of ancient Egyptian kings

333 *The B.M.:* British Museum, London

342–3 *Preferred ... common:* Preferred stock is stock on which dividends must be paid before those of common stock; it also has preference in the distribution of assets.

356 *bed-bolts:* bolts that secure the engines to their foundations

365 *Astor ... Straus:* financier John Jacob Astor (b. 1864), mining magnate Benjamin Guggenheim (b. 1865), Broadway producer Henry Birkhardt Harris (b. 1867), and Isidor Straus (b. 1845), owner of Macy's Department Store in New York. All died on the *Titanic.*

366 *Frohman:* Of the three Frohman brothers with theatrical interests, none was on the *Titanic;* but one, Charles Frohman (1860–1915), was drowned on the *Lusitania.*

368 *Hays:* Charles M. Hays (1866–1912), president of the Grand Trunk Railway
      Stead: William T. Stead (1849–1912), British spiritualist and editor

371 *Phillips:* Jack G. Phillips (1888–1912), first wireless operator on the *Titanic*

373 *Marconi valve:* vacuum tube used in radio, named after Guglielmo Marconi (1874–1937), Italian physicist, celebrated for his development of wireless telegraphy

389 *Bishop's Rock:* 'in the Scilly Islands on the approach to the English Channel' [*PUS*, p. 59]

395 *Beaucaire:* red wine from the area around the city of Beaucaire in France

400 *Moselle:* dry white wine from the Moselle Valley in France

425 *quarter:* 'aft section of the ship half-way between beam and stern' [*PUS*, p. 59]

434 *the highway which the Milkmaid passed:* the Milky Way

442 *taffrail log:* The taffrail is 'the rail around the stern' [*PUS*, p. 59]. The log rotator activated a counter on the taffrail, and a bell sounded after every knot or nautical mile of distance travelled.

450 *twenty after two:* The *Titanic* sank at 2:20 A.M., 15 April 1912.

452 *Hove-to:* brought to a standstill

464 *bridge induction light:* A panel on the bridge had a light for every section, the light glowing to indicate trouble in any section.

466 *reciprocating:* 'The *Titanic* was equipped with both reciprocating and turbine engines' [*PUS*, p. 59].

469 *pitch:* 'the wash made by the propeller' [*PUS*, p. 59]

473 *counter:* 'that part of the stern just above the rudder' [*PUS*, p. 59]

476 *Ace full:* 'three aces and a pair making a "full house"' [*PUS*, p. 59]

478 *roodles:* 'a jack-pot with everybody in and limit doubled' [*PUS*, p. 60]

484 *Open for ten:* 'begin the betting with a ten-dollar bet' [*PUS*, p. 60]

503 *see:* 'match the bet' [*PUS*, p. 60]

504 *call:* 'not raise the bet' [*PUS*, p. 60]

526 *Murdoch:* First Officer William M. Murdoch (1873–1912)

527–8 *Starboard ... port:* '"Starboard your helm" meant that the tiller would be put over to the starboard (right) side, which would turn the rudder to port (left)" [PUS, p. 60]. The ship would then heel, meaning lean over, to port.

540 *a sea:* ocean swell

558 *bilge turn:* 'the greatest point of curvature between the keel and the vertical part of the hull' [PUS, p. 60]

562 *C.Q.D.:* CQ (without periods since it is not an acronym) is the 'all stations' call. The addition of the *D* indicates special urgency. It is the 'older signal of distress' referred to a few lines later, which was being replaced about this time by SOS.

590 *Balkan scramble:* 'The captain's chief fear was that of panic in the steerage where hundreds from south-eastern Europe, ignorant of English speech, might not understand the orders of the officers' [PUS, p. 60].

598 *falls:* 'ropes' [PUS, p. 60]

615 *bore:* the distance across a pipe or tube

629 *chocks:* 'cradles on which boats rest' [PUS, p. 60]

630 *Welin davits:* Davits are cranes on the ship's sides for the lowering and raising of boats. The davits on the *Titanic* were supplied by the Welin Company, founded by the Swedish inventor Axel Welin in 1901.

663–4 *E-Yip ... I don't care:* from 'Yip-I-Addy-I-Ay' (words by Will D. Cobb and George Grossmith, Jr; music by John H. Flynn)

675 *gudgeon:* 'a part of the stern-post' [PUS, p. 61]
    stem: bow

700 *the exhaust from the condenser flow:* On the *Titanic,* sea water was used to cool the fresh-water steam in the condenser. The heated sea water was then sent back into the ocean through the exhaust.

726 *cargo ports:* openings in the side of the ship for loading or unloading cargo

737 *going by the head:* sinking at the bow

739 *warp of the bunker press:* The shifting coal in the bunker pressed the steel bulkheads out of shape.

769 *fo'c'sle:* 'forecastle; the forward decks housing the crew' [PUS, p. 61]

822 *fiddley:* 'passage-way from a stokehold' [PUS, p. 61]

831 *foremast root:* where the foremast is rooted in the deck

857 *I've ... Paris:* from 'The Man Who Broke the Bank at Monte Carlo' (words and music by Fred Gilbert)

866 *We've been together now for forty years:* from a popular song of the period, 'My Old Dutch' (words by Albert Chevalier, music by Charles Ingle)

867 *Whither you go, I go:* Ruth's words to Naomi. See Ruth 1.16.

876 *Millet:* Francis Davis Millet (1846–1912), a fashionable American painter

877 *Butt:* Major Archibald Butt (1865–1912), U.S. army officer, military aide to Presidents T. Roosevelt and Taft

896 *collapsibles:* collapsible rafts, which folded flat because they had canvas
   sides
959 *lop:* a state of the sea in which the waves are short and lumpy
970 *flying bridge:* part of the bridge extending over the side of the ship
1006 *shroud and stay:* wires or ropes supporting a mast or funnel
1011 *docking bridge:* aft bridge used when docking

THE BARITONE

date of composition: by December 1936
date of first publication: December 1936
19 *Giovinezza*] *Giovanezza*
29 periscopes,] periscopes.
19 *The Giovinezza:* (Ital.) 'youthfulness'; the anthem of the Italian fascists, usu-
   ally known in English as 'Song of the Blackshirts'
21 *stretto:* portion of a fugue in which one voice follows closely on the preceding
   one
22 *Dead March:* from Handel's sacred oratorio *Saul,* c. 1739. See 2 Samuel 1.17ff.
25 *codetta:* short coda

BRÉBEUF AND HIS BRETHREN

date of composition: from late 1939 to early June 1940
date of first publication: 15 July 1940
435 will – rejoined] will, rejoined
843 thou] Thou
1394/5 LINE SPACE] NO LINE SPACE
1948 He] he
   Jean de Brébeuf (1593–1649) was a Jesuit missionary who first came to Canada
in 1625. He went back to France in 1629 when Quebec was captured by the
English but returned to Canada in 1633, where he remained until his death. He
worked mostly with the Hurons, until his capture and death at the hands of the
Iroquois in 1649. His bones are buried at the Martyrs' Shrine near Midland,
Ontario. Pratt's main source is the Jesuit *Relations,* from which he quotes directly
at various points in the poem. For Pratt's comments on the story of Brébeuf, see
OHLP, pp. 46–7 and 114–26.
10 *St. Francis of Assisi:* 'St Francis of Assisi (1182–1226) left his father's home and
   devoted himself to a life of poverty and to the healing of the sick' [*TSP,* p. 145].

16 *Vincent de Paul:* 1580–1660, 'a French priest devoted to works of charity' [*TSP*, p. 146]

17–18 *Francis de Sales ... the Visitation:* 'Francis de Sales (1567–1622) established "the congregation of nuns of the Order of the Visitation"' [*TSP*, p. 146].

22 *City of God: De Civitate Dei,* by Saint Augustine (354–430)

24 *Imitatio:* 'The Imitation of Christ by Thomas à Kempis (1379–1471)' [*TSP*, p. 146]

28 *Theresa:* 'Saint Theresa (1515–82), reformer of the Carmelite Order' [*TSP*, p. 146]

29 *Carmelites:* members of a religious order founded in the twelfth century at Mount Carmel, Palestine

30 *John of the Cross:* 'a Spanish mystic (1542–91)' [*TSP*, p. 146]

33 *Xavier:* Francis Xavier (1506–52), Basque Jesuit missionary, called the Apostle to the Indies. He was an associate of Ignatius of Loyola, with whom he was involved in founding the Society of Jesus. He was renowned for his missionary work in the east, especially in India.

35 *Loyola, soldier-priest:* 'Ignatius Loyola (1491–1556), a Basque soldier who, after being wounded in the defence of Pampeluna (in Spain), went to the monastery of Montserrat and publicly renounced the profession of arms. His *Preludes* and *Spiritual Exercises* became the chief manual of instruction and inspiration for the Jesuits' [*TSP*, p. 146].

39 *Company of Jesus:* the Jesuits

47 *Magnificat:* a hymn of the Virgin Mary beginning 'My soul doth magnify (*magnificat* in Latin) the Lord' (Luke 1.46–55)
    Notre Dame: 'the cathedral in Paris' [*TSP*, p. 146]

58 *Bayeux:* near the coast of Normandy

62 *Via Dolorosa:* 'The Way of the Cross – the road leading to Golgotha over which Jesus passed on the way to the Crucifixion' [*TSP*, p. 146]

64 *the Real Presence:* a reference to the belief among certain Christians, especially Roman Catholics and some Anglicans, that the body and blood of Christ are actually present in the Eucharist

68 *per ignem et per aquam:* (Lat.) through fire and through water

74–5 *Champlain, Brulé, Viel, / Sagard and Le Caron:* '[Champlain] (1567–1635), founded Quebec in 1608, was the first governor of New France, [and] explored the Huron country, making it accessible to the missionaries and traders. It was under his direction that Brulé visited the Huron districts in 1611. Le Caron, Sagard, and Viel were Franciscan missionaries ... Viel was killed in 1625 by Indian traders from Huronia' [*TSP*, pp. 146–7].

83 *the manual:* Loyola's *Preludes* and *Spiritual Exercises*

88 *Deum laudet:* (Lat.) 'that he praise God'

104 *Hastings:* Battle of Hastings, 1066

105 *Howards:* family name of the Dukes of Norfolk

117 *Massé:* Father Enemond Massé (1575–1646), Jesuit priest and missionary to Acadia, 1611–13, and to Quebec from 1625 until his death
    Charles Lalemant: 1587–1674, first superior of the Jesuits in Quebec, responsible for setting up a Jesuit mission in Canada. He came to Quebec with Fathers Massé and Brébeuf in 1625.

120–1 *Notre Dame / Des Anges:* the first church erected by the Franciscans in Quebec, near Quebec City

121 *Daillon:* Father Joseph de la Roche Daillon (?–1656), priest of the Récollet order (a branch of the Franciscans) who came to New France in 1625 to assist Father Viel in his mission to the Hurons

122 *Three Rivers:* Three Rivers (Trois-Rivières) is located on the east shore of the mouth of the St Maurice River, midway between Quebec City and Montreal. At the time, it was an Algonquin settlement.

133 *Sault-au-Récollet:* Father Nicholas Viel, who was sent to the Canadian mission of the Récollets, was killed along with a convert at the last rapid above Montreal, thereafter known as Sault-au-Récollet.

150 *sagamite:* 'corn-mush mixed with dried fish' [*TSP*, p. 147]

153 *Turk's cap:* a flower, commonly called the American swamp lily

161 *de Noüé:* Father Anne de Noüé (1587–1646), Jesuit priest and missionary to the Hurons, 1626–7

191 *the island of the Allumettes:* in the Ottawa River

227 *Fort Richelieu:* Fort de Richelieu, on the site of present-day Sorel, was one of a series of forts established along the Richelieu River during the French regime.

229 *Neutrals:* The main villages of the Hurons were situated in what is now Simcoe County, the Algonquins being to the east and north, the Petuns (Tobacco Nation) to the southwest, and the Neutrals farther south in the general region north of Lake Erie.

251 *Arendiwans:* 'sorcerers' [*TSP*, p. 147]

262 *Richelieu:* 1585–1642, 'French statesman and cardinal' [*TSP*, p. 149]

263 *Cartier:* Jacques Cartier (b. 1491–1557) led three voyages of exploration to the St Lawrence region in 1534, 1535–6, and 1541–2. He is usually credited with discovering Canada, meaning the small region of Quebec he named Canada during his 1535 voyage.
    Magellan: Ferdinand Magellan (c. 1480–1521), Portuguese navigator; commander of the first expedition to circumnavigate the globe (although he died en route)

266 *Kirke:* 'Sir David Kirke [1597–1634] who sailed up the St Lawrence and captured Quebec in 1629' [*TSP*, p. 147]

282–4 *Summa of Aquinas, faith ... Reason slipped:* In the *Summa Theologica* (1267–73), Thomas Aquinas (1225–74) argued that the truths of faith complement those of reason.

305–6 *Thirty Years ... / La Rochelle and Fribourg:* The Thirty Years War (1618–48) was primarily a struggle of German Protestant princes and their allies against the Catholic powers represented by the Holy Roman Empire and the Hapsburgs. The French seaport of La Rochelle, a centre of Protestantism, was besieged and taken by Catholic forces. Fribourg, now in Switzerland, was on the French-German border during this period.

308 *Mazarin:* Jules Mazarin (1602–61), 'Prime Minister of France who continued the foreign policy of Richelieu' [*TSP*, p. 149]

Condé: Louis II de Bourbon Condé (1621–86), French general during the Thirty Years War

309 *Turenne:* Henri De La Tour D'Auvergne, Vicompte de Turenne (1611–75), French general during the Thirty Years War

314 *Le Jeune:* Father Paul Lejeune (1591–1664), Jesuit priest and missionary to the Hurons, 1639–49

Biard: Pierre Biard (1567–1622), Roman Catholic missionary who went to Acadia in 1611

319 *Chastellain:* Father Pierre Chastellain (1606–84), Jesuit priest and missionary to the Hurons, 1639–49

320 *Pijart:* Father Claude Pijart (1600–83), Jesuit priest and missionary to the Nipissings and Algonquins, 1637–44

Le Mercier: Father François-Joseph Le Mercier (1604–90), Jesuit priest and missionary to the Hurons, 1635–50

Isaac Jogues: 1607–46, Jesuit priest and missionary to the Hurons, 1637–42, and to the Iroquois from 1646 until his death at their hands

321 *The Lalemants:* Jérôme and Gabriel, brothers of Charles Lalemant. Father Jérôme Lalemant (1593–1673), a Jesuit priest, succeeded Brébeuf as superior of the Huron mission and served in that capacity until 1645. Father Gabriel Lalemant (1610–49), also a Jesuit priest, was a missionary to the Hurons from 1648 until his death at the hands of the Iroquois.

323 *Ragueneau:* Father Paul Ragueneau (1608–80), Jesuit priest, superior of the mission to the Hurons, 1645–50, and of the Jesuits in Canada

333 *Garnier:* Father Charles Garnier (c. 1605–49), Jesuit priest, missionary to the Hurons from 1636 until his death at the hands of the Iroquois

336 *Capuchin:* (Ital., 'hooded one') Roman Catholic religious order of friars, founded during 1525–8

342 *Chabanel:* Father Noell Chabanel (1613–49), Jesuit priest, missionary to the Hurons from 1644 until his death at their hands

370 *Chaumonot:* Father Pierre Joseph-Marie Chaumonot (1611–93), Jesuit priest and missionary to the Hurons, 1639–50

375 *the Lady of Loretto:* (also spelled 'Loreto') the Virgin Mary. Santa Casa, a famous chapel of the Virgin in Loreto, Italy, is a place of pilgrimage.

384 *Davost:* Father Amboise Davost (1586–1643), Jesuit priest and missionary to the Hurons, 1634–6

    Daniel: Father Antoine Daniel (1601–48), Jesuit priest and missionary to the Hurons from 1634 until his death at the hands of the Iroquois

437 *Fresh Water Sea:* Lake Huron

446 *arch-foes:* 'Iroquois' [*TSP*, p. 147]

491–2 *Le Capitaine / Du Jour:* (Fr.) 'the chief of the day'; the term used by the Hurons to refer to the clock

500 *oki:* 'a spirit or demon' [*TSP*, p. 147]

534–5 *Bird / Of Thunder:* The Thunderbird is a supernatural creature prominent in Indian myths which is responsible for thunder and lightning.

539 *Saint Joseph:* Saint Joseph was the patron of the Hurons. The house the Jesuits built at Ihonatiria was called St Joseph.

603 *Benedicite:* (Lat., 'bless') blessing

635 *Medici confession:* 'a reference to the methods of extracting testimony under certain rulers of the Florentine Medici in the fifteenth and sixteenth centuries' [*TSP*, p. 147]

675 *hatchet collar:* 'A form of torture was to place a ring of hot tomahawks around the neck of a victim' [*TSP*, p. 147].

692 *viscous melanotic current:* 'the stubborn, dark strain in the Indian temper' [*TSP*, p. 147]

756 *Saint Thomas:* Thomas Aquinas (1225–74), one of the greatest of the Catholic theologians

810 *Why hast Thou forsaken me:* Christ's last words: 'My God, my God, why hast thou forsaken me?' (Matthew 27.46; Mark 15.34).

823 *Du Peron:* Father François Du Peron (1610–65), Jesuit priest and missionary to the Hurons, 1639–49

827–8 *John / Of Patmos:* 'the writer of Revelation who was exiled to the island of Patmos in the Mediterranean' [*TSP*, p. 148]

899 *âmes damnées:* (Fr.) damned souls

932–4 *Thou shalt love ... thyself:* a paraphrase of Luke 10.27

941 *Oblates:* persons dedicated to the religious or monastic life

955/6 *Fort Sainte Marie:* Fort Sainte Marie, also known as Notre Dame de la Conception, was a fortified missionary centre, located near present-day Midland, Ontario. It was intended to be agriculturally self-sufficient and ultimately to become the nucleus of a Huron Christian community. Construction began in 1639.

968 *Poncet:* Father Joseph-Antoine Poncet De La Rivière (1610–75), Jesuit priest and missionary to the Hurons, 1639–40

969 *Le Moyne:* Father Simon Le Moyne (1604–65), Jesuit priest and missionary to the Hurons, 1638–49

Charles Raymbault: 1602–42, Jesuit priest and missionary to the Hurons, 1637–40

René Menard: 1605–61, Jesuit priest and missionary to the Hurons, Algonquins, Nipissings, and Iroquois from 1641 until his disappearance in 1661

971 *Le Coq:* ?–1650, lay-assistant of the Jesuits; supervisor of buildings and equipment at Sainte-Marie-des-Hurons from 1634 to 1649

Christophe Reynaut: Jesuit lay-assistant who helped with building the fort

Charles Boivin: one of three brothers who came as lay-assistants of the Jesuits to help with building the fort in 1640

972 *Couture:* Guillaume Couture (?–1701), lay-assistant who served in Huronia from 1641 to 1642

Jean Guérin: lay-assistant who helped with building the fort

1069 *the Manitou:* the supreme being or supernatural force in the traditional religion of the Algonquian peoples

1073 *breathings:* the practice by medicine men of curing disease by blowing or exhaling their breath

1192 *Sillery:* first Canadian Indian reserve, established in 1637 near Quebec City

1210–11 *the feast / Of St. Ignatius:* 31 July

1214 *Eustache:* Ahatsistari Eustache (1602–42), Huron warrior, baptized Eustache in 1642. He was killed by the Iroquois while accompanying Father Jogues back to Huronia.

1224 *Goupil:* René Goupil (1608–42), surgeon, possibly a Jesuit lay-assistant, who accompanied Father Jogues into Huron country in 1642, where he was captured and killed by the Iroquois

1356 *Fort Orange:* Dutch trading post on the Hudson River, on the site of present-day Albany

1422 *livres:* French currency, originally equivalent to a pound of silver

Ossernenon: 'now Auriesville, New York State' [*TSP*, p. 148]

1449 *Lalande:* Jean Lalande (?–1646), lay-assistant

1459/60 *Bressani:* Father François-Joseph Bressani (1612–72), Jesuit priest and missionary to the Hurons, 1644–5

1547 *Garreau:* Father Leonard Garreau (c. 1609–56), Jesuit priest and missionary to the Hurons, 1644–54

1553–7 *Rumours of treaties / ... Iroquois Confederacy / Might enter:* 'The Iroquois Confederacy consisted of the "Five Nations" – Mohawks, Oneidas, Onondagas, Cayugas, and Senecas' [*TSP*, p. 148].

1644 *The Passage:* 'the North-West Passage – the route for ships from the Atlantic to the Pacific by way of North America' [*TSP*, p. 148]

1678 *Bonin, Daran, Greslon:* Fathers Jacques Bonin (1617–?), Adrien D'Aran (1615–70), and Adrien Greslon (1617–97), Jesuit priests and missionaries to the Hurons, 1648–50

1932–3 *Palestrina's ... / The Assumpta est Maria:* Giovanni Pierluigi da Palestrina (c. 1525–94), choirmaster and composer for the papal choir in St Peter's. He was especially known for his masses, among the most famous of which was *Assumpta est Maria.*

1949–50 *This is my body ... / my blood:* recalling Christ's words at the Last Supper (Matthew 26; Mark 14; Luke 22; 1 Corinthians 11), which are repeated in the Mass

1996 *cidreries:* (Fr.) 'cider-houses'

2008 *Condé-sur-Vire:* home of Brébeuf in Normandy

2066 *Manresa:* 'a town in Spain near Montserrat, containing the church of San Ignacio built over the cave where Loyola lived and wrote' [*TSP*, p. 149]

2092 *Loyola's mountains:* 'the heights of sacrificial devotion to the cause of Christ' [*TSP*, p. 149]

2107 *the island of St. Joseph:* St Joseph Island, at the east entrance of the St Mary's River, connecting Lakes Huron and Superior; settled briefly after the destruction of Huronia in 1649 by fugitive Hurons and their Jesuit missionaries, who named it

COME AWAY, DEATH

date of composition: early autumn 1940
date of first publication: April 1941
46 breathing.] breathing
   The song 'Come away, come away, death' is sung by Feste, a clown in Shakespeare's *Twelfth Night* [2.1.52–68]. The poem was published in April of 1941, an exceedingly bleak point in the war. In this month there were heightened air attacks by Germany on London and other British cities, resulting in heavy civilian casualties. Simultaneously, German forces overran Greece, while British forces in North Africa lost Derna and Bardia.

1 *Willy-nilly ... clown's logic:* See the chop-logic of the First Clown, the gravedigger, in *Hamlet* 5.1.16–19: 'If the man go to this water and drown himself, it is, will he, nill he, he goes, mark you that. But if the water comes to him and drown him, he drowns not himself ...'

3 *mused rhyme:* See Keats's 'Ode to a Nightingale,' l. 53.

7 *poppy seeds:* The narcotic properties of the poppy have been associated with

death since ancient times. The poppy is associated with the war dead (see John McCrae's 'In Flanders Fields').

13 *acanthus leaf:* a plant whose leaves are the basis of the ornamentation used on the capitals of Corinthian columns. In Christian art, the acanthus symbolizes heaven.

14 *hyacinth:* flower associated in Greek mythology with the youth Hyacinthus, beloved by Apollo and accidentally killed by him

19 *mediaeval grace:* Compare Edward Arlington Robinson's 'Minniver Cheevy,' ll. 23–4: 'He missed the mediaeval grace / Of iron clothing.'

30 *the gride of his traction tread:* With the First and Second World Wars, death came in a new and mechanical form – the tank.

31 *one September night:* possibly a double allusion: the Second World War began on 3 September 1939 after the invasion of Poland by Germany. However, the poem was prompted by the Battle of Britain of August and September 1940. On 7 September, the date of the heaviest raid, four hundred bombers struck London.

52 *Piltdown:* 'a place in Sussex, England, from which were unearthed the remains of a prehistoric man' [*TSP*, p. 137]. In 1953, twelve years after this poem was written, the skull was exposed as a fake.

53 *Java:* Java man, *Pithecanthropus*, a genus known from skulls discovered in Java; considered one of the links between the apes and man

THE TRUANT

date of composition: from around spring to mid-August 1942
date of first publication: December 1942
27/8 LINE SPACE ADDED AFTER For the ballet of the fiery molecules.'

1 *Panjandrum:* a mock title for an official of imaginary or exaggerated importance or power

2 *Master of the Revels:* a person (permanently or temporarily) appointed to organize or lead revels, especially in the Royal Household or the Inns of Court

46 *cosmoscope:* Pratt's coinage

54 *coprophagite:* eater of dung (Pratt's coinage)

57 *sporozoan:* a spore-producing microbe, one form of which is responsible for malaria

71 *jacinth:* a reddish-orange gem, a kind of zircon

103 *Light-year:* an astronomical unit of distance. Pratt uses it as if it were a unit of time.

124 *Leo ... Taurus ... Bears:* northern constellations

125 *inverse squares:* referring to the relationship of two quantities, one of which

varies inversely as the square of the other: in this case the force of gravity, which varies inversely as the square of the distance from its source

127–8 *your rings / Of pure and endless light:* See Henry Vaughan's 'The World,' ll. 11–12.

155 *Lucretian atoms:* In *De Rerum Natura,* the Roman poet Lucretius presents the view that the world is constructed of atoms without any divine purpose or meaning.

159 *Chaos and Old Night:* See John Milton, *Paradise Lost* 1.543.

169 *The degradation of your energy:* entropy, the tendency of the universe towards increasing disorder

180 *cat-and-truncheon bastinades:* 'Cat' is short for 'cat-o'-nine-tails,' a rope whip with nine knotted lashes, once used for flogging. A 'bastinade' is a blow with a stick or whip, especially on the soles of the feet.

190 *Rood:* an archaic word for 'the cross of Christ'

THE GOOD EARTH

date of composition: January 1950
date of first publication: summer 1950

23 *germinating teeth:* a reference to the legend of Cadmus, founder of Thebes. Misfortune followed his family because he killed the sacred dragon that guarded the spring of Ares. Athena told him to sow the dragon's teeth, and from these sprang the Sparti (sown men), ancestors of the noble families of Thebes.

TOWARDS THE LAST SPIKE

date of composition: from 7 January 1950 to late October 1951
date of first publication: 27 June 1952

277/8 NOVEMBER 3, 1873] *November 3,1873*

1102/3 (*Onderdonk builds the* Skuzzy *to force the passage.*)] (ONDERDONK BUILDS THE "SKUZZY" TO FORCE THE PASSAGE.)

For Pratt's comments on *Towards the Last Spike* and especially on the extensive research he undertook in preparation for the poem, see OHLP, pp. 145–53.

40 *Thomas:* doubting Thomas. See John 20.25ff.

75 *fell of Grampian rams:* hide of rams in the Grampians, Scottish mountains

82 *Bannockburn:* In the Battle of Bannockburn, Scotland, on 24 June 1314, the Scots under Robert Bruce defeated the English forces of Edward II.

83 *Culloden:* On 16 April 1746, England's Duke of Cumberland defeated the Scots under Prince Charles Edward Stuart at Culloden, Scotland.

83 *the warnings of Lochiel:* See 'Lochiel's Warning,' by Thomas Campbell
(1777–1844). The hero of the poem is Donald Cameron, 'the gentle
Lochiel,' who, against his better judgment, supported Prince Charles at
Culloden.

88 *Scots wha hae:* See the 1793 poem 'Scots, Wha Hae,' by Robert Burns (1759–
96).

89 *Angus:* Richard B. Angus (1836–1922), banker and financier. A former general
manager of the Bank of Montreal, he helped to form the Canadian Pacific Rail-
way syndicate in 1880 and remained a director until his death.

90 *Fleming:* Sir Sandford Fleming (1827–1915), appointed chief engineer to the
Canadian Pacific Railway in 1871

91 *Hector (of the Kicking Horse):* Sir James Hector (1834–1907), geologist; discov-
erer, in 1857, of the Kicking Horse Pass
Dawson: Simon James Dawson (1820–1902), road builder, commissioned in
1868 to build a corduroy road between Lake of the Woods and the Red River,
which became known as the Dawson Route

92 *'Cromarty' Ross:* James Ross (1843–1913), engineer born in Cromarty, Scot-
land. In 1883 he took charge of the construction of the Canadian Pacific Rail-
way west of Winnipeg.
Beatty: Henry Beatty (1834–1914), a Scot who in 1882 resigned as manager of
the Northwest Transportation Company to take charge of a Great Lakes
steamship line being organized by the Canadian Pacific Railway

93 *Bruce:* James Bruce, eighth Earl of Elgin (1811–63), Governor-General of Can-
ada from 1847 to 1854
Allan: Sir Hugh Allan (1810–82), financier who with the backing of American
financiers founded the Canadian Pacific Railway Company in 1871, of which
he was president from 1872 to 1873, when the Pacific Scandal broke in the
House of Commons
Galt: Sir Alexander Tilloch Galt (1817–93), first minister of finance in the new
Dominion, a man with strong interests in the Grand Trunk Railway
Douglas: Sir James Douglas (1803–77), the 'Father of British Columbia,' first
governor of the province from 1858 to 1863

94 *Stephen:* Sir George Stephen (1829–1921), president of the Canadian Pacific
Railway during 1881–8. A Montreal businessman, president of the Bank of
Montreal, he, along with Richard Angus and Donald Alexander Smith,
formed the syndicate that organized the Canadian Pacific Railway in
1880.
Smith: Sir Donald Alexander Smith, Lord Strathcona (1820–1914), commis-
sioner of the Hudson's Bay Company, 1870–4. As independent MP for Selkirk,
1871–88, he voted against Macdonald in the debate over the Pacific Scandal.

As a member of the syndicate, he gave crucial support to the Canadian Pacific Railway in 1880 and drove the last spike in 1885.

100 *Sir John A.:* Sir John A. Macdonald (1815–91), first prime minister of Canada

112 *bull's beef:* bully beef, salt beef in barrels

114 *anchor-waist:* Pratt's point seems to be that Macdonald himself was the anchor: that is, the rope was around his waist in the tug-of-war.

131 *Tupper:* Sir Charles Tupper (1821–1915), premier of Nova Scotia during 1864–7, a Father of Confederation, and MP during 1867–84. As minister of railways and canals, 1879–84, he introduced the bill that gave the Canadian Pacific Railway its charter in 1881.

   Cartier: Sir George Etienne Cartier (1814–73), joint premier of United Canada, 1857–62, and a Father of Confederation; one of Macdonald's chief supporters in building the Canadian Pacific Railway

151 *Hudson, Davis, Baffin, Frobisher:* Henry Hudson (flourished 1607–11), John Davis (1550?–1605), William Baffin (1584?–1622), and Sir Martin Frobisher (1535?–94) were all English explorers who unsuccessfully sought the Northwest Passage.

152 *Franklin:* Sir John Franklin (1786–1847), British naval officer and arctic explorer. Franklin died, along with all his crew, on an expedition to discover the Northwest Passage.

   Ross: Alexander Ross (1783–1856), fur trader, author; celebrated the way of life of the Red River Settlement

   Parry: Sir William Edward Parry (1790–1855), rear admiral, arctic explorer; played an important role in the exploration of the Arctic and the eventual discovery of the Northwest Passage and the North Pole

154 *Kellett, McClure, McClintock of The Search:* Sir Henry Kellett (1806–75), Sir Robert John Le Mesurier McClure (1807–73), and Sir Francis Leopold McClintock (1819–1907) were all arctic explorers who participated in various unsuccessful missions to rescue Sir John Franklin and his crew (1846–50).

159 *Dead March:* from Handel's sacred oratorio *Saul*, c. 1739. See 2 Samuel 1.17ff.

160 *strychnine:* commonly used as a rat poison; a powerful stimulant in small doses

171–4 *Capella, Perseus / ... Cassiopeia ... / Aries ... Cygnus:* northern constellations

180 *Selkirk:* Lord Selkirk's Red River Colony, known also as the Selkirk Settlement, was settled by Scottish immigrants in 1812.

181 *Port Moody:* a city in British Columbia, at the head of Burrard Inlet

198 *the massacre at Seven Oaks:* near Winnipeg, 19 June 1816, in which the Métis killed Robert Semple, the governor of the Red River Colony, and twenty of his men

199 *Pemmican War:* the conflict between the North West Company and the Red

River settlers. Pemmican, originally a native Indian food, was dried meat, together with melted fat and dried fruits, pounded into a paste and made into cakes.

217 *from sea to sea:* See Zachariah 9.10.

228 *Tamales ... Cazadero ... Mendecino:* California towns (usual spelling 'Mendocino')

230 *Santa Rosa ... Santa Monica:* California towns

239 *San Diego:* short for San Diego de Alcala, a Spanish saint after whom San Diego, California, is named

257 *Disraeli:* Sir John A. Macdonald resembled Benjamin Disraeli, Earl of Beaconsfield (1804–81), prime minister of England in 1868 and from 1874 to 1880.

264/5 *Moberly:* Walter Moberly (1832–1915), engineer, who in 1853 sought a route through British Columbia for a transcontinental railway and in 1865 discovered Eagle Pass. In 1870 he took charge of mountain surveys for the Canadian Pacific Railway.

 Huntingdon: Lucius Huntingdon (1827–86), Canadian Liberal MP

 Blake: Edward Blake (1833–1912) was premier of Ontario during 1871–2. He became federal Liberal party leader in 1880, being succeeded by Laurier in 1887.

303 *Knights of Malta:* originally known as Knights Hospitallers; organized in the eleventh century to aid Christian pilgrims in Palestine

330–1 *damning correspondence ... / Montreal-Chicago understanding:* the correspondence between Sir Hugh Allan of Montreal and George W. McMullen of Chicago. McMullen and his Chicago group wanted a large part of the Canadian Pacific Railway to be in the United States and controlled by Northern Pacific. In 1871 Allan, who wanted to control the line, signed an agreement with the Chicago group that the line would run from below Sault Ste Marie, Ontario, through the United States and thence up to Winnipeg.

351/2 *Mackenzie:* Alexander Mackenzie (1822–92), Liberal prime minister, 1873–8

356–7 *The years were rendering up / Their fat:* a reference to the seven fat years followed by seven lean years which Joseph prophesied in Genesis 41

368–70 *loaves and fishes ... / Where are the multitudes:* See Luke 9.

419 *Emerson:* in southern Manitoba, just above the U.S. border

476 *the Pass had its ambiguous meaning:* double pun on the pass through Rockies and the 'pass' of legislation through the House

487 *the title of their wings:* In 1865 Walter Moberly saw eagles flying through a pass in the Gold Range of the Rockies, and named it Eagle Pass.

497 *Onderdonk:* Andrew Onderdonk (1848–1905), engineer and contractor who

received from the Canadian government in 1879 the contract to build the railway through the Thompson and Fraser canyons. His headquarters for the project was in Yale, British Columbia.

543 *Chatham:* William Pitt, first Earl of Chatham (1708–78)

544 *Burke:* Edmund Burke (1729–97), leader of the Whig party in England in the eighteenth century, an opponent of William Pitt and his Tory government's policy on the American colonies

576 *Fundy Tide:* The tides in the Bay of Fundy, an Atlantic inlet between New Brunswick and Maine on the west and Nova Scotia on the east, are the highest in the world.

580/1 *Pope:* John Henry Pope (1819–89), Macdonald's minister of agriculture

McIntyre: Duncan McIntyre (1834–94), a native of Scotland who came to Canada in 1849. A financier and railway builder, owner of the Canada Central line, he was one of the signatories to the preliminary agreement of 14 September 1880, for construction of the Canadian Pacific Railway.

588–90 *when a king ... / His Royal Charter:* charter granted to the Hudson's Bay Company on 2 May 1670 by Charles II

612–13 *The fleur-de-lis went to half-mast, the Jack / To the mast-head:* the Seven Years War, as a result of which France (*fleur-de-lis*) lost Canada to the British (Union Jack)

614 *Nor'-Westers at the Hudson's throat:* members of the North West Company, established by Montreal traders who in 1776 pooled resources to reduce competition among themselves and to resist inland advances of the Hudson's Bay Company

632 *Moses, Marco Polo, Paracelsus:* Moses caused water to flow from a rock in Horeb, by striking it [Exodus 17.6] ('To smite the rock and bring forth living water'); Marco Polo (c. 1254–1324) wrote accounts of his travels in China ('fabulize a continent'); Phillipus Aureolus Paracelsus (1493?–1541) was a Swiss physician and alchemist ('transmute ... to gold').

636 *rat-skins:* muskrat pelts

637 *Tadoussac:* in Quebec, near the junction of the Saguenay and St Lawrence Rivers

662 *Kitson:* Norman Wilfred Kittson (1814–88), a fur trader who developed the line of Red River steamers in the 1860s and later became an associate of James Hill in railway building

Kennedy: Sir John Kennedy (1838–1921), chief engineer of the Great Western railway system, president of the U.S. Great Northern Railway, 1893–1907, member of the board of the Canadian Pacific Railway, 1880–3

663 *Jim Hill:* James Jerome Hill (1838–1916), railway builder

673/4 *William Cornelius Van Horne:* Van Horne (1843–1915) was appointed general manager of the Canadian Pacific Railway in 1882, was vice-president in 1884, president during 1888–9, and chairman from 1890 to 1910.

689 *Agassiz:* Louis Agassiz (1807–73), Swiss-American zoologist and geologist, noted for his work on fossils and glaciation

691 *Crinoids:* Crinoid means 'lily-shaped' and is a term applied to fossils resembling sea urchins.

732 *Zuyder Zee:* (alternate spelling 'Zuider Zee') Dutch for 'Southern Sea,' a former shallow inlet of the North Sea now split in two by a dam

733 *the new Amsterdam:* New Amsterdam was a Dutch settlement at the mouth of the Hudson River and on the southern end of Manhattan Island. When it was captured by the British, it was renamed New York.

771 *Perry:* Albert Perry, a mountaineer who assisted Walter Moberly and was credited by him with discovering in 1866 the pass later explored by and named after Major Rogers

773 *Rogers:* Major A.B. Rogers (1829–89), explorer of Rogers Pass in 1881

777 *Gold Range:* a range in the Monashee Mountains, British Columbia. Eagle Pass provided a corridor through the Gold Range.

Coastal Mountains: The Coast Mountains extend for about 1,600 kilometres from the mountains of Alaska near the Yukon border to the Cascade Range near the Fraser River.

804 *Yellowhead:* The Yellowhead Pass crosses the continental divide between Alberta and British Columbia, 25 kilometres west of Jasper. It was originally proposed by Sandford Fleming as the route for the Canadian Pacific Railway, but was rejected.

826 *Shaughnessy:* Thomas George, first Baron Shaughnessy (1853–1923), president of the Canadian Pacific Railway, 1899–1918. Having joined the company as a purchasing agent in 1882, he was credited with maintaining the flow of supplies during the construction period.

863 *substance of things unseen:* 'Now faith is the substance of things hoped for, the evidence of things not seen' [Hebrews 11.1].

962 *Magellan:* Ferdinand Magellan (c. 1480–1521), Portuguese navigator; commander of the first expedition to circumnavigate the globe (although he died en route)

980 *chain:* a measuring line, used in land surveying, formed of one hundred iron rods called 'links' jointed together by eyes at their ends

transit: transit-compass, an instrument, resembling a theodolite, used in surveying for the measurement of horizontal angles

1009 *Paul Bunyan:* legendary American lumberjack, the hero of many 'tall tales'

1059 *ponderosa pine:* a large conifer, *Pinus ponderosa* or western yellow pine, native to western North America

1062 *Lyell larches:* The Lyall (correct spelling) or Lyall's larch is a small timberline tree that is found between Montana and British Columbia, and is used for telephone poles, mine timbers, and railway ties.

1069 *Balkan boundary:* The Balkan Peninsula includes Albania, Greece, Bulgaria, part of Turkey, most of the former Yugoslavia, and southeast Roumania. As a crossroads for European and Asian civilizations, it has been politically volatile as states sought to extend their boundaries.

1096 *Hell's Gate:* a rocky gorge of the Fraser River Canyon south of Boston Bar

1102/3 *Skuzzy:* steamboat which served on the Fraser between Lytton and Boston Bar; named after a stream draining into the Fraser

1111 *Chinese:* Onderdonk recruited thousands of labourers from China to work on the railway.

1124 *gaskets at the royal yards:* small ropes at the highest mast

1279 *leather-leaf:* a low evergreen shrub with leathery leaves

1290 *The Lady's face was flushed:* Contemporary political cartoons identified the province of British Columbia as a reluctant lady pursued by eager suitors, both American and Canadian.

1329 *brachiapods:* (Lat., 'arm-footed') usual spelling 'brachiopods'; two-shelled water creatures, so-called because each has two spirally coiled arms around its mouth

1401 *A shot fifteen years after it was fired:* the Red River Rebellion in 1870. See note to Riel below.

1404 *Riel:* Louis Riel (1844–85), Métis leader of the Red River Rebellion in 1870 and of the Riel Rebellion in 1885. Riel was hanged in 1885.

1409 *Scott:* Thomas Scott (c. 1842–70), Protestant Irish immigrant executed on Riel's orders during the Riel Rebellion

1411 *that young, tall, bilingual advocate:* Sir Wilfrid Laurier (1841–1919), later prime minister of Canada (1896–1911)

1419 *buffalo wallows:* areas of hard, bare ground on the prairies produced when bison roll in the soil ('wallow') in an effort to groom themselves, regulate their temperature, and provide protection against insects

1458 *under double-reef:* to sail under double reef is to reduce the spread of a sail by taking in two reefs

1473/4 *Revelstoke ... Baring:* Lord Revelstoke, British peer, after whom Revelstoke, British Columbia, was named to honour him for the role of his banking house, Baring's, in financing the Canadian Pacific Railway

1485 *Athanasian:* Athanasius (c. 296–373) championed the authorized Christian faith against all other interpretations; hence the saying *Athanasius contra mundum* ('Athanasius against the world').

1499 *shad-flies:* flies, especially mayflies, that appear when the shad, fish common on the Atlantic coast, are running

1593 *Flodden:* In the battle of Flodden in Northumberland, 9 September 1513, English soldiers defeated the forces of James IV of Scotland.

1604 *Egan:* John M. Egan (1811–57), general superintendent of the Canadian Pacific Railway's western division in 1885

1605 *Cambie:* Henry I. Cambie, a government engineer engaged in building the Canadian Pacific Railway

   Marcus Smith: 1815–1905, engineer-in-chief of the Canadian Pacific Railway during the absence of Sandford Fleming, 1876–8

   Harris of Boston: George R. Harris, a director of the Canadian Pacific Railway

1608 *Dug McKenzie:* Dugald McKenzie, locomotive engineer

   John H. McTavish: land commissioner, among those present at the ceremony on 26 September 1885

Selected Bibliography

WORKS BY PRATT

The latest edition of Pratt's *Collected Poems* to be published in his lifetime was:

The Collected Poems of E.J. Pratt. 2nd ed. Ed. and introd. Northrop Frye. Toronto: Macmillan 1958

The following volumes have so far appeared in the *Collected Works*, being published by University of Toronto Press:

E.J. Pratt on His Life and Poetry. Ed. and introd. Susan Gingell. 1983
E.J. Pratt: Complete Poems. 2 vols. Ed. Sandra Djwa and R.G. Moyles. Introd. Sandra Djwa. 1989
Pursuits Amateur and Academic: The Selected Prose of E.J. Pratt. Ed. and introd. Susan Gingell. 1995

Two further volumes in the *Collected Works* are currently being edited in both print and hypertext format: a second edition of *E.J. Pratt: Complete Poems*, by Sandra Djwa and Zailig Pollock; and the *Letters*, by D.G. Pitt and Elizabeth Popham. The URL for the hypertext editions is www.trentu.ca/pratt.

BIBLIOGRAPHY

Lila and Raymond Laakso. 'E.J. Pratt.' In *The Annotated Bibliography of Canada's Major Authors*. Vol. 2. Ed. Robert Lecker and Jack David. Toronto: ECW Press 1980, pp. 147–220
Lila Laakso. 'Descriptive Bibliography.' In *E.J. Pratt: Complete Poems*. 2 vols. Ed.

Sandra Djwa and R.G. Moyles. Introd. Sandra Djwa. University of Toronto Press 1989, 2:373–497

BIOGRAPHY

Ralph Gustafson. 'Portrait of Ned.' *Queen's Quarterly* 74 (Autumn 1967), 437–51
David G. Pitt. *E.J. Pratt: The Truant Years, 1882–1927*. Toronto: University of Toronto Press 1984
– *E.J. Pratt: The Master Years, 1927–1964*. Toronto: University of Toronto Press 1987
Mildred Claire Pratt. *The Silent Ancestors: The Forebears of E.J. Pratt*. Toronto: McClelland and Stewart 1971

CRITICAL STUDIES

Earle Birney. 'E.J. Pratt and His Critics.' In *Masks of Poetry*. Ed. A.J.M. Smith. Toronto: McClelland and Stewart 1962, pp. 72–95
E.K. Brown. 'E.J. Pratt.' In *On Canadian Poetry*. Toronto: Ryerson 1944, pp. 143–64
Peter Buitenhuis. 'E.J. Pratt.' In *Canadian Writers and Their Works*. Poetry Series. Vol 3. Ed. Robert Lecker, Jack David, and Ellen Quigley. Toronto: ECW Press 1987, pp. 111–60
Glenn Clever. *On E.J. Pratt*. Ottawa: Borealis 1977
W.E. Collin. 'Pleiocene Heroics.' In *The White Savannahs*. Toronto: Macmillan 1936, pp. 119–44
Robert G. Collins. *E.J. Pratt*. Boston: Twayne Publishers 1988
Roy Daniells. 'The Special Quality.' *Canadian Literature* 21 (Summer 1964), 10–12
Frank Davey. 'E.J. Pratt: Apostle of Corporate Man.' *Canadian Literature* 43 (Winter 1970), 54–66
– 'E.J. Pratt: Rationalist Technician.' *Canadian Literature* 61 (Summer 1974), 65–78
Sandra Djwa. *E.J. Pratt: The Evolutionary Vision*. Toronto and Montreal: Copp Clark/McGill-Queen's University Press 1974
Louis Dudek. 'Poet of the Machine Age.' *Tamarack Review* 6 (Winter 1958), 65–80
Northrop Frye. 'Letters in Canada: Poetry.' *University of Toronto Quarterly* 22 (April 1952), 97–103
– Introduction. *The Collected Poems of E.J. Pratt*. 2nd ed. Ed. Northrop Frye. Toronto: Macmillan 1958, pp. xiii–xxviii
– 'The Personal Legend.' *Canadian Literature* 21 (Summer 1964), 6–9

Susan Gingell. 'The Newfoundland Context of the Poetry of E.J. Pratt.' *Essays on Canadian Writing* 31 (Summer 1985), 93–105

R.D. MacDonald. 'E.J. Pratt: Apostle of the Techno/Corporate Culture?' *Canadian Poetry* 37 (Fall/Winter 1995), 17–41

Patrick O'Flaherty. 'Emigrant Muse.' In *The Rock Observed: Studies in the Literature of Newfoundland.* Toronto: University of Toronto Press 1979, pp. 111–26

Desmond Pacey. 'E.J. Pratt.' In *Ten Canadian Poets.* Toronto: Ryerson 1958, pp. 165–93

Catherine McKinnon Pfaff. 'Pratt's Treatment of History in *Towards the Last Spike.' Canadian Literature* 97 (Summer 1983), 48–69

Magdalene Redekop. 'Authority and the Margins of Escape in *Brébeuf and His Brethren.' Open Letter* 6.2–3 (Summer/Fall 1985), 45–60

John Sutherland. *The Poetry of E.J. Pratt: A New Interpretation.* Toronto: Ryerson 1956

Henry W. Wells and Carl F. Klinck. *Edwin J. Pratt: The Man and His Poetry.* Toronto: Ryerson 1947

Milton Wilson. *E.J. Pratt.* Toronto: McClelland and Stewart 1969

COLLECTIONS OF ARTICLES

Glenn Clever, ed. *The E.J. Pratt Symposium.* Ottawa: University of Ottawa Press 1977

D.G. Pitt, ed. *E.J. Pratt.* Toronto: Ryerson 1969

Index of Titles

Index of First Lines